The Church Speaks

Volume 2

For Both —
With affection,
admiration &
appreciation

James I. Cook

edited by

James I. Cook

Love —

Jim

Copyright 2002 by Wm.B.Eerdmans Publishing Co.
255 Jefferson Ave., S.E., Grand Rapids, Mich., 49503

Printed in the United States of America

ISBN 0-8028-0980-4

The Historical Series of the Reformed Church in America

No. 40

The Church Speaks

Volume 2
Papers of the Commission on Theology Reformed Church in America, 1985-2000

edited by
James I. Cook

Wm. B. Eerdmans Publishing Co.
Grand Rapids, Michigan

The Historical Series of the Reformed Church in America

The series was inaugurated in 1968 by the General Synod of the Reformed Church in America acting through the Commission on History—communicating the church's heritage and collective memory reflecting on our identity and mission encouraging historical scholarship which informs both church and academy.

General Editor

The Reverend Donald J. Bruggink, Ph.D.
Western Theological Seminary

Commission on History

The Rev. James Brumm, M.Div., Blooming Grove, New York
The Rev. Lynn Japinga, Ph.D., Hope College, Holland, Michigan
The Rev. Melody Meeter, M.Div., Brooklyn, New York
Jesus Serrano, B.A., Norwalk, California
The Rev. Robert Terwilliger, M.Div., Kalamazoo, Michigan
Jeffrey Tyler, Ph.D., Hope College, Holland, Michigan

*To the men and women
who have served
on the Theological Commission
of the
Reformed Church in America,
1985-2000*

Al Alicea
Johnny Alicea-Baez
Douglas Anderson
Michael Andres
Roy Anker
Thomas Boogaart
Steven Bouma-Prediger
James Brownson
Juan Carmona
John Chang
David Chen
Livingstone Chen
Robert Coughenour
George Cruz
Samuel Cruz
Eileen Esmark
David French
Paul Fries
Earle Hall
Amy Jo Hawley
I. John Hesselink
Carolyn Holloway

Renee House
Lynn Japinga
Christopher Kaiser
Norman Kansfield
Hugh Koops
David Landegent
Louis Lotz
Rodwell Morgan
Marchiene Rienstra
Kathryn Roberts
Leslie Seaton
David Timmer
Charles Van Engen
Leonard Vander Zee
Richard Veenstra
Petronella Verwijs
Dennis Voskuil
David Waanders
Martin Wang
Wilbur T. Washington
Merold Westphal
Robert White

The Editor

James I. Cook received his undergraduate education at Hope College, Holland, Michigan. In addition to earning the M.A. degree from Michigan State University, the B.D. degree from Western Theological Seminary, Holland, Michigan, and the Th.D. degree from Princeton Theological Seminary, Princeton, New Jersey, he has pursued post-doctrinal studies at the Hebrew University, Jerusalem, and the University of Durham, England. Until retirement he was a member of the Society of Biblical Literature.

Dr. Cook, an ordained minister of the Reformed Church in America, was pastor of the Blawenburg Reformed Church, Blawenburg, New Jersey, from 1953 to 1963. He has also served as a member of the Theological Commission from 1967 to 1973 and as member and moderator of the commission from 1979 to 1985. In 1982 he was elected president of the General Synod of the Reformed Church in America.

Dr. Cook is the author of *Edgar Johnson Goodspeed: Articulate Scholar* (1981), *One Lord One Body* (1991), and *Shared Pain and Sorrow: Reflections of a Secondary Sufferer* (1991). He is the contributing editor of *Grace Upon Grace: Essays in Honor of Lester J. Kuyper* (1975), and *Saved by Hope: Essays in Honor of Richard C. Oudersluys* (1978). A founding editor of the journal *Perspectives*, Mr. Cook was editor of the *Reformed Review*, 1987-2002. In 1985 he edited *The Church Speaks: Papers of the Commission on Theology, Reformed Church in America, 1959-1984*.

Dr. Cook joined the faculty of Western Theological Seminary, Holland, Michigan, in 1963, and is presently Professor of New Testament Emeritus.

Contents

The indices are for both volume one and volume two of *The Church Speaks*. References to volume one are indicated by Roman numeral I and to volume two by Roman numeral II.

Bibliographical Note
to the Reader

Regarding citations of published works the editor has imposed a uniformity upon the varied usage which appears in the original format of the commission papers. All such citations have therefore been divided into two categories.

The first is restricted to the following publications that are especially integral to the faith and life of the Reformed Church in America:

Minutes of the General Synod, RCA (MGS)
The Book of Church Order (New York: Reformed Church Press) (*BCO*)
Liturgy and Psalms (New York: Board of Education, 1968) (*Liturgy and Psalms*)
The Belgic Confession, 1561 (BConf)
The Heidelberg Catechism, 1563 (HCat)
The Canons of the Synod of Dort, 1618-1619 (Dort)
(Note: Although earlier translations of the above doctrinal standards exist, the current official translations appear in *Liturgy and Confessions*, 1990.)
John Calvin, *Institutes of the Christian Religion* (Philadelphia: Westminster Press, 1960) (*Institutes*)

References to all other publications belong to the second category. The appropriate bibliographical data for them appear in the notes.

Preface

No event could be more consonant with the life and purpose of the Commission on Theology than the collection and publication of its papers. Since its inception in 1959 the commission has sought to serve the church by articulating its theological understanding of contemporary issues. This has been accomplished in the first instance through annual reports made to the General Synod and printed in the synodical minutes. All too often commission papers were thus fated to become matters of historical record rather than handy resources. Occasionally the desire to be heard beyond a synod and its minutes found expression through recommendations that papers be made available to the churches in some form. That at least once the commission had a larger vision is indicated in its 1975 report:

> The commission has made a study regarding various papers which have become a part of General Synod minutes. The commission feels that several of these papers should be made available to pastors. The commission will be presenting a plan to the Synod of 1976 regarding means to print these papers, and in that way, make available to pastors theological guidelines which have been approved by the church.

Unhappily there is no further reference to this plan in reports to subsequent synods.

To the General Synod of 1981, however, the commission announced its intention to collect and issue its papers as a volume in the Historical Series of the Reformed Church in America. That volume, edited by James I. Cook, was published in 1985 under the title, *The Church Speaks: Papers of the Commission on Theology, Reformed Church in America, 1959-1984.* The papers of this second volume, produced from 1985 to 2000 have been gathered into chapters according to six categories: scripture, faith, sacraments, ministry, witness, and sexuality. Chapters begin with an introduction which sketches the historical background and summarizes the contents of each paper. With joy and thanksgiving, these studies which arose out of the life of the church, are now returned to it in permanent form.

From 1985 to 2000, a significant number of persons, both clergy and lay, have served on the Theological Commission. The papers they have written reflect both their learning and their love of the Lord, the Scriptures, and the church. To this company we are all indebted. In addition, appreciation is particularly expressed to Marilyn Essink not only for her expert assistance in preparing the manuscript, but also for her personal and collegial commitment to this kingdom project; to Russell L. Gasero for the preparation of the index, and to Donald J. Bruggink for his service as the general editor of the Historical Series of the Reformed Church in America.

James I. Cook, Editor

Historical Introduction

The Commission on Theology was born out of the struggle of the Reformed Church in America with the problem of the unity of the church. Among the recommendations made to the General Synod of 1958 by the Committee on Approaches to Unity was "that General Synod give serious consideration to the appointment of a theological commission to make a long term study looking toward the production of a document that will give expression to our Christian Faith on the basis of Scripture, the historic creeds, and the Reformed Standards of Unity, in the light of present day needs and experiences" (*MGS*, 1958:355). This recommendation was referred to the Special Committee on Approaches to Unity which reported that it was more than sympathetic toward the request:

> Indeed it is our conviction that such a task should always be at the centre of the life of a Church which claims to be Reformed according to the Word of God. Not only is the Reformed Church, as one of the smaller Communions in our country, constantly in need of interpretation to those unacquainted with its life and work, but, more importantly, those who form its membership must always be rediscovering the relevant vitality of the faith which they profess. A Reformed Church whose theological inheritance no longer speaks to its members in the

places where they live and work is, in the deepest sense of the word, no longer Reformed.

We can, therefore, see a real place for such a commission, not to re-write or alter our historic creeds and confessions, but to bring them into living relationships with the Church as it confesses its faith in the present day (*MGS*, 1958:357).

The synod then adopted the following recommendations regarding the creation of a theological commission:

a. That the Committee on Approaches to Unity be re-constituted as the Committee on Confessional Interpretation and given the task of preparing a preliminary survey of this question;

b. That this survey, to be presented to the next General Synod, seek to ascertain the mind of the Church in this important matter, to prepare an outline of the areas and problems requiring study, to suggest the personnel of such a theological commission, and whatever else in the opinion of the Committee be involved in the presentation of such a full outline to Synod;

c. That in carrying out this task the Committee be encouraged to consult with both missionaries and lay persons, as well as any others who may have a contribution to make (*MGS*, 1958:357f.).

The following year (1959), the newly-appointed Committee on Confessional Interpretation gave its report. The committee chose to focus on synod's charge to prepare a preliminary survey looking toward the appointment of a theological commission. Included in the report were the following significant paragraphs:

Your committee has given some thought and study to this mandate of Synod. We believe that this mandate of Synod is very important and can result in great spiritual benefit to the Reformed Church in America. In recent years many questions have been brought to the Synod. Synod has tried to deal with these questions by appointing various committees to study the questions and problems which have arisen. They have given their reports so that Synod could act. Recent instances are found in the appointment of committees to study the Ordination of Women and Approaches to Unity. Questions regarding Biblical

Interpretation are currently under discussion and the clarification of our doctrinal position is a pressing need.

A Theological Commission is envisaged which should prepare a Handbook of Instruction of the Reformed Faith We Confess. Such a project will require the labors of Theological Professors as well as men in the pastorate. We believe that this commission should be charged with the task of formulating a handbook which will embody the teaching of Scripture, the historic creeds of Christendom and the Reformed Standards of Unity. Such a study ought to set forth plainly Historic Christianity in terms that are relevant to the present day situations and challenges . . . .

Such a commission should be prepared to organize itself for a long term study and should be organized with a President, Vice President, and Secretary so that it may function properly.

The commission should be free to determine its own mode of procedure but within the general framework suggested by this committee and approved by General Synod.

Your present committee which was first organized as "The Committee on Approaches to Unity" is of the opinion that its work is ended and that the committee is to be dissolved. The committee feels, however, that its original work is not completed and recommends that the new commission include in its study and consideration of the doctrine of the Church the problem of the Unity of the Church.

Since General Synod has suggested that names be given for consideration by the nominating committee who will present the nominees to General Synod, your committee suggests that the committee be so constituted that there be a number of teachers from our Theological Schools, a number of men who are in the pastoral work of the Church, and that pastors, as much as possible, be selected from all the areas of the Church. We further suggest that the committee be composed of ten men: four men from our two Theological Schools and six men who are active in the pastoral life of the Church . . . .

It is the conviction of your committee that the commission ought to set as its goal a concise and practical "Handbook of

Instruction of the Reformed Faith We Confess" which shall be presented to the General Synod for consideration at the end of its study. This handbook should present a comprehensive statement of the historic Reformed Faith in the context of our current day needs and problems. We realize, of course that there can and will be specific facets of our beliefs which will need special consideration by the commission. We believe that should the need arise the General Synod can request or direct the commission to give special consideration to pressing theological problems of the denomination.

We believe that this study should have as its point of departure the historic, ever-living and exalted Lord Jesus Christ. Christ occupies a central place in the revelation and prophecy of the Old Testament. The New Testament presents His life, His work, and His program. The person of Jesus Christ is God with us. In Him God reaches out to seize and to liberate lost sinners. He is the foretoken and pledge of the complete realization of the Kingdom of God (*MGS*, 1959:363ff.).

To that same synod of 1959 came three overtures of particular theological importance. One, from the Classis of South Grand Rapids, requested "that General Synod affirm positively the historical character of the Genesis Account and appoint an appropriate committee to investigate and report this entire matter of Biblical Criticism commonly referred to as Higher Criticism." A second, from the Classis of Raritan, requested the synod to establish a permanent commission for theological studies. A third, from the Classis of Paramus, requested that "General Synod have its president appoint a commission to study the matter of the Inspiration of Scripture; and that the commission submit to the next General Synod for approval a deliverance on the subject of the Inspiration of Scripture; and, in particular, a deliverance regarding the right of a classis to require candidates for licensure and/or ordination to subscribe to, or to reflect in their replies to questions, the 'verbal inspiration' view." Upon the recommendation of the Overtures Committee, the General Synod of 1959 immediately referred the three overtures to the new Theological Commission it had created.

Thus began the life of the Commission on Theology. In terms of size, the commission has experienced little change. From 1969 to 1981, its membership was reduced from its original ten to nine, but in 1982 it was enlarged to ten once more. In terms of makeup, however, the years have brought significant change. According to the 2000 edition of the *Book of Church Order*, the commission's membership shall include three persons from among the Reformed Church seminary faculties, two persons from among the faculties of the Reformed Church colleges, three pastors, and two laypersons. In addition, there shall also be two ecumenical observers: one from other reformed bodies, and one from the Evangelical Lutheran Church in America.

In light of the synod's clear instruction that the Theological Commission prepare a "Handbook of Instruction of the Reformed Faith We Confess," it is remarkable that that specific project was never carried out. The contemporary description of the commission's responsibilities is to study theological matters arising in the life of the church and referred to it by the General Synod or initiated by the commission itself. The papers collected in the two volumes of *The Church Speaks* are the results obtained in the discharge of those responsibilities.

1

Church and Scripture

Introduction

The Use of Scripture in Making Moral Decisions

In response to an overture from the Classis of New York, the 1992 General Synod instructed the Commission on Theology to prepare a study of the use of Scripture in moral decision-making (*MGS*, 1992:470). The commission submitted a paper, "The Use of Scripture in Making Moral Decisions," to the General Synod of 1993 (*MGS*, 1993:418-27). Upon recommendation of the Advisory Committee on Theology, the paper was referred back to the commission "for further study and report to the 1994 General Synod" (*MGS*, 1993:427). After considering the issues of both substance and presentation of the paper raised by the advisory committee, the commission presented a revised paper to the General Synod of 1994.

Affirming the Reformed conviction that the Bible is the very foundation of the Christian moral life, and recognizing that Christians disagree on how the Bible is to be interpreted in Christian moral decision-making, the paper provides principles and guidelines for the use of Scripture in the making of ethical decisions in today's complex world. In the process it addresses the authority, character, and focus of Scripture; the Bible and

1

the Christian community; the Christian's moral identity; moral rules and ethical principles; the formation of Christian identity in the world; and the task of moral discernment. The study concludes that the more focused Christians are upon reading Scripture as the book which leads them to God and which forms Christ in them, the more clearly they will also be able to discern who they are and what they are to do.

The synod voted to commend the paper to the congregations of the Reformed Church in America for study; to encourage them to send comments and suggested revisions to the commission; and to request the commission to submit a revised paper to the 1995 General Synod. To that synod, however, the commission reported that since the some dozen responses from the congregations taken together did not disclose any clear direction for emendation and resubmission, it did not intend to submit a revised version of the paper at that time.

The Paper

The Use Of Scripture
In Making Moral Decisions

Introduction

The title of this report reflects the Reformed conviction that all moral decisions must be made in light of Scripture. The Bible is not merely an accessory to the Christian moral life, but its very foundation. Despite agreement on this presupposition, however, a substantial portion of the controversy and debate which exists today among Christians centers precisely around this topic. In particular, Christians disagree on how the Bible is to play this central role and how it is to be interpreted in the process of Christian moral decision-making.

The commission neither expects nor intends that this report will resolve all those disputes. The commission's intention is more modest: to lay out what it believes to be helpful "ground rules" for Christians who wrestle with Scripture and with difficult moral judgments. The commission believes there is a store of wisdom to be found in Reformed tradition and in the best of biblical scholarship, which can enable Christians to keep their bearings as they struggle with difficult questions. This collective wisdom may also make it easier to talk with each other and to really hear each other as Reformed Church in America members struggle with their differences.

The commission is attempting in this report to walk a careful path between two extremes. On the one hand, the commission rejects any form of relativism which would deny God's self-revelation in Scripture and the moral implications of that self-revelation. The commission believes that God has not set Christians adrift without a moral compass to guide them. Scripture is sufficient to guide Christians in living a moral life which is pleasing to God. On the other hand, the commission rejects all simplistic attempts to apply scriptural rules to the lives of Christians apart from a careful and theologically sound process of interpretation.

In contrast to both these distortions, Reformed Christians confess that the primary purpose of Scripture is to lead them to the living God. Encounter with God, guided and informed by Scripture, directs a Christian's moral decision-making. A Christian's ultimate allegiance is not to a book, but to the living Christ, to whom Scripture directs a Christian's attention, faith, and obedience. Christians make moral decisions in union with Christ, in the fellowship and power of the Holy Spirit, in prayer and communion with God's people, to the glory of God. Scripture is given to help Christians fulfill this calling. In what follows, the commission hopes to describe how Scripture helps Christians toward this great purpose.

The Authority, Character, and Focus of Scripture

Together with the whole church, the Commission on Theology affirms the Scriptures of the Old and New Testaments as inspired by God and as the only final authority for the faith and practice of the people of God. The making of Christian moral decisions is therefore directly linked to the role that Scripture plays in the life of the church. According to Article Two of the Bélgic Confession, Scripture is primarily a means "by which we know God." Scripture is, above all else, the means by which God is revealed to us. The question of human response and moral behavior emerges only within the context of God's self-revelation. First God meets people, then people respond. Every attempt, therefore, to discern a morality in Scripture must be grounded in this context of life before God.

The Heidelberg Catechism has the same relational emphasis. It begins by declaring that "I am not my own, but belong, body and soul, in life and in death, to my faithful savior Jesus Christ.... Because I belong to him, Christ, by his Holy Spirit, assures me of eternal life and makes me wholeheartedly willing and ready from now on to live for him" (Q/A 1). The central purpose of our salvation is the reconciliation of people to God. In summarizing the central thrust of his faith, Paul writes simply, "I want to know Christ" (Phil. 3:10). Augustine expresses a similar perspective: "The sum of all we have said since we began to speak of things thus comes to this: it is to be understood that the plenitude and the end of the Law and of all the sacred Scriptures is the love of a Being which is to be enjoyed and of a Being that can share that enjoyment with us."[1]

Reformed Christians confess that God's self-revelation appears in its greatest fullness and clarity in the story of the life, death, and resurrection of Jesus Christ. Here one sees the full scope of the gracious character and purpose of God (John 5:39; 14:8-11; Eph. 1:9,10; Heb. 1:1-3). One also sees in Christ the clearest model of the appropriate human response to God's gracious character and purpose (Phil. 2:1-11; Heb. 2:10-18). Therefore all Christian moral judgments must ultimately be grounded in Christ, who models God's disposition toward us and our appropriate response toward God. In Christ one discovers the full character of the life-before-God to which Scripture calls us.

The moral context for human life that is revealed in Christ is always eschatological and transformational in character. That is, Christian moral discernment is not in essence pragmatic or utilitarian. Christians do not seek only to preserve or restore the status quo in a given situation. Rather, they always seek to view each situation in light of God's revealed saving purpose for the world, and in light of the surprising, transforming power of the Spirit. "If anyone is in Christ, there is a new creation: everything old has passed away; see, everything has become new!" (2 Cor. 5:17). At the same time, Christian moral discernment does not naively assume either that one's creaturely limitations can or should be transcended, or that one's struggle with sin is ever complete in this life. Christians continue to experience the "first fruits of the Spirit" while awaiting the full renewal of the whole creation (Rom. 8:22, 23).

---

[1]   *On Christian Doctrine* (New York: Liberal Arts, 1958), 30.

The Bible and the Christian Community

This life-before-God of which Scripture speaks is essentially covenantal and communal. God's purpose throughout Scripture is to call forth a redeemed community to live in God's presence as a sign of God's redemptive purpose for the world. 1 Peter 2:9 declares, "you are a chosen race, a royal priesthood, a holy nation, God's own people, in order that you may proclaim the mighty acts of him who called you out of darkness into his marvelous light." For the same reason, Scripture regularly uses the image of the body as a central metaphor for the life of the church (1 Cor. 12:12 ff.; Eph. 4:15, 16). Hence every attempt to discern a morality in Scripture must be grounded in this communal context of life before God.

This covenantal life-before-God of which Scripture speaks is always specific, historical, and particular. Scripture reveals what covenantal life-before-God is by showing the way in which the word of God confronted specific groups of people in specific cultural contexts. This life-before-God does not consist only in abstract principles. It encompasses a host of practices, traditions, rituals, values, and behaviors. Scripture reveals multiple forms in which covenantal life-before-God takes shape. Such life is always worked out, in all its complexity, in specific historical and cultural circumstances. God spoke to people in their own language, addressed their own culture, and utilized their specific gifts to the praise of God's glory.

This is seen most clearly in the many contrasts between different times and places in the history of God's covenant people. Even within the New Testament, different Christian churches spoke different languages, struggled with different problems, and followed different customs and practices. One should not view this pluralism of culture within the Bible and the history of Christianity as an unfortunate problem, but rather as a fulfillment of God's purposes. Revelation 5:9 celebrates this reality: "by your blood you ransomed for God saints from every tribe and language and people and nation." Therefore, when Scripture is used in making moral decisions one must consider the specific historical and cultural contexts in which God's self-revelation took place.

Because the life-before-God to which Scripture calls us in Christ is always historical and particular, there is no single "Christian culture" which Scripture calls for. In the New Testament, for example, Paul never demands that Jews cease circumcision and kosher observance; their life in Christ could and should be Jewish in character. Yet Paul also insists that a different form of life was appropriate for Gentiles, and Christians should not all be forced to share the same culture. Paul writes: "To the Jews I became as a Jew, in order to win Jews. To those under the law I became as one under the law…so that I might win those under the law. To those outside the law I became as one outside the law…so that I might win those outside the law" (1 Cor. 9:20, 21). The coming of the gospel of Christ shattered the cultural exclusivity of the people of God and opened the way for those of "every nation and tribe and language and people" (Rev. 14:6) to live out in diverse ways the multi-colored grace of God (see I Pet. 4:10).

Although Christian faith takes diverse cultural forms, it does not follow that Scripture supports every cultural practice. Instead, one should observe how God's will relates to human cultures in a dynamic tension of affirmation and judgment. Because God calls each community to respond in distinctive ways to God's self-revelation in Christ, the full richness of human diversity, both at the individual and cultural level, is affirmed as a valid and beautiful means for glorifying God. At the same time, every community is called to repentance and conversion to a new pattern of life before God.

An example of this dynamic tension is found within the New Testament, where one finds lists of virtues and vices which have marked similarities to lists in the writings of Hellenistic moralists, particularly Stoic philosophers (see Eph. 5:21-6.9; Col. 3:18-4.6; 1 Pet. 2:11-3.12). At the same time, however, the New Testament writers place these elements from their culture in a new setting by interpreting them in light of the gospel of Christ. Likewise, every culture will find itself both affirmed and called to repentance in the face of God's self-revelation in Scripture. The particular pattern of affirmation and critique may vary extensively, however, from one setting to another.

The Christian's Moral Identity

Scripture reveals a form of life before God in Christ which may receive different cultural expressions. This fact helps in understanding an important aspect of Scripture: even within Scripture, specific moral rules may vary according to place, time and circumstance. In the Old Testament, for example, the practice of polygamy by the patriarchs is accepted without question. By contrast, the New Testament presupposes a monogamous ethic. Paul writes that for Christians with weak consciences, the act of eating meat offered to idols is to be regarded as sinful. For others, however, it would not be a sin (1 Cor. 8:4-13). This diversity at the level of specific moral rules is seen throughout Scripture: in contrasting forms of piety, in different approaches to family life, in differing approaches to church discipline, etc. Rather than supplying a universal set of abstract moral rules which is equally binding upon all people in all cultures, the Bible challenges all people to live out—often in a variety of ways—the particular life which is theirs in Christ.

Of course, not all the moral rules of Scripture vary from one culture to the next. Nevertheless, some rules do vary, and other rules are interpreted differently in different places within Scripture. The fact that these kinds of variations occur poses an important question as one attempts to determine which rules in Scripture apply and how they should apply. Scripture also supplies a way of answering that question. By disclosing the character of God and the dynamics of life before God, Scripture provides enduring *identity*. That identity takes shape in response to the faithful character of God. It unfolds in every context where people gather to respond to God's mercy in covenantal loyalty. It defines who people are as Christians in the most basic way. It consists of the set of perspectives, dispositions, intentions, values and principles that grow out of a person's life before God. Out of this identity, and informed by the Holy Spirit's leading, Christians discover how to glorify God in their historical and cultural settings, and how Scripture should address that setting.

Christian identity as spoken of here is not the introspective and individualistic notion of "identity" which is pervasive in North American culture. It is more corporate than individual, more cultural than psychological. It is not discovered through introspection of the isolated individual, but rather passed on within the Christian community through worship, instruction, and example. It is less a matter of what rules we are to follow than of what kind of people we ought to be in light of the gospel. Out of this sense of identity, and informed by the leading of the Holy Spirit, Christians acquire the moral discernment which enables them to discover how it is they may glorify God in their distinctive historical and cultural setting.

This Christian identity grows from our covenantal life before God; it is conformed to the image of Christ; it is based upon the transforming power of the Spirit and issues in a life of faith, hope, and love. It is an identity that is profoundly moral in character. Yet Christian moral identity does not flow directly from moral rules, but rather from our life in Christ, lived out before God in the power of the Spirit. Paul writes, "if you are led by the Spirit, you are not subject to the law" (Gal. 5:18).

Reformed theology has always distinguished between the law as a requirement and the law as a guide for grateful living. According to John Calvin, the "third use" of the law, as a guide for grateful living, "finds its place among believers in whose hearts the Spirit of God already lives and reigns."[2] It is the presence of the Spirit, creating and confirming our identity as God's people, which determines "the proper use of the law."[2] This principle lies at the heart of the Bible's notion of the freedom of the redeemed Christian. Galatians 5:1 states, "For freedom Christ has set us free. Stand firm, therefore, and do not submit again to a yoke of slavery." Similarly, Colossians 2:20 states, "If with Christ you died to the elemental spirits of the universe, why do you live as if you still belonged to the world? Why do you submit to regulations?"

As Christians, people find themselves called to obey many specific moral rules found in Scripture. It is important, however, to understand the logic of such obedience. One does not obey a moral directive simply because it is found in Scripture; indeed, there are many directives in Scripture that do not apply to Christians for a variety of legitimate reasons. For instance, some aspects of ritual law are superseded in Christ, while other directives are specific to one culture, such as the Old Testament requirement that one may not wear wool and linen woven together (Deut. 22:11) or the New Testament injunction to avoid the braiding of hair (1 Tim. 2:9).

When a person does apply moral rules from Scripture directly to his or her life, it is because of a belief that the moral rules appropriately express one's moral identity in Christ. This identity is informed by Scripture and shaped by one's encounter with the God revealed in Scripture. Christians do not live by the letter; all moral responses flow from a living response to the God revealed in Scripture. Hence, the moral rules in Scripture

2   *Institutes,* 2.7.12.

inform one's life in Christ, but they do not by themselves constitute one's life in Christ.

Therefore, in the making of concrete and specific moral decisions, some scriptural rules function authoritatively, but as an indirect source. Scripture as a whole is a direct source for a Christian's knowledge of God, for the revelation of all a person must know for the glory of God and for salvation. Scripture is a direct source for the formation of Christian identity and world view. Out of this Christian identity and world view, then, one makes specific moral decisions, guided by the example of moral judgments found in Scripture. At the same time, however, a believer neither restricts his or her moral decisions to a repetition of specific moral mandates found in Scripture (for that would leave the believer without guidance in many areas of our modern world), nor does one feel bound to every moral directive of Scripture (for that would deny the diversity and historical character of the moral codes found in Scripture itself).

It is important to emphasize that even where one may not feel obligated to obey particular moral directives of Scripture, those moral directives are still important for the shaping of Christian identity in a more general way. For example, the law of "levirate marriage" (Deut. 25:5-10) required the brother of a man who died without an heir to marry the widow and raise up a son for the deceased man. Christians today do not regard this rule as directly binding on them. Nonetheless, they may recognize in it the pattern of covenantal faithfulness which they are called upon to emulate in their own circumstances. A somewhat different example is evident in the commandment to leave forgotten sheaves in the field at harvest time, so that the orphans and widows may be provided for (Deut. 24:19-22). In today's context, this injunction hardly requires that modern farmers leave behind a row of corn which was missed by the tractor; yet the commandment still challenges Christians to find creative ways to share their plenty with those in need, in ways which give dignity to the needy.

Moral Rules and Ethical Principles

Another way of clarifying a Reformed use of Scripture is to distinguish between moral rules and ethical principles. Moral rules focus upon specific behaviors, whereas ethical principles focus upon the values and dispositions which are expressed by those rules. Moral rules answer the question, "What must I do?" Ethical principles answer the question,

"What kind of person must I be?" Scripture is authoritative in the formulation of ethical principles—principles which flow out of the Christian identity and knowledge of God disclosed in Scripture. At the level of specific moral rules, however, the authority of Scripture is not always prescriptive; sometimes it is exemplary or illustrative.

The distinction between ethical principles and moral rules does not mean Christian moral judgment is either arbitrary or relativistic. The ethical principles of Scripture, expressing the character of God and the identity of God's people, call all people to love, to holiness, to fidelity, to a concern for building up the community of believers, to advocacy for the oppressed, and to a deep compassion. Likewise they consistently condemn lying, cheating, stealing, murder, adultery, blasphemy, and the like. The ethical principles of Scripture reveal a pattern of life in which human beings can flourish; we would expect no less from the God revealed there, who loves us and longs for our flourishing. Hence, in the vast majority of human situations, these principles will translate directly into binding moral rules.

Nor is an appeal to ethical principles a way of evading obedience in concrete human situations. When Jesus in the Sermon on the Mount goes beyond the specific moral stipulations of the law (e.g., do not kill, do not commit adultery) to a more encompassing interpretation (e.g., be a reconciler, be chaste in your attitudes), he is moving the discussion to the arena of ethical principles, and at the same time intensifying the scope and impact of those principles upon the lives of people (Matt. 5:17-48). The challenge to obedience is not lessened through an appeal to ethical principles, but rather intensified.

However, some still may wonder: doesn't the appeal to ethical principles in Scripture rather than moral rules make moral decision-making more complicated and subjective? Three responses may be helpful: First, the focus in this paper is on difficult moral decision-making where there is conflict or disagreement, even among Christians. In such contexts, it is particularly important not merely to quote "proof-texts," but to make decisions on the basis of broad ethical principles in Scripture. Secondly, a pastoral perspective suggests people tend to move from decisions based on moral rules to those based on ethical principles as they mature in the Christian life. For younger children and newer Christians, the simplicity of moral rules may be helpful. As one grows, however, one's ability to make complex moral decisions based on principles also grows. Finally, the appeal to ethical principles will not be overly subjective so long as people commit themselves to a thorough encounter with Scripture and hold themselves accountable to one another in their decision-making.

By considering the ethical principles which underlie moral rules, people are enabled to determine how moral rules should be expressed and lived out differently in diverse cultural contexts. It is only by appealing to ethical principles, for example, that one can determine if the Bible has any relevance to the complex moral questions raised by modern technology, since these problems are nowhere specifically addressed in Scripture. Likewise, it is an appeal to broader ethical principles that enables Christians to recognize that in this cultural setting, polygamy or slavery would be morally wrong, regardless of whether they were sanctioned by Scripture during the time of Abraham.

An example from the New Testament may serve to clarify the point. When confronted with the question of the observance of special days in Romans 14:5, Paul casually writes, "Some judge one day to be better than another, while others judge all days to be alike. Let all be fully convinced in their own minds." When confronted with a similar problem in Galatia, the observance of "special days, and months, and seasons, and years" (Gal. 4:10), Paul condemns the practice categorically as an abandonment of Christian faith. In each specific situation, an ethical principle—that God is to be served freely and sincerely—had to be brought to bear in differing ways because of the different needs, circumstances, and dynamics of each community.

It is important to note that even appeals made to ethical principles in Scripture must never be abstracted from their larger context of Christian life before God, as if principles by themselves were sufficient to guide. This becomes clear when one encounters "boundary situations" in which ethical principles may actually come into conflict with each other, or in which one may be uncertain which principle to apply (such as wartime situations or times of dramatic cultural change). In all moral reasoning, and especially in such cases, it is neither principles nor rules alone which guide; these principles and rules must finally be addressed within the context of a deeply internalized sense of Christian identity shaped by a Christian community's ongoing encounter with Scripture.

Forming Christian Identity in the World

This sense of Christian identity that forms the ground and context for moral judgment is a dynamic reality which emerges within the context of growing, continuing, and developing traditions, built upon Scripture and embodied in the life of believing communities. All Christian communities have various customs, practices, and norms which are neither commanded nor forbidden by Scripture, but which form an important part of the moral framework of that community. One thinks, for example, of the various ways in which couples in different cultures move toward marriage, and of the various customs and practices which are part of that movement. Such practices must not be automatically rejected as nonbiblical, nor should their legitimacy be assumed without question. Rather, they must be considered as part of the total fabric of Christian identity which takes shape in a given context. Although all such confessions and traditions must finally stand under the authority of Scripture, each may help to clarify the meaning of Christian identity, and therefore of Christian moral discernment, within particular historical or cultural contexts.

In addition to the resources which the larger Christian community provides in guiding moral decisions, one should also note the importance of spirituality in shaping Christian identity and understanding of Scripture. Only lives characterized by prayer, worship, spiritual disciplines, the sacraments, and other means of grace can reliably discern the Word of God in Scripture. Even the most dutiful and conscientious appeals to Scripture in the making of moral decisions will become arid and stale if they are not enlivened by a living Christian identity which is informed by the "practice of the presence of God."

The human sciences—psychology, sociology, anthropology, and the like—may also be of assistance in clarifying the sense of Christian identity which is the context and ground of moral discernment. For example, in its desire to pursue economic justice, the church may benefit from various forms of economic analysis in order to help it to understand the implications and impacts of various moral stances it may take. Cultural anthropology may help the church to understand the role of specific elements of a moral code within the overall context of a given culture. Psychology may deepen understanding of the factors conditioning human dispositions and behaviors. Such approaches may help to clarify human interactions in a given setting. This growth in awareness can enable one to be more precise, informed, and focused in the attempt to respond to God's self-disclosure in every dimension of the Christian's life. Yet human knowledge can never become a substitute for Christian identity based on Scripture. Its role is always to clarify that identity and the situation in which that identity is expressed.

The Task of Moral Discernment

Because the context of moral decision-making is a communal life lived before God in response to God's self-revelation in Scripture, moral decisions are inherently communal decisions. The ethical principles derived from Scripture apply across a wide range of historical or cultural settings. However, the moral discernment required to apply those principles to specific cases emerges "from the ground up," out of a specific social and cultural context. The ones best qualified to make concrete moral judgments for a community are the mature and tested members of that community. The early Christian practice of choosing and installing office-bearers within particular congregations, which has been preserved in Reformed polity, reflects this same principle. This practice assumes the gifts or charisms, including that of discernment, are to be recognized by the community within which they are exercised. It follows, then, that the making of moral judgments needs to be done within the context in which such decisions will be lived out.

Within Christian communities whose identities are shaped by Scripture and the Christian tradition, the Holy Spirit often gives particular gifts of insight and discernment to certain members. Such people have a deeply internalized sense of Christian identity. This equips them to guide the community in discerning how it should respond when facing especially complex or difficult moral dilemmas and choices. These people are able to bring from Scripture a word from God which illumines their situation, and to bring from their situation elements which illumine the Scripture, thereby guiding the community in hearing and responding to the Word.

This becomes clear in the life of the early church as described in the New Testament. The apostle Peter is equipped to guide the community toward the inclusion of Gentiles (Acts 10) and to sort out the resulting tensions between Jewish and Gentile believers (Acts 15:6-11). One thinks of Barnabas, who takes the risk of identifying with the newly converted

Saul of Tarsus, introducing him to the apostles, and protecting him from harm (Acts 9:27). Later Paul takes a similar risky leadership role, encouraging Philemon to receive back Onesimus, not as a slave, but as a brother in Christ (Philem. 16).

Christian identity emerges not only from within communities, but also from relationships among believing communities. Although the moral context of each Christian community will have distinctive elements, there is much that they will share with other parts of the same denomination and with the Christian church as a whole. The moral discernment of particular Christian communities is enhanced and corrected when Christians engage in a common life and dialogue with members of other Christian communities, testing their own discernment of ethical principles and moral rules against the discernment embodied in other communities. These attempts at common life and dialogue must always be characterized both by a respect for differences and by a desire for mutual learning.

The so-called "Jerusalem council" described in Acts 15 is an especially apt example. Here the moral judgments of specific communities (the church of Antioch and the church of Jerusalem) were tested against the backdrop of a larger collective wisdom. In the course of the deliberations, passages from the Scriptures were brought to bear on the question of Gentile inclusion in the church, in a way that produced a revolutionary new insight into God's purposes for the people of God.

The Word of God comes in both affirmation and judgment to all human communities, including Christian communities. Occasionally the moral framework and Christian identity of a community is corrupt, deficient, or distorted. Not every community which claims a Christian identity makes sound moral judgments! Therefore the church must continually be open to reforming its moral rules through a deeper encounter with the Word of God. This may at times result in dramatic shifts in the pattern of moral decisions made by a community. For example, in the time of the Reformation, the church in Europe protested against corruption in the church and called for a deep transformation of moral perspective. In the middle of the nineteenth century, the church in America began to struggle in a deeper way with the problem of slavery. In this century, the church in South Africa has had to grapple with the challenge of apartheid.

There may also be situations within the life of a community in which Christians are unable to come to agreement, at least in the short run, on what specific moral judgments constitute the most appropriate way to live out the community's life before God. In such circumstances, the community should test the different options to determine whether they do indeed flow out of a biblically informed sense of Christian identity; they should consult with other believers of the past and present; they should look for signs that a particular option results in the deepening of spiritual life; and they should continue to pray and reflect. In such cases, neither abrupt anathemas nor easy tolerance are called for, but rather love, patience, and honest confrontation.

Conclusion

The purpose of this study has been to provide principles and guidelines for the use of Scripture in the making of ethical decisions in today's complex world. This is not as simple as it might first appear. The Bible provides many laws, rules, and specific exhortations to live the Christian life, but even within Scripture there are contrasting viewpoints and considerable openness and flexibility. There is also the problem of deciding which laws and requirements—particularly in the Old Testament, but also in the New—still apply to Christians today. Moreover, new situations arise with technological and cultural changes that are not addressed by any specific biblical commandments or injunctions.

This is why it is important to discern within the Bible broad principles that can guide us in our decision-making. It is also important to bear in mind that God's will as expressed in various directives and commandments cannot be encapsulated in a set of commandments. The law is given within the context of a covenant of grace. This colors and influences one's whole understanding of the law and points to Christ, the one in whom the law is both completed and fulfilled (Rom. 10:4). In Christ one sees the incarnate expression of God's love and grace. Ultimately, one's moral vision is guided by Christ and informed by the guidance of the Spirit, not only as an individual, but above all as a participant in a Christian community.

Living the Christian life is not first of all a matter of following certain rules or commandments, but rather of developing a Christian identity which is molded by a life lived in Christ before God, in the context and with the help of the Christian community, the church. To live before God in love and holiness is to live in a way which reflects the will of God as revealed in Jesus Christ, "the way, the truth, and the life" (John 14:6). The goal of the Christian life, therefore is to "do justice, and to love kindness, and to walk humbly with your God" (Mic. 6:8) as we have the image of the true human, Jesus Christ, restored in us.

This report therefore ends where it also began, with the reality and presence of God, from whom, through whom, and to whom are all things (see Rom. 11:36). God's truth, mercy, and righteousness forms the basis of all our moral judgments. God's saving purpose is the goal toward which all our moral efforts reach. The more focused we are upon reading Scripture as the book which leads us to God and which forms Christ in us, the more clearly we will also be able to discern who we are to be and what we are to do.

Select Bibliography of Recent Titles

This bibliography is not a comprehensive listing, nor does it represent any kind of endorsement on behalf of the Commission on Theology. The commission provides it merely to inform those who may wish to do further study on this topic.

Birch, Bruce C., and Rasmussen, Larry L. *Bible and Ethics in the Christian Life*. Minneapolis: Augsburg, 1976.

Chilton, Bruce, and McDonald, J.I.H. *Jesus and the Ethics of the Kingdom*. Grand Rapids: Eerdmans, 1987.

Fowl, Stephen E., and Jones, L. Gregory. *Reading in Communion: Scripture and Ethics in Christian Life*. Grand Rapids: Eerdmans, 1991.

Goldsmith, Dale. *New Testament Ethics: An Introduction*. Elgin, IL: Brethren Press, 1988.

Hesselink, I. John. *Calvin's Concept of the Law*. Alison Park, PA: Pickwick Publications, 1992.

Jones, L. Gregory. *Transformed Judgment: Toward a Trinitarian Account of the Moral Life*. Notre Dame, IN: University of Notre Dame Press, 1990.

Lohse, Eduard. *Theological Ethics of the New Testament*. Tr. by M. Eugene Boring. Minneapolis: Fortress, 1991.

Mouw, Richard J. *The God Who Commands*. Notre Dame, IN: University of Notre Dame Press, 1990.

Nelson, Paul. *Narrative and Morality: A Theological Inquiry*. University Park, PA: The Pennsylvania State University Press, 1987.

Ogletree, Thomas W. *The Use of the Bible in Christian Ethics*. Philadelphia: Fortress, 1983.

Sampley, J. Paul. *Walking Between the Times: Paul's Moral Reasoning*. Minneapolis: Fortress, 1991.

Schrage, Wolfgang. *The Ethics of the New Testament*. Philadelphia: Fortress, 1988.

Verhey, Alan. *The Great Reversal: Ethics and the New Testament*. Grand Rapids: Eerdmans, 1984.

2
Church and Faith

Introduction

The Challenge of Liberation Theology

The General Synod of 1986 received the draft of a study of liberation theology initiated within the Theological Commission itself. This current understanding of the presence of the power of God in our world, together with its study guide, was presented to the church for study. The synod voted to distribute both paper and study guide to consistories and classes, and to request their written responses by the following June. To the General Synod of 1988 the commission brought its final study, revised in the light of the church's response.

Because liberation theologians call the church to rediscover neglected biblical motifs, a list of biblical texts is prefixed to the paper. Liberation theology's central claim that "God is on the side of the poor and oppressed" confronts the church with a challenge to sweeping and fundamental change. Fearsome as this revolution is, Reformed Christians would seem impelled by their very identity to take the challenge seriously. The paper's purpose, therefore, is not to offer a critique of liberation theology, but rather to ask what the Reformed Church can learn from it.

To reach the heart of the matter necessitates a discussion of the mixing of religion and politics that is grounded in the distinctive view of the biblical God revealed in the Exodus encounter of that God with Pharaoh. This leads to the suggestion that traditional, orthodox Christianity has seriously misunderstood the nature of God. The concluding section explores in detail the disturbing possibility that orthodox Christianity has the capacity of transforming theology into idolatry and ideology. Thus, as the paper progresses, it becomes increasingly clear that the most fundamental question raised by liberation theology is: Who do we really think God is?

The General Synod chose not to adopt the commission's recommendation to "accept" the study. Instead, it voted to distribute it for information only, calling attention to the paper's concluding suggestion and its accompanying study guide.

Confessing the Nicene Creed Today

To the General Synod of 1989, the Commission on History recommended that the Reformed Church in America rectify a longstanding historical error concerning the sixth-century insertion of the *filioque* (and the Son) clause into the Nicene Creed by confessing that creed in the form adopted in the Council of Constantinople in A.D. 381. The synod referred this recommendation to the Commission on Theology for study and report to the General Synod of 1990. In 1990, however, the commission promised their report in 1991. This brief 1991 paper set forth the issues involved, the rationale for a decision, and the conclusion that the Nicene Creed should be preserved in the form that the fourth-century church gave it. The 1991 General Synod agreed and adopted the commission's recommendation to that end.

The Nicene Creed and the Procession of the Spirit

Accompanying the 1991 brief piece, "Confessing the Nicene Creed Today," was a full study of the issue complete with biblical and historical details. The paper begins by contrasting the role of the Nicene Creed in the Reformed Church in America with its role in the Eastern Orthodox and Roman Catholic churches. In the former, acceptance of the Nicene Creed is required at ordination (along with the other five confessional standards), but ministers do not make much use of it thereafter. In the latter, however, the early creeds define the conditions of salvation and admittance to the Lord's Table. Therefore, the difference in wording between the Eastern and Western versions of the Nicene Creed is a matter of utmost importance.

Once the question of which form the Reformed Church should use to confess the Nicene Creed is set in the historical and theological context of the church catholic, a series of issues is involved. Thus, the paper responds in turn to (1) whether the procession of the Spirit in the creed is temporal or eternal; (2) what Scripture teaches about the procession of the Spirit; (3) what theological issues are involved (providing an historical/ theological survey from the fourth-century fathers to Karl Barth and George Hendry); and (4) whether the *filioque* should be bracketed or footnoted.

The study concludes that pending the decision of some future ecumenical council called to deal with such matters of faith and practice in a comprehensive fashion, the Reformed Church should bracket the *filioque* and add an explanatory footnote. The synod affirmed this conclusion and voted to make the two commission papers available to Reformed Church pastors and congregations upon request.

Confirmation and the Reformed Church

In 1990, the General Synod, after having referred a proposed liturgy for the "confirmation of baptismal vows" back to the Commission on Christian Worship for further study and review, instructed the Commission on Theology to study, clarify, and define "confirmation" as both a concept and as Reformed Church in America congregations practice it; to pay particular attention to the relationship of confirmation to baptism, to membership in the body of Christ and in a congregation; and to report their findings to the 1992 General Synod (*MGS,* 1990:212).

After defining "confirmation" as inclusively as possible, the paper traces three stages in the development of its practice in the Reformed Church from 1906 to 1990. Thus, although confirmation officially came into practice in 1991, some Reformed Church congregations have been practicing it unofficially for a long time. A history of confirmation in the Church Catholic reveals that the earliest attestation of the ceremony which came to bear that name dates from the end of the second century. Eventually confirmation became one of the seven sacraments of the

Roman Catholic Church. It was thus among the five Roman sacraments rejected by the Reformers. In the Reformed tradition, "profession of faith" came to replace confirmation. The continuing interest in confirmation among Reformed churches is put down to the entrance into the Reformed Church in America of German evangelical congregations, and to the influence of "liturgal renewal" and American revivalism. The paper concludes with eight theological benchmarks offered to guide the Reformed Church away from the supplementary rite of initiation called "confirmation."

The synod voted to make the paper available through the Reformed Church Distribution Center to encourage individuals, consistories, regional synods, and racial/ethnic councils of the Reformed Church in America to study the issue of confirmation and communicate their findings to the commission by January 1, 1994. The Office for Christian Education and Youth Ministries was also requested to consider the conclusions and implications of the paper in the discharge of its educational task. By 1993, the commission had began to receive responses, and commission members had met with various groups to discuss the issues raised in the paper. The commission anticipated the submission of recommendations regarding confirmation to a future General Synod. A year later responses were still being gathered.

Book of Church Order Conscience Clauses

The 1996 General Synod voted "to instruct the Commission on Theology, in consultation with the Commission for Women, to study the *Book of Church Order* (BCO) conscience clauses...in the light of Reformed theology, with report of their findings, with recommendations, to the 1997 General Synod" (*MGS,* 1996:313, R-11).

In 1997, the commission reported finding confusion in the Reformed Church in America surrounding the original intention of the "conscience clauses," and some inconsistency in their application. Some applications of the clauses may have violated their original intent, and some appeals to them may have violated other articles of the *Book of Church Order.* Four basic areas of concern were identified in this preliminary study (*MGS,* 1997:398).

The commission's final report was made to the 1998 General Synod. It offered an analysis of the conscience clauses and a discussion of three deeper theological issues they raise. Their analysis revealed that there is a Reformed understanding of conscience in the clauses; that they rightly limit the nature and scope of objection; that they assume, but fail to provide, a process for determining whether an objector's conscience has been biblically informed; and that their close tie to a particular moment in Reformed Church history renders them problematic for the denomination today. Theologically, the Reformed Church needs to face the questions of whether or not the conscience clauses undermine the historic, Reformed understanding of Christ's delegated authority and its respect for office holders functioning in the name of Christ; of how, as a denomination, the Reformed Church in America handles dissent; and of whether the historical particularity of the clauses is inconsistent with the spirit of the *Book of Church Order.*

The commission's recommendation that the General Synod request the Commission on Church Order to clarify if and how the understanding of the authority of office holders implicit in the conscience clauses (*BCO,* chap. 1, part 1, art. 5, sec. 2h; chap. 1, part 2, art. 13, sec. 7; and chap. 1, part 2, art. 13, sec. 14) is consistent with the understanding of office holders in the Preamble of the *Book of Church Order* was not adopted. However, the synod did adopt its recommendation to request the Commission on Church Order to formulate a more general process of dissent for inclusion in the *Book of Church Order.*

"The Crucified One Is Lord": Confessing the Uniqueness of Christ in a Pluralistic Society

The 1996 General Synod directed the Commission on Theology to prepare a study on "Christian Witness to the Uniqueness of Christ among People of Other Faiths" (*MGS,* 1996:403, R-3). In response, the commission presented the paper, "'The Crucified One Is Lord': Confessing the Uniqueness of Christ in a Pluralistic Society." The synod directed that this paper be sent to the congregations, to the lower judicatories, and to the commissions, agencies, and institutions of the Reformed Church in America for provisional use for instruction and study, with a request for response to the commission. After gathering and discussing the numerous responses, the commission revised the paper for presentation to the General Synod of 2000.

As revised, the paper addresses in detail three basic concerns: What do we believe about Jesus Christ? How do we interpret and live out these beliefs in a pluralistic world? How are we to understand the implications of these beliefs for the adherents of other religions? Regarding the first concern, the paper not only affirms that "Jesus is Lord," but explains what that most basic of Christian confessions means. In addressing the second concern, it seeks to lay to rest contemporary fears about the use and abuse of authority by emphasizing that in the Bible authority is an affirmation of divine grace, and that this gracious authority never expresses itself in domination, but rather in service. With regard to the third concern, the paper maintains that Christian faith is incompatible with a general affirmation of all religions because of a fundamental difference in understanding what religion is: For Christians, it is not our quest for God, but our response to God's quest for us in Christ. Thus, the church's mandate is to be the agents through which God extends his salvation to the world through witness to Jesus Christ in word and deed, while confessing with humility that it does not know the limits of God's grace. The synod voted to approve the paper and to distribute it to congregations, classes, regional synods, agencies, and institutions of the Reformed Church in America for study and use in the church, and to instruct the Commission on Theology to prepare a brief study guide that would attend to some continuing concerns raised by the paper.

The Papers

1
The Challenge of Liberation Theology

Like the Reformers, the liberation theologians call us to rediscover biblical motifs that have been neglected by the church in one way or another. The following texts are of special importance for understanding liberation theology and this essay. It is suggested that they be read in conjunction with this paper. The list is intended to be illustrative and not exhaustive.

Old Testament	New Testament
Exodus 1:1-3:10	Matthew 25:31-46
Leviticus 25	Luke 1:46-55
Deuteronomy 8:1-18	4:16-30
1 Kings 21	6:20-26
Psalm 82	7:18-23
Isaiah 1:10-23	16:19-31
3:14-15	18:18-27
10:1-4	Corinthians 8-9
58:3-12	James 5:1-6
Jeremiah 22:13-17	Revelation 17-18
Amos 2:6-8	
5:21-6:7	

Introduction

"God is on the side of the poor and oppressed." This is the central claim of liberation theology. Like Luther's "justification by faith alone," it is reverberating throughout the church and shaking the foundations. As the pivotal and pervasive theme of the many different Asian, African, Latin America, and even North American theologies which have come to bear the liberation label, this claim is seen by friend and foe alike to portend changes in the church as sweeping as those of the Protestant Reformation. Little in our theory and practice of the faith could remain unaffected by taking seriously this claim that the God of the Exodus and the Incarnation, of the Old Covenant and the New, has a special concern for the little people of the world, the marginalized, the excluded, in biblical language: the widows and orphans. Gustavo Gutierrez has said, "A radical revision of what the church has been and what it now is has become necessary," and Jose Miguez Bonino suggests that if liberation theology is on the right track, "it demands a total overhaul of Christian piety, ecclesiastical institutions, discipline, and theological reflection."[1]

We are naturally fearful in the face of change, especially sweeping and fundamental change. There is the danger that we shall lose something of real values, and there is the even more threatening danger that we shall be called to repentance. So the temptation is strong to escape this challenge. When we find that we can no longer ignore it, we seek to find sufficient fault with the liberation theologies to render them discredited. God does not take sides, we say. Or, with the Pharisees, we say that God is on the side of the righteous. Or, speaking more carefully, we say that God is on the side of repentant sinners. Or, we admit that the God of the Bible is on the side of the poor and oppressed, but insist that there is more to the story than that.

Of course there is more to the story than that, and there is truth in all of these responses (though the first two are quite dangerous). But if we use such responses to dismiss the challenge of liberation theology before we have listened to it carefully, humbly, and openly, we abuse the truth rather than serve it. For there are several powerful reasons why we should rather look this challenge straight in the face and take it very seriously.

In the first place, as Reformed Christians we are not permitted to find our security in the way things are, even in the church. Our only comfort in life and in death is to be found elsewhere.[2] Since we profess to be the church "reformed and reforming," we realize that reformation can never simply be a past event. Like our personal growth in Christ, the reformation of the church must be a process which continues until Christ returns and God's will is finally done on earth as it is in heaven.

1   Gustavo Gutierrez, *A Theology of Liberation: History, Politics and Salvation*, trans. Sister Caridad Inda and John Eagleson (Maryknoll: Orbis Books, 1973), 251, and Jose Miguez Bonino, *Doing Theology in a Revolutionary Situation* (Philadelphia: Fortress Press, 1975), xxiv. Cf. Juan Luis Segundo, S.J., *The Liberation of Theology*, trans. John Drury (Maryknoll: Orbis Books, 1976), 97.
2   The Heidelberg Catechism opens with this question and answer: What is your only comfort, in life and death? That I belong – body and soul, in life and in death – not to myself but to my faithful Savior, Jesus Christ...."

Beyond this general openness to ongoing reform in the church, there are three specific features of liberation theology which relate it directly to our Reformed identity:

1. It makes its appeal to the Bible, challenging all Christians to take another long, hard look at its message.
2. It expresses a worldly piety in the context of a sweeping social vision of liberty and justice.
3. It is one of two or three major current developments within the worldwide church of Jesus Christ.

As Christians who profess to take the authority of Scripture seriously, who have our roots in the worldly piety of John Calvin's own sweeping social vision, and who pride ourselves on our ecumenical participation in the worldwide church, we would seem to be impelled by our own identity to take this challenge seriously. The purpose of this paper, therefore, is not to offer a critique of liberation theology, but rather to ask what we can learn from it.

Liberation theology can be described as the systematic attempt to take seriously the claim of Jesus that his messiahship, his anointing, was "to preach good news to the poor...to set at liberty those who are oppressed" (Luke 4:18; cf. 7:18-23). Consequently its interpretation of the biblical story addresses itself primarily not to the questions of the *non-believer*, but rather to the needs of the *non-person*. When seeking to address the gospel to the marginal people of the world, "the poor in Third World countries, and...exploited groups in rich countries," the theological task becomes "how to proclaim to non-persons that God is personal, and that all human beings are truly sisters and brothers."[3] Of course, the least of Christ's sisters and brothers are not non-persons in the eyes of God, in whose image they are created. But they are treated as if they were non-persons by the kings and merchants of Babylon, the political and economic leaders of those kingdoms which are not the kingdom of God (Rev. 18, especially vv. 11-13). As a result, they become in one sense non-

---

3   Robert McAfee Brown, Gustavo Guitierrez, *Makers of Contemporary Theology* (Atlanta: John Knox Press, 1980), 45-46, and *Theology in a New Key: Responding to Liberation Themes* (Philadelphia: Westminster Press, 1978), 62-64.

persons, for the opportunities for their personhood to fulfill its God-given destiny are severely restricted.

At the same time these theologies address us, who are not numbered among "the wretched of the earth," inviting us to read the Bible and hear the gospel through the eyes and ears of the least of Christ's sisters and brothers.[4] It is an invitation to discover what Karl Barth has called a "strange new world within the Bible."[5] Because "the word of God is living and active" (Heb. 4:12), we, like the Reformers, can find the biblical message to be both strangely new and wonderfully liberating in our own time. This is why Barth has wisely reminded us that "no one can claim to have heard the gospel already."[6]

In this connection we do well to remember that during Jesus' earthly lifetime the strongest and ultimately fatal resistance to recognizing him as the Christ, the Son of the living God, came from devoutly religious people, not unlike ourselves, who were convinced that they had already heard God's word to them, that their task of listening and understanding was finished. Whatever did not fit into their tidy theology and habitual practice could safely be rejected as blasphemous and of the devil (Mark 2:1-7, Luke 3:22, John 10:31-39, Matt. 26:62-66). It was precisely the absolutes and the certitudes of popular biblical theology which made it both impossible for "the righteous" to recognize Jesus as the Christ and necessary to see him as a criminal threat.[7] With his parable of the Grand Inquisitor in *The Brothers Karamazov,* Dostoyevsky reminds us that the possibility of crucifying the Son of God afresh while sincerely professing to serve God's kingdom belongs to every age.

This study takes that danger seriously. That is why it opens with a plea for openness. On the positive side, the church in North America can be greatly enriched if we can learn to listen to our brothers and sisters in the Third World. We would be wonderfully renewed and revitalized if we

---

4 See Robert McAfee Brown, *Unexpected News: Reading the Bible with Third World Eyes* (Philadelphia: Westminster Press, 1984). The bibliography to this volume includes numerous resources for such reading. See especially *The Gospel in Solentiname,* 4 vols. Orbis Books, 1976-82, containing the transcripts of village Bible studies in Nicaragua.
5 Karl Barth, *The Word of God and the Word of Man,* trans. Douglas Horton (New York: Harper & Brothers, 1957), Ch. 2.
6 Karl Barth, *The Epistle to the Romans,* trans. Edwyn C. Hoskyns (New York: Oxford University Press, 1968), p. 34. Cf. *Church Dogmatics,* IV/3, ed. Bromiley and Torrence (Edinburgh: T & T Clark, 1961-62, 817-19.
7 Segundo, 77-81.

were widely and regularly exposed to preaching which incorporated what is best in liberation theology. For that reason, this study addresses itself primarily to those entrusted with the responsibility for preaching in the church: pastors, elders (who oversee the preaching ministry of the church), and our seminary professors and students (who together prepare for the future of the preaching ministry).

Toward this end of real listening and of learning to read the biblical message afresh, the present study will draw on both the Latin American and South African traditions of liberation theology. Latin America is its primary home and the focus of most discussion. But the inclusion of South Africa has real advantages. By noting the real and important differences between these two families of liberation theology, we will be better enabled to perceive the common ground on which they meet above their differences and thus avoid treating as primary those issues which are secondary.

Liberation theologies are contextual theologies and need to be read in light of the histories and social situations in which they arise. The colonial histories of Latin America and South Africa are quite different, and racism has come to play a far more dominant role in the poverty and oppression of the latter than of the former. The setting in Latin America is predominantly Roman Catholic, while the setting in South Africa is primarily Protestant, with our own Dutch Reformed tradition the most important Protestant presence. The Latin American theologies, while critical of Marx's overall worldview, often affirm the value of Marxist analyses of poverty and oppression and often describe the alternative they seek as some form of socialism; these elements are not typical in South Africa. Until recently, one of the most important differences has been that Latin American theologies have been less reluctant than South African theologies to accept violence as a means of last resort in the struggle for liberation. Perhaps this is due to the lingering influence of Mahatma Gandhi, who gave birth to non-violent resistance in South Africa. But as the situation in South Africa has worsened, this difference has lessened. The acceptance by many liberation theologies of violent revolution as a last resort against violent oppression has been offensive to many North American Christians. Without pretending to address the issue substantively, we note how odd it is for American Christians who see the Fourth of July as a day of national celebration rather than of national repentance to insist that the Third World find its way to freedom nonviolently. Surely *if* there is ever justification for violent revolution, the contexts in which liberation theologies are spawned provide vastly stronger justification than the American colonists ever experienced under George III.

Even within Latin America or South Africa, liberation theology has no single, monolithic meaning, and it is no accident that we have begun to speak of liberation theologies. In spite of important differences, however, there are fundamental agreements that make it also possible to speak of liberation theology. And it is in the convergence of liberation theologies that we must look for the real heart of liberation theology.

The first step toward discovering the heart of the matter is the realization that liberation theology is political theology. Hence, the next section of this paper is "The Mixing of Religion and Politics." The second step is understanding this "mixing" to be grounded in the distinctive view of the biblical God expounded in the section entitled, "Who Is the God of the Bible? Ask the Pharaoh!" This leads to the suggestion that traditional, orthodox Christianity has seriously misunderstood the nature of God, and thus to the section entitled, "The Capacity of Orthodoxy for Idolatry and Ideology." The concluding section, "Three Paths by Which Theology Becomes Idolatry and Ideology," explores this disturbing possibility in more detail. It becomes increasingly clear as the paper progresses that the most fundamental question raised by liberation theology is the question: Who do we really think God is?

The Mixing of Religion and Politics

Our search for the core of liberation theology begins when we notice a very conspicuous feature shared by these traditions. They are offensively political. From Jesus' perspective this offense is to be expected. When John the Baptist sent a delegation to find out if Jesus was indeed the long-awaited Messiah, Jesus gave an extraordinarily this-worldly (materialistic, horizontal) answer. "Go and tell John what you have seen and heard: the blind receive their sight, the lame walk, lepers are cleansed, and the deaf hear, the dead are raised up, the poor have good news preached to them." There is nothing offensive about these references to the blind, the lame, the lepers, the deaf, and even the dead. But that the poor have good news preached to them is another matter, and no doubt this is why Jesus went on immediately to say, "And blessed is he who takes no offense at me" (Luke 7:18-23).

That good news to the poor is a decisive hallmark of Jesus as the Christ will be especially offensive if this is understood as Mary understands the messianic fulfillment of the covenant promises in her *Magnificat:*

> You [the Lord, God my Savior] have shown strength with your
>   arm,
>   scattered the proud in their conceit.
> You have brought down rulers from their rank,
>   and lifted up the lowly.
> The hungry you have filled with good things,
>   the rich you have sent empty away. (Luke 1:51-53)

Perhaps Jesus had learned this interpretation of Hannah's song (1 Sam. 2:1-10) from Mary herself. Was it she who pointed out to him, for example in Psalms 9-10, the linkage between pride and power and wealth and, most importantly, that the victims of this unholy trinity can expect God to come to their aid? In any case the gospel story prepares us to find that the social meaning of the kingdom will offend the arrogance of power and wealth.

So it is not surprising that when a Roman Catholic archbishop in Brazil, Dom Helder Camara, and an Anglican bishop in South Africa, Nobel Peace Prize winner Desmond Tutu, actively and articulately side with the poor and oppressed, the Pharaohs, the Herods, and the chief priests of the world are displeased. When these bishops (along with many other pastors) find they cannot announce the good news of the kingdom without denouncing the political, economic, and ideological systems which sustain misery in their parishes, the beneficiaries of those systems are offended.8 Generalities about justice and human dignity would probably be tolerated but these bishops get specific and call these systems by their names. They identify the political systems which oppress their people both as military dictatorships and as the "democracies" which exclude the masses from effective participation, and then rely on military and police violence, including torture, to repress dissent. They identify the

---

8 On the link between *announcing* the Kingdom and *denouncing* the principalities and powers, see Gutierrez, 233-34 and 268-69.

economic systems which sustain poverty in northeastern Brazil and in the townships and "homelands" of South Africa as capitalism, the neocolonial impact of multinational corporations, and the institutional frameworks of international trade and banking. They identify the ideological systems which legitimate these structures as anticommunism, the theory of development, the idea of the national security state, and the Christian theology in unholy alliance with these other systems.[9]

At this point there is a loud protest against the mixing of religion and politics. For example, when the South African Council of Churches (SACC) issued its *Message to the People of South Africa* in 1968, strongly denouncing apartheid and the theological legitimation of it, Prime Minister Vorster warned those "who wish to disrupt the order in South Africa under the cloak of religion" that they should not try to do what Martin Luther King did in America (note the acknowledged absence of any threat of violence) but should rather "cut it out, cut it out immediately for the cloak you carry will not protect you if you try to do this in South Africa." In an open letter to SACC leaders he wrote, "It is your right, of course, to demean your pulpits into becoming political platforms to attack the Government and the National Party.... I again want to make a serious appeal to you to return to the essence of your preaching and to proclaim to your congregations the Word of God and the Gospel of Christ."[10]

We learn a great deal about liberation theology by listening to its response to this entirely typical criticism. Each of the three following replies will take us closer to its center. The first response is an *ad hominem* one. It points out the double standard employed by those who raise this objection. Bishop Tutu writes, "A familiar remark which has become almost a parrot cry is 'Don't mix religion with politics!' It is a remark which is made not because a politician in his election campaign introduces a moral or religious element. No, we almost always hear it when a particular political, social, or economic fact of life is criticized as being inconsistent with the Gospel of Jesus Christ.... If the Church demonstrates a concern for the victims of...neglect or exploitation...then the Church

9   A particularly good example of this kind of specificity is Dom Helder Camara, *Revolution through Peace,* trans. Amparo McLean (New York: Harper & Row, 1971).
10 Quoted in John W. De Gruchy, *The Church Struggle in South Africa* (Grand Rapids: Eerdmans, 1979), 118-19.

will be accused of meddling in affairs it knows very little about. This kind of criticism will reach crescendo proportions if the Church not merely provides an ameliorative ambulance service, but aims to expose the root causes; if it becomes radical (which refers to the roots of the matter), then it will arouse the wrath of those who benefit from the particular inequitable status quo....If the South African Council of Churches were to say now that it thought apartheid was not so bad, I am as certain as anything that we would not be finding ourselves where we are today. Why is it not being political for a religious body or a religious leader to praise a social political dispensation?"[11]

In the same vein Mexican bishops expose the by no means disinterested nature of efforts to preserve the "purity" and "dignity" of religious activity uncontaminated by "political" involvement. "Frequently this false zeal veils the desire to impose a law of silence when the real need is to lend a voice to those who suffer injustice and to develop the social and political responsibility of the people of God."[12] Allan Boesak unites Tutu's point about the double standard with the bishop's point about its political function in a letter to the South African minister of justice. "The only conclusion that I can come to is that you do not really object in principle to the participation of the clergy in politics—as long as it happens on *your* terms and within the framework of *your* policy.... Or perhaps there are some who fear that should Christians in South Africa perform their duty in being more obedient to God than to humans, the idolized nature of this state will be exposed."[13]

The second response of liberation theology to the charge of meddling in politics instead of preaching the gospel can be called the situational response. It suggests that political neutrality can never be more than a hypocritical and self-deceptive pretense because it is, at least in situations with great discrepancies of power and wealth, impossible to achieve. The circumstances are so structured that choosing not to take sides is one way of taking sides.

---

[11] Desmond Tutu, *Hope and Suffering: Sermons and Speeches,* ed. John Webster (Grand Rapids: Eerdmans, 1984), 36-37, 170.
[12] Quoted in Gutierrez, 115
[13] Allan Boesak, *Black and Reformed: Apartheid, Liberation, and the Calvinist Tradition,* ed. Leonard Sweetman (Maryknoll: Orbis Books, 1984), 34-35.

When the United States State Department stated that it would not take sides in the struggle between black and white in South Africa, Bishop Tutu put the point most graphically. "Admirable impartiality, but how can you be impartial in a situation of injustice and oppression. To be impartial and not to take sides is indeed to have taken sides already. It is to have sided with the status quo. It is small comfort to a mouse, if an elephant is standing on his tail, to say, 'I am impartial.' In this instance, you are really supporting the elephant in its cruelty. How are you to remain impartial when the South African authorities evict helpless mothers and children and let them shiver in the winter rain, as even their flimsy plastic covers are destroyed?"[14]

Where white racism prevails, to be color-blind is to be pro-white. Moreover, it is to be morally blind. For to profess neutrality where it is not possible is to adopt a naïve "pseudo-innocence" which serves "to blind people so that they do not see the atrocities of the present."[15] And not only those of the present. The past also has a bearing on the possible neutrality of the church, as Archbishop Camara reminds us. "Let's get rid of the idea that the Church, after having committed so many atrocities, can now afford it sit back."[16] Every theology is political, and those theologies which insist upon remaining unaware of this are "always bound up with the status quo."[17] In at least one sense this is worse than openly siding with those in power. As Allan Boesak puts it, addressing Christians in the Netherlands (and us, too) directly, "Neutrality, as you know, is the most abominable demonstration of partiality because it means choosing the side of power and injustice without assuming responsibility for them. This you can no longer do. You, too, must make a choice."[18]

The *ad hominem* response and the situational response to the charge of mixing religion and politics are part of liberation theology's challenge to us, but they do not take us to the central issue. They challenge us not to apply a double standard on the issue, accepting the mixture of religion and politics when it sanctifies our own advantage but protesting against it

14 Tutu, 115. Cf. 39.
15 Boesak, 60. Also *Farewell to Innocence: A Socio-Ethical Study on Black Theology and Power* (Maryknoll: Orbis Books, 1977), 3-4.
16 Quoted in Miguez Bonino, 46.
17 Segundo, 74.
18 Boesak, *Black and Reformed,* 134. Cf. 75.

when our perceived interests seem threatened. They challenge us to careful self-examination lest our apparent impartiality or uninvolvement in social conflicts mask a silent complicity with injustice. But they do not get to the heart of the matter because the issue is a theological one and these are not theological replies.

After having himself made these first two responses, Segundo takes us on to the third and crucial response when he says, with reference to Jesus' "commandment of love and his countless examples and admonitions concerning it in the Gospels," that to "attempt to inculcate an apolitical love today" would be "to seriously distort the gospel message." [19] The ultimate issue is the very meaning of the gospel. When the privileged and powerful (such as Prime Minister Vorster) urge the church to quit meddling in politics and get back to preaching the gospel, the most basic reply is a question: Which gospel, the gospel of white supremacy, the gospel of the national security state, or the gospel that is good news to the poor?

Who is the God of the Bible? Ask the Pharaoh!

This question about the nature of the gospel is the second step toward discovering the heart of liberation theology. The deepest reason why it is offensively political is the conviction that God is revealed throughout the Bible to be on the side of the poor and oppressed. Gutierrez writes, "Within a society where social classes conflict, we are true to God when we side with the poor, the working classes, the despised races, the marginal cultures."[20]

Liberation theologians are fond of quoting Karl Barth on this point. "The human righteousness required by God and established on obedience—the righteousness which according to Amos 5:24 should pour down as a mighty stream—has necessarily the character of a vindication of right in favor of the threatened innocent, the oppressed poor, widows, orphans and aliens. For this reason, in the relations and events in the life of His People, God always takes His stand unconditionally and passionately on this side and on this side alone: against the lofty and

---

[19] Segundo, 71. For his version of the first two responses see 70 and 127 and 13, 74, and 130 respectively.

[20] Gustavo Gutierrez, "The Poor in the Church," in *The Poor and the Church*, ed. Norbert Greinacher and Alois Müller (New York: Seabury Press, 1977), 15.

on behalf of the lowly; against those who already enjoy right and privilege and on behalf of those who are denied it and deprived of it."[21]

Calvin expresses the bond between the God of the Bible and the victims of human injustice even more strongly in his commentary on Habakkuk 2:6. "Tyrants and their cruelty cannot be endured without great weariness and sorrow.... Hence almost the whole world sounds forth these words, How long, how long? When anyone disturbs the whole world by his ambition and avarice, or everywhere commits plunder, or oppresses miserable nations, when he distresses the innocent, all cry out, How long? And this cry, proceeding as it does from the feeling of nature and the dictate of justice, is at length heard by the Lord.... *And this feeling, is it not implanted in us by the Lord? It is then the same as though God heard himself, when he hears the cries and groanings of those who cannot bear injustice.* "[22] God does not merely side with the poor and oppressed, but identifies so fully with them that their cries express divine pain. Scripture teaches us to equate our treatment of them with our treatment of God (Prov. 14:31, 19:17; Matt. 25:31-46).

This aspect of who God is can probably best be understood through the experience of parents. The parent who insists that an older, stronger child stop bullying a younger, weaker one clearly takes the side of the one child against the other. But only the bully, while still in a pout over this, will interpret this parental intervention as meaning that the parent does not love them equally. This simple analogy helps us to see that God's "partiality" for the victims of injustice is fully compatible with the claim that all persons are equally objects of divine love. We must not allow the message of God's love for the whole world as expressed in John 3:16 to blind us to the sustained biblical witness that God has a special concern for the widows and orphans, the little people, the victims, the excluded, the powerless.

The story of the Exodus plays the role of paradigm for this understanding of who the God of the Bible is. The God who chooses a people through whom to fulfill covenantal blessing to all humanity chooses a rabble of slaves and delivers them from their political and economic oppression. In giving the covenantal law to the covenantal people, God identifies

---

21 Karl Barth, *Church Dogmatics,* II/1, ed. Bromily and Torrance (New York: Charles Scribner's Sons, 1957), 386.

22 Quoted twice in Boesak, *Black and Reformed,* 23-24 and 63-64. Boesak's italics.

himself very specifically, by proper name and resume. "I am Yahweh your God, who brought you out of the land of Egypt, out of the house of bondage" (Exod. 20:2).

Bishop Tutu expresses this importance of the Exodus as revealing who God is. Having seen the suffering of the people and having heard their cries, God promised to deliver them. But "He is not just a talking God. He is not like Bishop Tutu who was warned by Mr. le Grange, the minister of police, 'Bishop Tutu talks too much and he must be careful.' This God did not just talk—He acted. He showed Himself to be a doing God. Perhaps we might add another point about God—He takes sides. [Note the movement from past to present tense, from what God did to what God does.] He is not a neutral God. He took the side of the slaves, the oppressed, the victims. He is still the same even today. He sides with the poor, the hungry, the oppressed, and the victims of injustice."[23] Through many variations on this theme, liberation theology suggests that if we would know who the God of the Bible is, we should ask the Pharaoh.

The centrality of the Exodus motif in a theology arising among and addressed primarily to the least of Christ's sisters and brothers is due in part to its obvious relevance to their suffering. But it is not simply a matter of finding an attractive part of the Bible. Once we see the importance of this event for revealing the nature and character of God, it is easy to see its themes throughout the whole of Scripture. Just as the Commission on Christian Action's study, "Biblical Faith and Our Economic Life," traces God's concern for the poor and oppressed through six key texts from the Law, the Psalms, the Prophets, the Gospels, the Epistles, and the Apocalypse (*MGS,* 1984:51-68), so liberation theology finds the God of the Exodus throughout the biblical story and especially in the life and teaching of Jesus. It challenges us, personally and corporately, to abandon all pretenses of neutrality and to take our stand unambiguously with the poor and oppressed, a pattern of life without which we cannot legitimately claim to be disciples of Jesus.

Not surprisingly, given that Abraham Kuyper's theology has been used in South Africa to help legitimize apartheid, Allan Boesak makes this latter point in Kuyper's own words. "When the rich and poor stand opposed to each other, Jesus never takes his place with the wealthier, but always stands with the poorer. He is born in a stable; and while foxes have

23 Tutu, 51. Cf. 80.

holes and birds have nests, the Son of Man has nowhere to lay his head.... Both the Christ, and also just as much his disciples after him as the prophets before him, invariably took sides *against* those who were powerful and living in luxury, and *for* the suffering and oppressed."[24]

When we look for liberation motifs in the gospel story, Mary's new version of the Song of Hannah, Jesus' reference of Isaiah 61 to himself in Luke 4, his reply to John the Baptist's inquiring disciples (see above for all three), his teachings about wealth and power, and the political character of his confrontation with the Jewish authorities—all begin to make sense and gain importance.[25]

The challenge to learn to reread the Gospels begins to take on content. We are invited to reexamine the biblical story to discover how central to biblical revelation are the deeds and the teachings in which God sides with the poor and oppressed. The claim of liberation theology is simple but powerful. So fundamentally is the God of the Bible a God who wills justice and liberation for the poor and the powerless, that to worship and proclaim any god, by whatever name, for whom this character is not essential and central is to worship and proclaim a false god, an idol. This is not to say that social injustice is the only form of sin, that social transformation is the whole meaning of salvation, or that God has no other concerns than the liberation of the poor. But it is to say that this concern is so basic to the God revealed in the Bible, that the god we worship is an idol if this concern is lacking or merely peripheral. That God is on the side of the poor and oppressed is a matter of orthodoxy, not "merely" of ethics and politics.

The Capacity of Orthodoxy for Idolatry and Ideology

Juan Luis Segundo speaks for the whole tradition when he says that "formal orthodoxy is not a sufficient guarantee against idolatry." He notes that polytheism and idolatry used to be easier to identify, since

---

24 Quoted in Boesak, *Black and Reformed*, 91.
25 For a typical brief sketch of the liberation motif throughout the Bible see Boesak, *Black and Reformed*, 64-65, 71-74. For more sustained exegetical studies see J. Severino Croatto, *Exodus: A Hermeneutics of Freedom* and Jose Porfirio Miranda, *Marx and the Bible: A Critique of the Philosophy of Oppression*, both from Orbis. For the political character of Jesus; encounter with the leaders of his people, see Segundo, 111-12 and Gutierrez, *A Theology of Liberation,* 228-32 against the background of Richard J. Cassidy, *Jesus, Politics and Society: A Study of Luke's Gospel* and *Political Issues in Luke-Acts,* ed. Richard Cassidy and Philip Scharper, both from Orbis.

different gods went by different names. But now we use the one term, God, to express experiences and conceptions which are quite diverse, even diametrically opposed to each other. This means that we "can recite all the creeds of theological history and still believe in an idol. And that fact should not surprise us. Jesus himself accused the most monotheistic people in history of idolatry, as did Paul. The 'adulterous generation' to which Jesus refers bitterly is the biblical image of an idolatrous people, a people who leave their true spouse and go out to worship false gods." This kind of idolatry leads to atheism, since these idols are easily exposed as unworthy of allegiance. When offered such unworthy gods, people readily give up on God altogether. Does not the church, just to the degree it succumbs to this idolatry, not only break the First Commandment but also give aid and comfort to the atheism it wishes to oppose?[26]

From the liberation perspective, traditional orthodoxy is doubly deficient. In the first place, many creeds of the church focus so exclusively on metaphysical and personal issues that they have little or nothing to say about God's concern for social justice. One would never guess from them what Pharaoh learned about the God of the Bible. That is why those Christians who have perpetrated atrocities against Jews, blacks, the indigenous peoples of the new world, and others from the Crusades to the Third Reich, from slavery to apartheid, and from the military-commercial *conquistadors* of the old colonialism to those of the new have almost always been impeccably orthodox by traditional criteria. Even when they acted from good intentions, their theology failed them dramatically in essential matters of biblical faith. When liberation theology points this out, its purpose is not to embed us in our hindsight with secure superiority, but rather to challenge us to examine our own theology. We need to write new creeds, new liturgies, new theologies, new church school curricula, and so forth, which incorporate the liberation themes which are so often conspicuous by their absence in traditional theology, teaching, and worship. (See Appendix.)

But it is not enough to learn to talk differently about God. The second deficiency of traditional orthodoxy is the primacy it gives to theory over practice, to belief over behavior. Even if our orthodoxy were enriched to include liberation within our concept of salvation, we might be no better

---

[26] Segundo, 45-47.

off than the demons, who also believe—and shudder (James 2:19). The warning from James that faith without works is dead becomes for the liberation theologians, who after all are theologians, the claim that "*orthopraxis*, rather than orthodoxy, becomes the criterion for theology."27

This claim is entirely compatible with the Reformed emphasis on justification by grace through faith. For orthopraxis is not made the ground of justification but the criterion for theology. The question here is not Luther's question: How can I be sure of God's forgiving acceptance? It is the question: What good is my theology?

Miguez Bonino, who formulates the point in this way, defends it by reference to the biblical concept of truth. The faith of Israel was not a *gnosis* so much as a walk or a way (Jer. 22:13-16). In the New Testament the Johannine concept of doing the truth (John 3:21; cf. 13:17 and James 3:21) is joined with the Pauline concept of the obedience of faith (Rom. 1:5). The result is that "correct knowledge is contingent on right doing. Or rather, the knowledge is disclosed in the doing."28 Segundo likewise affirms that right behavior is both the means of achieving and the criterion of identifying right belief "both in theology and in biblical interpretation."29 This insight stands at the very fountainhead of liberation theology. The sixteenth-century Spanish Bishop Las Casas, who took the side of the native Americans against the Spanish conquistadors, has had a powerful influence on Gustavo Gutierrez. An important reason is simply this. "He judges the theologies of his opponents by their political consequences: theologies that lead to murder and enslavement invalidate their claim to be Christian."30

For making sense out of this puzzling discovery that orthodoxy can be idolatrous, liberation theologians often turn to the concept of ideology as formulated by Karl Mannheim. For *idolatrous* theologies are inevitably *ideological* in his sense of the term, which focuses our attention on the function of our ideas, the role they actually play in our lives. Mannheim first directs our attention to ideas which we might call ideals, ideas which describe not how the world actually is but how it might be, how it ought to be. The biblical images of the messianic shalom would be good

27 Miguez Bonino, 81.
28 Ibid., 88-90.
29 Segundo, 32.
30 Brown, *Gustavo Gutierrez*, 23-24.

examples. Then he notes that such ideas can have two very different social uses. Sometimes they "take on a revolutionary function," they "pass over into conduct, tend to shatter, either partially or wholly, the order of things prevailing at the time." In this transformative social role, Mannheim calls them Utopias.[31]

On the other hand the very same ideas and images of a better world can be "effective in the realization and the maintenance of the existing order of things." This happens when the portrayal of the ideal serves to blind people to the cruel realities of the present or when the ideal is constantly postponed to some indefinite future. In this case Mannheim calls the ideas in question ideology. Because even, or better, especially those ideas which have utopian possibilities can serve an ideological function, "representatives of a given order have not in all cases taken a hostile attitude towards orientations transcending the existing order [ideals]. Rather they have always aimed to control those situationally transcendent ideas and interests which are not realizable within the bounds of the present order, and thereby to render them socially impotent,…. Every period in history has contained ideas transcending the existing order, but these did not function as utopias; they were rather the appropriate ideologies of this stage as long as they were 'organically' and harmoniously integrated into the world-view characteristic of the period (i.e., did not offer revolutionary possibilities). As long as the clerically and feudally organized medieval order was able to locate its paradise outside of society, in some otherworldly sphere which transcended history and dulled its revolutionary edge, the idea of paradise was still an integral part of medieval society. Not until certain social groups embodied these wish-images into their actual conduct, and tried to realize them, did these ideologies become utopian."[32]

This concept of ideology requires that we distinguish the *function* of our ideas from both their *content* and their *intent*. Traditionally theology has emphasized the *content* of our religious ideas and has been satisfied to ask whether they are correct. But a single set of ideas, which obviously has but a single truth value, can have two diametrically opposed *functions*. What Mannheim refers to as "the idea of paradise," the biblical concept of the

---

[31] Karl Mannheim, *Ideology and Utopia: An Introduction to the Sociology of Knowledge*, trans. Louis Wirth and Edward Shils (New York: Harcourt, Brace & World, 1936), 192-93.
[32] Mannheim, 192-93.

kingdom of God, can serve to pacify serfs, slaves, landless peasants, the unemployed, or to lead them to revolt, just as it can serve to assuage or rankle the consciences of those who benefit from various forms of economic oppression. Thus, Gutierrez insists, biblical eschatology is not the truth of God but an "evasion of reality" if it does not function as a utopia and lead to political action "in the present."[33] When we pray, "thy kingdom come, thy will be done, on earth as it is in heaven," and then do not do what we can do to make earth a bit more heavenly, a place where God's will is done as it is in heaven, we put a true idea in the service of a false reality, and our theology degenerates into ideology.

If liberation theologians imply that the fullness of God's kingdom can be realized by human agency alone, we shall have to resist them. But nothing of the sort is implied in the claim that our eschatology, our theology of the kingdom, serves as an ideological support of an unjust status quo if it does not challenge and direct us to replace unjust practices and institutions with more nearly just ones when and as we are able to do so.

It also becomes necessary to distinguish the public, social *function* of our theology from its private, personal *intent,* since intent is no more reliable an indicator of function than content. Mannheim writes, "The idea of Christian brotherly love, for instance, in a society founded on serfdom remains an unrealizable and, in this sense, ideological idea, *even when the intended meaning is, in good faith, a motive in the conduct of the individual. To live consistently, in the light of Christian brotherly love, in a society which is not organized on the same principle is impossible.*"[34] This historical point about feudalism raises an awkward question about contemporary society. Since the principle of capitalist society is possessive individualism rather than *agape,* can Christian love be consistently lived in North America today?

Sincere intent is no more able to protect our beliefs from ideological function than correct content. When a southern governor physically bars blacks from access to the state university and insists that he has no hatred in his heart for blacks, we need not challenge the sincerity of this claim. For those with a Calvinist understanding of sin, it will be no surprise that personal affection for blacks can factually coexist with public practices which are demeaning and unjust toward them. And if the governor's

33 Gutierrez, *Theology of Liberation,* 234.
34 Mannheim, 194-95. Our italics.

theology tends to hide rather than to expose this contradiction between his warm feelings and cruel behavior toward blacks, it functions as an ideology in support of the racist status quo.

Miguez Bonino appeals to the philosophy of language to underscore this failure of private intention to determine the operative meaning of our theology. If orthodoxy is to be judged by orthopraxy, "what are the criteria for judging a theology's commitment? Today we know enough about language, thanks to structural analysis, to realize that the meaning of a language is determined not simply by the intention of the speaker, but through the code or context of meanings which are already present and into which the pronounced word becomes inserted, independent of the speaker's intention…[Words] specify themselves through the cultural and political context in which they function.…*The question, therefore, is not what is intended with words, but how do they operate*…. Very concretely, we cannot receive the theological interpretation coming from the rich world without suspecting it and, therefore, *asking what kind of praxis it supports, reflects, or legitimizes.*"[35]

This question about how our theology functions is a reminder that we are quite skillful, personally and collectively, at managing not to notice facts about ourselves which conflict with our self-image and our professed values. Again, for those with a Calvinist understanding of sin, it should come as no surprise that "the heart is deceitful above all things, and desperately corrupt" (Jer. 17:9) or that we tend to think of ourselves "more highly than [we] ought to think" (Rom. 12:2). The challenge set for us Miguez Bonino is twofold. The first is to accept the Third World suspicion of our theology in humility and openness, free of the need to justify ourselves (Luke 10:29). The second is to practice the art of self-examination for ourselves, learning to ask the questions of suspicion about our own theology.

This means going beyond asking whether our beliefs are true and our conscious intentions respectable to asking the really hard questions. How does our theology function? What sort of relation does it establish between us and the poor, the powerless, the mentally and physically handicapped, those racially, ethnically, and educationally different from ourselves in our own communities and throughout the world? Does it reflect their interests and needs? What kind of institutions and social

[35] Muguez Bonino, 80 and 91. Our italics.

structures does it support? Does it permit us to use our vote to shape these by asking, as the politicians encourage us, if we are economically better off than we were four years ago? What injustice and suffering does it legitimize? Does it leave unchallenged the nationalism and materialism which lie at the heart of so much of the world's suffering?

In asking these questions about our theology, we need to think of theology in the broadest sense. It is simply the reflective side of our faith, the way we express and explain it to ourselves and to others. Theology occurs in the massive tomes of a Barth, a Berkouwer, or a Berkhof, and in the learned lectures of seminary professors. But it also occurs in every prayer. When we sing

> Jesus loves me! This I know,
> for the Bible tells me so

we express a simple but beautiful and powerful theology. In view of the fact that children are the primary victims of poverty in this country and throughout the world, the question becomes whether that theology functions harmoniously in our lives with the simple, beautiful and powerful theology of another song we may sing

> Jesus loves the little children,
> All the children of the world;
> Red and yellow, black and white,
> They are precious in his sight,
> Jesus loves the little children of the world

If our worship in the church and our service in the world are shaped only by the first theology while the second remains at the level of a sweet sentiment for children and idealists, our theology has become an ideology. In spite of the fact that its center is a profound biblical truth, the "praxis it supports, reflects, and legitimizes" will include systems of poverty and oppression rooted in racism. Since the gods who are indifferent to such systems—such deities as National Security and Economic Growth—are not the God of the Bible, our worship has become idolatrous.

Three Paths by which Theology Becomes Idolatry and Ideology

How is it possible for a theology, including ours, to function in a manner so contradictory to both its content and our intent? In challenging us to serious self-examination on this issue, the liberation theologians provide three answers. They can help us to be more critical of our own theology in order to be more faithful to our liberating Lord. The first is perhaps the most obvious and therefore usually not the most dangerous. When human ingenuity is combined with human sinfulness, it becomes possible to manipulate the message of God's shalom so that it seems to sanctify a sinful drive for power and wealth. Biblical justifications for the exploitation of serfs, slaves, and wage laborers have not been lacking in the church's history—nor have theological rationalizations for the colonial domination and even extermination of peoples of different color and culture. The most dramatic and tragic contemporary example has no doubt been the attempt in the white Dutch Reformed churches of South Africa to present apartheid as biblical mandate.[36] We might call this path along which theology prostitutes itself in the service of secular interests the path of Overt Espousal. Christian theology publicly takes the side of systems and practices which desecrate God's image in children and women and men, its only bearers in all of creation.

The second path along which theology becomes ideology we can call the path of Vague Generality. At first glance it seems to be just the opposite of the first. For in announcing the kingdom, theologies on this path denounce the evils of which the poor and oppressed are victims. But they do so in such abstract and general terms that there is no way to move from theory to practice. It is in these terms that liberation theology finds the political theologies of the north (Moltmann, Metz, Cox) to be far less radical than they sound. The student whose paper began, "On balance,

---

[36] See *Human Relations and the South African Scene in the Light of Scripture* (Capetown—Pretoria: Dutch Reformed Church Publishers, 1976). This is the official translation of a study, also known as the Landman Commission Report, approved and accepted by the General Synod of the Dutch Reformed Church (NGK). In 1986 the NGK moved cautiously away from this position, calling apartheid unjust and unacceptable on Christian terms. But they left the door open to some other form of "separate development" and rejected a proposal for the union of white and black churches. See *Sojourners* (January, 1987), 5

Plato believed good was better than evil," provides an example, admittedly extreme, of the problem here.

Theology enters the path of Vague Generality to avoid the scandal of specificity. Of course, one way in which specificity is scandalous is that it earns the ire (and often the persecution) of those whose interests are vested in the status quo. So there is a question of courage and cowardice here.

But there are other more respectable fears at work here. And so, in their repeated and united emphasis on the risk involved in being concretely and specifically on the side of the poor and oppressed, the liberation theologians emphasize not the political risks (of which they are keenly aware), but two theological risks.

The first of these is the risk of being wrong. We are, of course, never free from this possibility, but the chances of being wrong increase as we get specific. It is much safer to say, "God is love and wills all people to live together in peace and justice," than it is to apply this truth to the actual, current struggles for human dignity throughout the Third World. Since we cannot deduce from Scripture the answers to our questions about, for example, the role of capitalism in Latin America, the temptation arises to remain at the level of "hoary abstract certitudes" rather than to plunge into the uncertainty of concrete political and economic reality. It is especially on the questions of means that the movement from the absolutes of the biblical message to the relativities of historical situations is treacherous.[37]

The other theological risk, whose corresponding fear tempts theology toward the path of Vague Generality, is the risk of what Gutierrez calls a "Constantinianism of the Left,"[38] the blurring of the distinction between the kingdom and historical movements of liberation which may be seeking to embody it, giving uncritical support to historical agencies which, however hopeful they may appear, are nevertheless human and sinful. It is doubly ironic that this danger is sometimes cited to discredit the whole project of liberation theology. In the first place, those who offer this critique are often themselves not very careful to distinguish their own nation or political ideology from God's kingdom. In the second place, none have been more keenly aware of this danger than the liberation

---

37 Segundo, 69-72, 87, and 108.
38 Gutierrez, *Theology of Liberation*, 266.

theologians themselves. Gutierrez's own warning against this danger is eloquent. Our efforts toward liberation must avoid "becoming translated into any kind of Christian ideology of political action or a politico-religious messianism. Christian hope opens us, in an attitude of spiritual childhood, to the gift of the future promised by God. It keeps us from any confusion of the kingdom with any one historical stage, from any idolatry toward unavoidably ambiguous human achievement, from absolutizing any revolution. In this way hope makes us radically free to commit ourselves to social praxis, motivated by a liberating utopia.... And our hope not only frees us for this commitment; it simultaneously demands and judges it."[39]

The risk of being wrong and the risk of becoming uncritically and absolutely attached to our historical choices are serious risks. But while the liberation theologians take them seriously, they do not allow themselves to be scared away from their task. For the apparently safer path is even riskier. To remain safely at the level of Vague Generality is to condemn evil in the abstract while tolerating both in theory and in practice the concrete evils from which our sisters and brothers, especially the children, daily suffer and die.

The third way in which theology comes to support and justify what Jesus and the prophets would have denounced is a model of biblical interpretation which neutralizes the social and political message of the Bible. We can call this the path of Dualistic Hermeneutics. Along this path several interrelated dualities serve to separate human life into independent regions and to give religious primacy to the nonpolitical, noneconomic regions. The dualisms which make this possible include those of spiritual vs. material, future vs. present, personal and inward vs. social and public, and vertical vs. horizontal. With their help, the Bible is interpreted exclusively in innerworldly, otherworldly, and afterworldly terms, with the only social comment often being the claim that the social order is God-ordained and to be accepted. One of the most familiar symptoms of this practice is the church's overwhelming preference for Matthew's beatitudes (Blessed are the poor in spirit) over Luke's (Blessed are the poor).

By contrast, liberation theology insists on a holistic framework for theology. In *A Message to the People of South Africa* in 1968, the South African

---

[39] *Ibid.,* 238.

Council of Churches affirmed that the gospel of Jesus Christ "offers hope and security for the whole life of man; it is to be understood not only in a mystical and ethical sense for the salvation of the individual person, and not only in a sacramental and ecclesiastical sense within the framework of the Church. The Gospel of Christ is to be understood in a cultural, social (and therefore political), cosmic, and universal sense, as the salvation of the world and of human existence in its entirety. Further, the Gospel of Christ is not only the object of our hopes; it should be experienced as a reality in the present."[40] Thus Bishop Tutu insists that liberation concerns sin in all its forms, not just the sociopolitical forms. But he simultaneously insists that the latter are integral to the Gospel and cannot be excluded or made secondary. He is fond of quoting Archbishop Temple's claim that "Christianity is the most materialistic of the great religions."[41]

In view of the integral holism of biblical revelation, theologies grounded in Dualistic Hermeneutics turn out to be pagan by being polytheistic and thus idolatrous. Allan Boesak quotes a missionary from Uganda who notes that when we so spiritualize our theology that it loses its political involvement "we have drifted back into the old polytheism against which the prophets of the Lord waged their great warfare. The real essence of paganism is that it divides the various concerns of a man's life into compartments. There is one god of the soil; there is another god of the desert…. All this is precisely where the modern paganism of our secular society has brought us today. Certain portions of our life we call religious. Then we are Christians…. We turn to another department of our life called politics. Now we think in quite different terms. Our liturgy is the catchwords of the daily press…. Our incentive is the fear of—we're not sure what. But it certainly is not the fear of the Lord."[42]

With sadness Adeolu Adegobola describes how in Africa "in opposition to the biblical insight of our day and to the best traditions of the people in Africa…conversion to Christianity has meant, among other things, acceptance of the view that life can be divided into spiritual and material, worldly and heavenly; and God has been thought of as being in control

---

40 Quoted in *Apartheid is a Heresy*, ed. John W. de Gruchy and Charles Villa-Vicencio (Grand Rapids: Eerdmans, 1983), 154-55.
41 Compare Tutu, 169-70 and 176-77 with the statement quoted in de Gruchy, *The Church Struggle in South Africa*, 163.
42 Boesak, *Black and Reformed*, 88-89. Cf. 59.

only of the spiritual.... Catechumens have been led to repeat the Apostles' Creed, 'God the Father Almighty, Maker of heaven and earth,' and at the same time to behave as if the earth were outside God's sovereign control and better left in the hands of the 'princes of the world.'"[43]

Whether this happens in Africa, or in Latin America, or in North America, it has the political significance of making theology into an ideological support for the status quo, however unjust. How does it do this? Not by overtly espousing the evils of the social order but by defining the Christian life without reference to them. And since the Christian faith is represented as having nothing to say about them, the message clearly is that one can be a good Christian while continuing to participate in them as perpetrator or as beneficiary. The evil systems of the world seldom demand that the church actively support them. They are usually content with the church's silent complicity. This is why, in his 1965 call for a Confessing Church in South Africa, Beyers Naude mentioned sinful silence in the face of injustice as one of the striking parallels between the South African and German situations.[44]

In the 1981 Charter of the Alliance of Black Reformed Christians in South Africa (ABRECSA), we read the following: "The Reformed tradition in South Africa is seen as responsible for political oppression, economic exploitation, unbridled capitalism, social discrimination and the total disregard for human dignity. By the same token, being Reformed is equated with total, uncritical acceptance of the status quo, *sinful silence* in the face of human suffering and *manipulation* of the Word of God in order to justify oppression."[45] This manipulation of the Word of God is what we have described as Overt Espousal of systems of social evil. The sinful silence which liberation theology regularly views as the powerful partner of such manipulation comes in at least two forms, Vague Generality and Dualistic Hermeneutics. In the face of social injustice, the former is silent through its refusal to become specific, while the latter is silent through its asocial spirituality. With reference to this silence and this

---

[43] Quoted in Manas Buthelezi in "The Theological Meaning of True Humanity," *The Challenge of Black Theology in South Africa,* ed. Basil Moore (Atlanta: John Knox Press, 1974), 100.

[44] See John W. Du Cruchy, "Towards a Confessing Church: The Implications of a Heresy," in *Apartheid is a Heresy,* 75-76.

[45] Quoted in *Apartheid is a Heresy,* 164. Our italics.

manipulation, James Cone has said, "In both cases theology becomes *a servant of the state,* and that can only mean death to black people.[46]

The challenge of liberation theology is a matter of life and death—physical life and death for many of the poor and oppressed throughout the world, and spiritual life and death for the churches of privilege and power, including our own. As we examine our own theologies, however simple or sophisticated, to detect the presence of Overt Espousal, Vague Generality, and Dualistic Hermeneutics, we will do well to remember that ultimately the issue concerns our behavior, personal and corporate. We need to remember the concluding words of Gustavo Gutierrez in *A Theology of Liberation:* "To paraphrase a well-known text of Pascal, we can say that all the political theologies, the theologies of hope, of revolution, and of liberation, are not worth one act of genuine solidarity with exploited social classes. They are not worth one act of faith, love, and hope, committed—in one way or another—in active participation to liberate man from everything that dehumanizes him and prevents him from living according to the will of the Father."

The Commission on Theology thinks it is appropriate, therefore, that among the most frequent responses to an earlier draft of this paper was the question, What recommendations for action do you make? We are convinced that before the church(es) can respond to the challenge of liberation theology faithfully, we must first hear that challenge open-mindedly and understand it deeply. We therefore limit our suggestions at this time to those which might help us better to listen to the liberation theologians. We do so in the hope that this listening will come to fruition in the reformation of the church(es) spoken of in the opening paragraph of this paper. We address these suggestions primarily to those identified above as being responsible for the preaching and teaching ministries in the Reformed Church in America.

1. We suggest the widespread study of this paper, using its study guide, as an introduction to liberation theology and the challenges it addresses to us. We suggest seminary classes, consistory meetings

---

[46] Quoted by Segundo, 28. Cf. Charles Villa-Vicencio, "An All-Pervading Heresy: Racism and the 'English Speaking Churches,'" in *Apartheid is a Heresy,* 63.

or retreats, and adult education classes as the most suitable settings for such study.

2. We need a better understanding of the biblical witness to which liberation theology makes its appeal. To this end we suggest the study of the 1984 Christian Action Commission paper, "Biblical Faith and our Economic Life" (available from the Reformed Church Distribution Center with accompanying study guide) and Robert McAfee Brown, *Unexpected News: Reading the Bible with Third World Eyes* (which also includes discussion questions —see note 4).

3. We need a better understanding of the historical and social contexts from which liberation theologies emerge. To this end we suggest the study of such works as Jose Miguez Bonio, *Doing Theology in Revolutionary Situation*; William O'Malley, *The Voice of Blood: Five Christian Martyrs of Our Time*; Placido Erdozain, *Archbishop Romero: Martyr of Salvador*; John W. de Gruchy, *The Church Struggle in South Africa*; and de Gruchy and Villa-Vicencil, *Apartheid Is a Heresy* (see notes 1, 10, and 40; O'Malley and Erdozain are published by Orbis).

4. With this preparation, we suggest the study of some of the classics of liberation theology, such as:

    Gutierrez, *A Theology of Liberation*
    Segundo, *The Liberation of Theology*
    Miguez Bonino, *Faces of Jesus*
    Boff, *Jesus Christ Liberator*
    Boesak, *Black and Reformed: Apartheid, Liberation, and the Calvinist Tradition*
    Tutu, *Hope and Suffering.*

5. Throughout this study we suggest the sustained discussion of the questions found in the third paragraph from the end of the section of this paper entitled "The Capacity of Orthodoxy for Idolatry and Ideology."

Perhaps the commission is foolish to suggest listening by study at a time when we are told that reading is a dying art. But when we notice how many people are willing to take night courses in college or graduate school to enhance their professional skills and job opportunities, including ministers in D.Min. programs, we think it not unfair to challenge those with leadership responsibilities in the church(es) to engage in serious reading and discussion in response to this new call for reformation in the church(es).

Those who have ears to hear, let them hear what the Spirit says to the churches.

Appendix

Comparison of the following creed with the Apostles' Creed or the Nicene Creed will reveal the absence of political content in the creeds most often used in our liturgy. The language is general, as is appropriate to a creed for liturgical use, but it unmistakably serves to remind those who confess it of the political dimension of the gospel. It comes from the Presbyterian Church of Southern Africa, 1973. The wording has been modified for the sake of inclusive language. Quoted from *Apartheid is a Heresy*, 160.

Declaration of Faith

We believe in God the Father; who created all the world, who will unite all things in Christ and who desires all people to live together as sisters and brothers in one family.

We believe in God the Son, who became human, died, and rose in triumph, reconciling all the world to God, breaking down every wall that divides God's human children, every barrier of religion, race, culture, or class, to create one united humanity. Christ is the one Lord who has authority over all. He summons both the individual and society, both the Church and the State, to reconciliation, unity, justice, and freedom.

We believe in God the Spirit, who is the pledge of God's coming Kingdom, who gives us power to proclaim God's judgment, and forgiveness of individuals and nations, to love and serve all people, to struggle for justice and peace, and to summon all the world to recognzie God's reign here and how.

* * * *

A similar but longer attempt to write a new creed is The Confession of 1982 of the Dutch Reformed Mission Church of South Africa, also known as "The Belhar Confession." For the Reformed Church in America response to this creed, see *MGS,* 1986:300-301.

Study Guide to Accompany
"The Challenge of Liberation Theology"

Introduction

The central claim of liberation theology is that God is on the side of the poor and oppressed. For the church to follow its Lord in this regard would require "a total overhaul of Christian piety, ecclesiastical institutions, discipline, and theological reflection" (Jose Miguez Bonino). Though we are naturally fearful in the face of such potentially sweeping and fundamental change, as Reformed Christians we cannot with integrity ignore this challenge. For reformation is not only a past event but an ongoing reality to the church "reformed and reforming." Moreover, since we profess to practice a biblical, worldly, and ecumenical piety, we are triply open to the liberationists' challenge a) to reexamine the Scripture, b) to make our faith relevant to the realities of daily life, and c) to do so in a global and ecumenical context. We cannot assume that we are immune to repeating what happened during Jesus' earthly life, namely, that the strongest opposition to his proclamation of the kingdom came from "the righteous," the devoutly religious members of God's covenant people. For that reason this study is directed, not toward a critique of liberation theology, but toward hearing the challenge which comes to us from both its Latin American and South African versions.

1. To what degree do we celebrate major change in the church—the Reformation—when it is safely behind us, and fear major change that might occur in our lifetime? What can be done to counteract this tendency?

2. Is Miguez Bonino right in suggesting that for the church to side decisively with the poor and oppressed would require a "total overhaul" of its life? If not, why not? If so, what changes would be involved?

3. What does it mean to say that "no one can claim to have heard the gospel already?"

4. Do North American Christians, few of whom espouse nonviolent resistance, have the right to demand that liberation theologians denounce violent revolution?

5. What is the significance for our relation to liberation theology of the reminder that the decisive opposition to Jesus came from the devoutly religious, or, as Barth has put it, that it was the church and not the world that crucified him?

6. What steps can we take to counteract our natural tendency, in the face of a theology which challenges our own theory and practice, to seek first to criticize and discredit it rather than submit to honest and humble self-examination?

7. Is reference to the oppressed redundant in the phrase "poor and oppressed"? In other words, are there in our society those who though not poor are second class citizens, victims of discrimination, and in that sense oppressed?

The Mixing of Religion and Politics

Though liberation theologies differ on many important issues, they agree that if the gospel is to be good news to the poor the church will have to be offensively political, that it will have to imitate its Lord in visibly taking sides with the victims of social injustice. In response to the charge that this involves an illegitimate mixing of religion and politics, liberation theologians make three replies, each of which moves us closer to the heart of the matter. First, they point out that those who make this charge are often quite willing to mix religion and politics in the service of their own interests. Second, they argue that in situations of great inequality and injustice there is no neutrality or impartiality on political and economic issues. Not to side with the oppressed is to side with the oppressors. This silent complicity is said to be the worst form of taking sides, for it does so without accepting responsibility for doing so. Finally, and most importantly, liberation theologians argue that the issue concerns the very nature of God, that the God of the Bible does not practice or permit neutrality in the face of oppression. When told to quit meddling in politics and get back to preaching the gospel, they ask: Which gospel, the biblical gospel which is good news to the poor or some human gospel which is not?

1. Is the mixing of politics and religion compatible with the separation of church and state?

2. What economic, political, and ideological systems are the special focus of concern for liberation theologians? How do you respond when you hear them called oppressive? How much validity do you see in these claims?

3. Reflect on your own church's experience in relating religion and politics. Have they been mixed? If not, why not? If so, has this mixture taken account of the biblical emphasis on God's concern for "nonpersons"?

4. What steps has the Reformed Church in America taken to free itself from the pretense of "impartiality"? How involved is your local church in these denominational efforts? What more could/ should be done at the denominational level? At the local level?

5. The secular media has sharply criticized the Moral Majority for mixing religion and politics. How would the liberation theologians respond? How do you respond?

Who is the God of the Bible? Ask the Pharaoh!

The deepest reason why liberation theology is offensively political is the dual conviction that God is revealed throughout the Bible to be on the side of the poor and oppressed and that the church, if it would be faithful, must be actively on their side as well. The story of the Exodus plays the role of a paradigm in this respect. Far from treating it as an isolated, favorite story, liberation theologians find in it a key which points to a dominant and recurring theme of both the Old and New Testament. While they like to quote such Reformed theologians as Calvin, Barth, and Kuyper to this effect, the core of their appeal is to Scripture itself. Their conclusion is a strong one. So fundamentally is the God of the Bible a God who wills justice and liberation for the poor and the powerless, that to worship and proclaim any god, by whatever name, for whom this character is not essential and central is to worship and proclaim a false god, an idol. A triune God who justifies sinners by grace through faith but who is indifferent to social injustice is simply not the God of the Bible.

1. If God were to reenact the Exodus today, how and where might it happen? Would you/your local church/the Reformed Church in America be excited or dismayed by such an event? How might our lives be changed by a new exodus?

2. "Within a society where social classes conflict, we are true to God when we side with the poor, the working classes, the despised races, the marginal cultures." How does the RCA side with these groups in our society? in the Third World? How does your local church do so?

3. "It is then the same as though God heard himself, when he hears the cries and groaning of those who cannot bear injustice." How is this aspect of who God is presented in our preaching? our hymns? our prayers? our celebration of the sacraments? our Christian education programs? our church budgets? our family life? our family budgets?

4. Reflect on Pharaoh's encounter with the God of the Bible. What would he say if asked to write the portion of a creedal statement on the nature of God?

5. "I am Yahweh your God, who brought you out of the land of Egypt, out of the house of bondage." If you were writing a commentary on this verse, what would be the main points you would want to make?

The Capacity of Orthodoxy for Idolatry and Ideology

In liberation perspective formal orthodoxy is no guarantee against idolatry, for orthodoxy has traditionally been defined in metaphysical and personal terms with little or no reference to issues of social justice. Just as Jesus and Paul accused the most monotheistic people in history of idolatry, so liberation theologians challenge us to inquire whether in spite of our orthodoxy we worship an unbiblical god. They see traditional orthodoxy as doubly endangered. First, because of the way in which orthodoxy has been defined, one would never guess from many of its creeds and much of its theology what the Pharaoh learned about the covenantal God. Second, because of the primacy given to theory over practice, even a more genuinely biblical theology might not translate into faithful behavior. *Orthopraxis* (right action) needs to become the criterion of our theology, not just orthodoxy (right belief).

The concept of ideology is helpful in understanding this latter point. A single idea or theory can function in more than one way. For example, the idea of God's heavenly kingdom can serve to reconcile slaves to their slavery on the grounds that in the life to come their suffering will be replaced by joy. But it can also lead them to try to make the earth a bit less hellish now by the abolition of slavery. A theory, including a theology, becomes an ideology when it functions to justify a given social order, rendering its injustices immune from criticism and change. When liberation theology asks us to see whether our theology has become an ideology, the issue is not the truth of our ideas, but their function. The question concerns not the content of our theology, nor the subjective intent with which we hold it, but the objective impact it has social behavior. What sort of social order does it support, justify, and legitimize?

1. According to liberation theologians, the Apostles' Creed may be deficient in two ways. What are these? What biblical support could be offered in support of this claim?
2. How is the South African creed, found in the Appendix, like the Apostles' Creed? How is it different? Should we use it in our churches?
3. What does it mean to say that *orthopraxis*, or right action, should become the criterion of our theology?
4. "To live consistently, in the light of Christian brotherly love, in a society which is not organized on the same principle is impossible." Is this true? If so, why? If not, why not?
5. How is it possible for biblical ideas to have an ideological function, that is to serve to support and justify social systems of injustice and oppression?
6. How *might* relief aid to hungry people in the Third World *function* to turn our faith into an ideology? What is the difference in such a case between intent and function?

Three Paths by which Theology Becomes Idolatry and Ideology

How is it possible for a theology, even an orthodox theology, to become idolatrous and to provide the ideological support for social structures of poverty and oppression? Liberation theology provides three answers to this question, answers which can be aids to corporate self-examination if we will let them. First, there is the path of Overt Espousal. Oppression in the form of anti-Semitism, or slavery, or apartheid is explicitly declared to be God-ordained, and scriptural justifications are developed and propagated. The second path along which theology becomes ideology is the path of Vague Generality. Evil is denounced, but at a level so abstract and general as to be entire innocuous. The concrete evils from which actual people suffer every day are not mentioned, and people can be "good Christians" while remaining indifferent to poverty and oppression or even helping to perpetrate them. In this way theology avoids the danger of being wrong, which increases as it gets concrete about the evil it opposes. And it diminishes the danger of becoming uncritically supportive of social movements for change. But it thereby becomes uncritically supportive of present social structures and ends up with a God so unbiblically tolerant of actual evil as to be an idol and not the living God. The third way in which theology supports and justifies what Jesus and the prophets would have denounced is the path of Dualistic Hermeneutics. Along this path several interrelated dualities serve to compartmentalize life and to give religious primacy to the non-political, non-economic regions. These dualisms include spiritual vs. material, future vs. present, personal and inward vs. social and public, vertical vs. horizontal, and so forth. A gospel interpreted in these terms becomes an innerworldly, otherworldly, and afterworldly affair. At times its only social comment is the claim that the social order is God-ordained and therefore to be accepted. If Overt Espousal is a form of manipulating the gospel to justify injustice, Vague Generality and Dualistic Hermeneutics achieve the same effect by rendering the gospel silent on concrete social evils.

1. Which of the three paths to idolatry and ideology is least dangerous in your church? Which is most dangerous? What can be done to protect against the latter?

2. The paper names the risks involved in moving from Vague Generality to concrete and specific ways of talking about God's concern for social justice. What risks are there in not making this move? How do we decide which risks outweigh the others?

3. As you understand the Reformed tradition, is it friendly or unfriendly to Dualistic Hermeneutics?

4. What is your response to the suggestion that Dualistic Hermeneutics is polytheistic and thus idolatrous?

5. Does the Apostle Paul practice Dualistic Hermeneutics when he says nothing to the Roman government about slavery while he urges Christians to experience *spiritual* freedom? How might he

respond to this charge in his proclamation that "Jesus is Lord"?
What can we learn from this?

6. How can a proper understanding of the three paths to idolatry and
ideology lead to a richer experience of God and the Christian
faith?

2
Confessing the Nicene Creed Today

At issue are the words "and (from)"[1] the Son" (the *filioque* clause), added
to the third article of Western versions of the Nicene Creed in the early
Middle Ages. The original wording of the creed was, "And I believe in the
Holy Spirit, the Lord and Giver of life, who proceeds from the Father,
who with the Father and the Son together is worshipped and glorified,
who spoke by the prophets." In the expanded Western form, as presently
confessed in the Reformed Church in America, the second attributive
phrase reads: "…who proceeds from the Father *and the Son*" (the added
phrase is italicized). The original purpose of the addition was to bring the
Nicene Creed into line with the Western, Augustinian theology of the
Spirit and to differentiate the definition of orthodoxy in the Roman
Catholic Church from that in the Eastern (Greek) Orthodox Church. (A
full study paper on this issue with biblical and historical details, "The
Nicene Creed and the Procession of the Spirit," follows this paper.)

The procession of the Spirit in eternity is as much a mystery as the
eternal generation of the Son. Biblical texts indicate that the Spirit is sent
to us from the risen Christ as well as from the Father (Mark 1:8; Luke
24:49a; John 1:33; 4:14; 15:26; 16:7, 20:22; Acts 2:33b; 16:7; Rom. 8:9b;
Gal. 4:6; Phil. 1:19; 1 Pet. 1:11). On the other hand, Christ was sent and
empowered by the Spirit as well as by the Father (Matt. 1:18, 20; 3:16; 4:1;
12:15-18, 28; Luke 1:35; 4:14-19; 5:17; 6:19; John 1:32; 3:34; Acts 10:38).

---

[1]The literal translation of the Latin word "filioque" is "and from the Son." The Western
form as presently confessed in the Reformed Church in America is "and the Son."

An examination of the biblical texts alone does not decide the issue, however. Some scholars, including prominent Reformed theologians, have argued that the eternal origin of the Spirit must be understood to be from the Son as well as from the Father in order ensure the unity and equality of the Father and Son or the distinctness of the Son and Spirit. Others, including prominent Reformed theologians, have argued that the Spirit proceeds from the Father alone or "from the Father *of* the Son" (rather than "from the Father *and* the Son"). Within the Reformed tradition as well as from a biblical perspective, it is possible to affirm either the double (biune) procession of the Spirit (from the Father *and* the Son) or that both the Son and the Spirit proceed directly from God the Father. The important point, in either view, is that the deity of the Spirit is maintained.

Calvin accepted the later Western form of the Nicene Creed which included the words "and (from)* the Son." He did not mention other versions or discuss their relative adequacy. But he stressed that the essential points of the doctrine of the Trinity were the unity of God and the distinction and equal deity of the three persons (*Institutes* 1.13.3). He also pleaded for the unity of the church based on these fundamentals of trinitarian faith—not including the double (biune) procession of the Spirit.

Therefore, the Reformed Church in America is entitled to confess the double (biune) procession of the Spirit as a distinctive belief of the Western church, one that the Reformed Church shares with most other Protestants and Roman Catholics. The Reformed Church does so in the words of the Athanasian Creed (line 23) and the Belgic Confession (Art. 8). The recommendation from its Commission on History before the 1989 General Synod (*MGS*, 1989:366) did not call these confessions into question. It applied only to the wording of the Nicene Creed.

The status of the Nicene Creed is different from that of the other creeds and confessions of the Reformed Church. It is the only credal statement originally composed in Greek (the ecumenical language of the time) rather than Latin. It is the only credal statement composed by ecumenical councils (Nicea and Constantinople). It is the only credal statement that is accepted as normative by all major branches of the Christian church— Protestant and Catholic; Eastern and Western; Chalcedonian and non-Chalcedonian. In the words of the Nicene Creed, the confession of faith is not what it means to be Reformed, or even what Western Christians (Protestant and Catholic) believe, but what the Reformed Church in America and other Western Christians with *all* branches of the church believe to be essential to the faith.

In the words of the Nicene Creed the Reformed Church confesses neither what was discovered by the Reformers in the sixteenth century, nor even what was argued by Augustine in the fifth century, but what was established by the first two ecumenical councils (Nicea and Constantinople) in the fourth century. Therefore, it should be preserved in the form that the fourth-century church gave it.

At one level the issue at stake is merely one of following the best early texts of the Nicene Creed as the Reformed Church does with modern translations of the Bible and the Reformed standards. Late additions to the text of the New Testament are normally placed in footnotes along with a brief explanation for the change. Additions to the Heidelberg Catechism are normally bracketed or placed in footnotes. The same should be done with the Nicene Creed as a matter of historical accuracy.

At a deeper level, what is at stake is the Reformed Church in America's understanding of itself in the larger world. Is the Reformed Church exclusively a Western church or one that identifies itself with the church universal while at the same time affirming its distinctively Western contributions to that church? Is the Reformed Church basically a modern (post-medieval) movement or the revival of an ancient one—one that goes back to the ecumenical (pre-medieval) church of the first four centuries? Is the Reformed Church a church that looks primarily to Rome as its antecedent and partner, or one that looks also to the indigenous churches of Eastern Europe, Africa, and Asia? The handling of a few words in one particular creed is not a small matter. These few words say a lot about the Reformed Church as believers particularly to other fellow believers for whom the Nicene Creed is the one universal definition of a saving faith in Father, Son, and Holy Spirit.

3
The Nicene Creed and
the Procession of the Spirit

Introduction

At the 1989 General Synod, a recommendation, originating from the Commission on History, read as follows: "To confess the Nicene Creed in the form adopted in the Council of Constantinople in A.D. 381."[1] The primary concern for the recommendation was the fact that the form in which the Reformed Church in America presently confesses the Nicene Creed[2] differs from the original (Greek) wording attributed to the Council of Constantinople and hence separates the Reformed Church and other churches in the West from the practice of the indigenous Eastern Christian churches (other than those that have accepted the authority of Rome), particularly the Eastern Orthodox Church.[3]

The principal difference in wording between the two versions of the Nicene Creed occurs in a phrase describing the eternal procession of the Holy Spirit.[4] The original wording of the creed in both Greek and Latin

---

1   *MGS*, 1989: 366, R-5.
2   "Nicene Creed" is the name generally used for the creed of the First Ecumenical Council (Nicea, 325) as officially amended by the Second Ecumenical Council (Constantinople, 381) and attested by the Fourth Ecumenical Council (Chalcedon, 351). The material of concern here is part of what was added at the Council of Constantinople in 381. It was taken from a baptismal creed already known to Epiphanius in 374: P. Schaff, *Creeds of Christendom* (New York: Harper and Row, 1931), 34. For problems related to documenting the association of this material with the Council of Constantinople, see J.N.D. Kelly, *Early Christian Creeds* (London: Longman, 1972), 305-31.
3   Eastern churches that confess the Nicene Creed in the same form as the Eastern Orthodox include the Coptic Orthodox, the Syrian (Jacobite) Orthodox, the Nestorian, the Armenian Orthodox, and the Mar Thoma Church in South India. The Maronite Church was originally in agreement with the other Eastern churches but has accepted the Western form of the creed since its reunion with Rome in 1181: A. S. Atiya, *A History of Eastern Christianity* (London: Methuen, 1968), 58, 201, 224, 294-95, 344, 384, 401.
4   This is not the only difference in wording between the two versions of the Nicene Creed. With respect to the church, the Greek version reads (in translation): "And I believe...in one, holy, catholic, and apostolic church." Latin versions leave out the word, "in." The significance of the Latin wording was stressed by Augustine (*On Faith and the Creed* X.21) and Calvin (*Institutes*, 4.1.2) though probably without awareness of the Greek alternative. However, the 1989 Report of the Commission on History only raises a question concerning the words about the procession of the Spirit (*MGS*, 1989: 365-66).

versions[5] was (in translation): "who proceeds from the Father; who with the Father and the Son together is worshiped and glorified." The wording to which the Reformed Church presently subscribes is: "who proceeds from the Father *and the Son*; who with the Father and the Son together is worshiped and glorified." The added words, italicized here, are traditionally referred to as the *filioque*—a Latin phrase, meaning "and (from)* the Son."[6] The recommendation before General Synod in 1989 was to omit these words (the *filioque*) from the Reformed Church's version of the Nicene Creed. In response, the 1989 General Synod referred this matter to the Commission on Theology for further study (*MGS*, 1989: 306).

Confessional Standards in the Reformed Church in America

The Nicene Creed is one of six confessional standards adhered to by the Reformed Church in America. Three of these standards articulate the distinctive doctrines of the Reformed churches of Germany and the Netherlands from which the first Reformed Church congregations originated. These three Reformed standards are the Heidelberg Catechism, the Belgic Confession, and the Canons of Dort.

Three other standards are creeds that the Reformed churches inherited from the Roman Catholic Church and which date back to the first millennium.[7] In the order of their formulation, they are the Apostles' Creed (third century),[8] the Nicene Creed (fourth century), and the

---

[5] Early Latin versions of the Nicene Creed like that attributed to Dionysius Exiguus (c. 500-550) do not contain the disputed addition: Schaff (1931), 2:57-58. In fact, the earliest uncontested evidence of its inclusion dates from the late eighth century (section 4 below): Kelly (1972), 362; J. Pelikan, *The Christian Tradition: A History of the Development of Doctrine* (Chicago: University of Chicago Press, 1971-89), 2:184.

[6] Properly speaking, the Latin term, *filioque*, refers only to the words "and (from) the Son," in the Nicene Creed. The doctrine that the Spirit proceeds from the Son as well as from the Father (as confessed, for instance, in the Athanasian Creed and the Belgic Confession, is sometimes referred to as the "double procession" of the Spirit. This terminology (like that of "three persons" in the Trinity) raises unnecessary problems for biblical monotheism. In order to avoid this possible misunderstanding, this paper refers to the doctrine of the "biune procession" of the Spirit in analogy with the doctrine of a "triune God."

[7] These "ecumenical creeds" were first cited as a group of three in the thirteenth century: J.N.D. Kelly, *The Athanasian Creed* (London: Adam & Charles Black, 1964), 44.

[8] The Apostles' Creed was not written by the twelve Apostles. The textus receptus, including the phrase, "he descended into hell," dates from the early eighth century. However, the main body of the creed, the old "Roman Symbol" (in both Greek and Latin versions), goes back to the early third century: Kelly (1972), 113, 128.

Athanasian Creed (fifth century).[9] These creeds are not exclusively Reformed standards. Issues that separated the Reformers from Rome were largely ones that had arisen in the later Middle Ages. Consequently, the Reformers could find nothing unbiblical in the earlier creeds. Calvin did not accept the usual interpretation of the phrase, "he descended into hell," but he never suggested that it be omitted from the Apostles' Creed. In fact, Calvin and the other Reformers affirmed all three of these creeds as an indication of their orthodoxy and solidarity with the early church. The Belgic Confession referred to them as the "three ecumenical creeds" and deferred to their authority on issues concerning the doctrine of the Trinity (Art. 9). They are standards of basic Christian orthodoxy as understood by Protestants and Catholics alike. Hence, they may be said to characterize the faith of all Western churches (and churches deriving from their missions) even though they differ at significant points from the faith of most Eastern churches.

In practice, only the Apostles' Creed is regularly used in Reformed churches. The order of worship in the Reformed Church hymnbook, *Rejoice in the Lord*, calls for the use of either the Nicene or the Apostles' Creed following the sermon and prior to the passing of the peace and the offering (564-66), but the fact that most Reformed Church members know the Apostles' Creed by heart tilts the balance against usage of the Nicene Creed.

These observations on the use of the Nicene and Athanasian creeds are important for the question at hand: it is the point at which the Reformed Church differs most strikingly from several other branches of the Christian church. For the Reformed Church the Nicene Creed is a convenient summary of early Christian teachings. Reformed Church ministers of the Word are expected to accept it in order to qualify for ordination, but they do not make much use of it thereafter. There is generally more concern about the views of Reformed Church ministers of the Word concerning the sacraments and justification by faith.

---

9   The Athanasian Creed was not written by Athanasius (d. 373). Written in Latin in late fifth or early sixth century Gaul (possibly at the monastery of Lerins), it was largely based on the theology of Augustine: Kelly (1964), 123. The mistake in attribution was not realized until the mid-seventeenth century. Consequently, both the Reformers and their Catholic contemporaries accepted the creed as the authentic work of Athanasius.

Eastern and Western Versions of the Nicene Creed

For the Eastern Orthodox and Roman Catholic churches, however, the early creeds define the conditions of salvation and admittance to the Lord's Table.[10] Anyone who does not accept their teachings is judged to be a heretic in danger of eternal damnation. Typically creeds were followed by anathemas against those who did not accept their contents (as the Canons of Dort also do). Even when the anathemas were not recited liturgically, they were understood to apply. As the Athansian Creed states in its conclusion: "This is the Catholic faith, which a person must believe faithfully in order to be saved."

Therefore, the difference in wording between Eastern and Western versions of the Nicene Creed is a matter of utmost importance to the Roman Catholic and Eastern Orthodox churches. Long before the Reformation, each had anathematized the other for deviating from what it considered to be the correct wording.[11] The problem arose only with respect to the Nicene Creed for several reasons: of the Western (Latin) creeds, only the Nicene was a direct translation from the Greek language; only the Nicene Creed had originated from universally accepted, ecumenical councils (Nicea, 325; Constantinople, 381); only the Nicene Creed had been further endorsed by ecumenical councils (beginning with Chalcedon, 451); and only the Nicene Creed was officially recognized by the Eastern Orthodox Church.[12]

---

[10] The recitation of the Nicene Creed was placed just before the Lord's Prayer—hence introductory to communion—in the Byzantine and Mozarabic rites: Kelly (1972), 352.

[11] The Third Council of Toledo (589) anathematized anyone as an Arian who might refuse to confess that the Spirit "proceeds from the Father and the Son," but it is not clear whether these words were included in its version of the Nicene Creed: Kelly (1972), 361-62 (see section 4 below). Patriarch Photius of Byzantium called a council in 867 to excommunicate Pope Nicholas on the grounds of heresy for his adherence to the Latin wording of the creed. Photius was anathematized in turn by Rome in 869. After several temporary reverses, Photius secured the formal anathematization of anyone who added "illegitimate words" to the Nicene Creed at the Council of Constantinople held in 879-80. Controversy over the wording of the creed was one of several factors that led to the schism between East and West in 1054: Every (1965), 9-11. In 1274, the Second Council of Lyons anathematized all those who denied that the Spirit proceeds from both Father and Son. The mutual excommunications of 1054 were annulled in 1965.

[12] At the Council of Florence (1438-45), the Greek Orthodox delegates declared that they were unaware of the existence of the Apostles' Creed: J.H. Leith, *Creeds of the Churches* (Atlanta: John Knox Press, 1982), 24.

One is confronted, then, with three distinct traditions regarding the added phrase in question: the Eastern Orthodox tradition, which rejects the *filioque*; the Roman Catholic tradition, which not only accepts the *filioque* but makes it a test of orthodoxy; and the Reformed tradition, which accepts the *filioque* on the basis of received tradition, but in principle rejects any tradition that does not agree with Scripture.

The Issues

On the basis of the foregoing, the recommendation before General Synod in 1989 and referred for further study, actually involves a series of issues: (1) Does the procession of the Spirit confessed in the Nicene Creed refer to the sending of the Spirit at Pentecost or to the eternal origin of the Spirit within the triune God? (2) What, if anything, does Scripture say about this procession of the Spirit? In particular, does Scripture teach the biune procession of the Spirit (eternal procession from the Father and the Son together)? (3) What theological issues are involved in an affirmation about the Spirit's eternal procession? Are there broader biblical principles that may decide the matter even in the absence of definitive biblical texts? Are these biblical and theological grounds sufficient to make belief in the biune procession of the Spirit a test of orthodoxy? (4) When and why was the *filioque* (in English, the words, "and the Son") added to the statement about the eternal procession of the Spirit in Western versions of the Nicene Creed? Was this addition justified? Was it ecumenically binding? (5) Given the fact that it was added (and later accepted by the Reformers), should the *filioque* now be bracketed or footnoted for biblical, theological, or ecumenical reasons? (6) Should the Reformed Church now unilaterally bracket or footnote the *filioque* in accordance with the recommendation presented at the 1989 General Synod?

Responses to the Issues

To anticipate the conclusions drawn below: (1) The procession of the Spirit in the creed refers to its eternal origin within the Godhead. (2) The New Testament does not teach that the Spirit proceeds from the Father and the Son. It would be more biblical to say that the Spirit proceeds from the Father of the Son. (3) The theological reasons traditionally given for the biune procession of the Spirit are speculative and debatable. They are not sufficiently cogent to warrant making the biune procession of the

Spirit a test of orthodoxy. (4) The addition of the *filioque* to the Nicene Creed was not theologically justified and is not ecumenically binding. (5) In spite of the fact that the Reformers accepted it, the *filioque* should be bracketed or footnoted in present-day versions of the Nicene Creed just as late additions to the text of the New Testament are footnoted in modern editions of the Bible. (6) Pending the decision of an ecumenical council, the Reformed Church should bracket the *filioque* in its present-day versions of the Nicene Creed.

(1) Whether the Procession of the Spirit in the Creed is Temporal or Eternal:

The questions that led to the formulation of the Nicene Creed were rather different from those we encounter in the pages of the New Testament. Most of what the New Testament says about the origins of Christ and the Spirit concerns their being sent into the world (see next section, "What Scripture Teaches About the Procession of the Spirit"). In the fourth century, however, questions arose concerning their eternal origin. The Arians viewed Christ as a mere creature and later the Macedonians or Pneumatomachians ("Spirit-fighters") accepted the deity of Christ but denied the proper deity of the Spirit.

Against the Arians, the Council of Nicea (325) affirmed that Christ was "begotten from the Father...begotten not created." The council went on to say that it was "for us and for our salvation," that Christ "came down and was made flesh and became human."[13] These two sets of phrases clearly referred to two different stages in the story of the eternal Son of God: the origin in eternity ("begotten from the Father") and the primary mission in history ("came down from heaven").[14]

Against the Macedonians, the Council of Constantinople (381) added that the Spirit "proceeds from the Father," a phrase taken from an earlier baptismal creed.[15] The council went on to say that the Spirit "spoke

---

[13] For the text of the original creed of the Council of Nicea, see Schaff (1931), 60; Kelly (1972), 215-16; Leith (1982), 30-31.

[14] To the first of these phrases, the Council of Constantinople added the words "before all worlds," based on a baptismal creed used by Cyril of Jerusalem and Epiphanius: Schaff (1931), 31, 33. The reason for the addition was the heresy of Marcellus of Ancyra, who accepted the deity of Christ but regarded him as only a temporary manifestation of deity.

[15] The first formula of Epiphanius in 374: Schaff (1931), 34.

through the prophets" and that the church is "one, holy, catholic, and apostolic."[16] The reference to the prophetic activity of the Spirit in Israel points to the belief that the church's experience of the gifts of the Spirit—the basis of its unity, holiness, catholicity, and apostolicity—was a renewal of this ancient work of God, a belief attested in the New Testament by reference to the prophecy of Joel (Joel 2:28-9; Acts 2:16-18, 33, 38).[17]

As in the case of the statement about Christ, we have two phrases referring to two stages in the story of the Holy Spirit: the origin in eternity ("proceeds from the Father") and the mission in history ("spoke through the prophets"). The fact that the words describing the procession of the Spirit directly parallel the earlier description of the eternal generation of the Son,[18] and the fact that they were directed against the Macedonians, who regarded the Spirit as a creature, make it clear that the idea of the procession from the Father referred to the eternal origin of the Spirit, not just its being poured out at Pentecost.

(2) What Scripture Teaches about the Procession of the Spirit:

In spite of all the theological debate about the procession of the Spirit, there is only one place in the entire New Testament where the Spirit is explicitly said to "proceed" from God. It occurs in John 15:26, where Jesus makes the following promise to his disciples: "But when the Counselor comes, whom I shall send to you from the Father, even the Spirit of truth, who proceeds from the Father, he will bear witness to me." The Greek verb used here to describe the procession of the Spirit is *ekporeuomai*, which means to go or flow out of something as a word comes from the heart or a river flows from its source (Matt. 4:4; Rev. 22:1). It is the same verb used to describe the procession of the Spirit in the Nicene

16 The phrase "who spoke through the prophets" dates back to the Catechetical Lectures of Cyril of Jerusalem (c. 350). Like the phrase "who proceeds from the Father," it was taken by the Council of Constantinople from the baptismal creed of Epiphanius (374): Schaff (1931), 32, 34.

17 A second formula given by Epiphanius states that the Spirit is the one "who spoke in the Law and preached through the prophets, and came down [on Jesus] at the Jordan, who speaks in Apostles, dwells in saints': Schaff (1931), 37. The fact that phrases like these were not adopted at Constantinople indicates that they were understood to be implicit in what was already said about the Spirit and the church.

18 The prepositional phrases describing the generation of the Son and the procession of the Spirit are identical—in Greek, *ek tou patros*; in Latin, *ex Patre*—in both cases.

Creed. Jesus' words in John 15:26 undoubtedly provided the scriptural basis for the creed's assertion that the Spirit "proceeds from the Father."[19] The meaning in both cases is that the Spirit has its ultimate source in the Father.

In addition to the fact that the Spirit proceeds from the Father as its ultimate source, John 15:26 also states that it is sent from the Father by Jesus. So the Spirit is clearly sent to the church by the Son as well as by the Father. This much is beyond dispute. The question is whether this fact can be used as the basis for saying that the Spirit proceeds from the Son as well as from the Father, in eternity as well as in time. The Western churches argue that the sending of the Spirit by the Son in time implies that the Spirit proceeds from the Son in eternity. The Eastern churches argue that the sending of the Spirit is strictly an historical relationship of Christ and the Spirit and does not necessarily reflect their eternal relations.

Clearly there are hazards in both approaches. Not everything that the divine persons have done in history can be read directly back into their proper natures and relationships. In fact, Reformed theology has traditionally made a fairly clear distinction between appearances on earth and the realities in heaven—particularly with respect to the incarnation and ascension. In a human view of things, Christ once came down from heaven and then returned to heaven after the resurrection. But from the perspective of God, Christ had never left heaven in the first place.[20] One has to leave some room for uncertainty and paradox in all matters concerning the deity.

On the other hand, a denial of any relationship between historical appearances and eternal reality would undercut the value of all revelation. As Karl Barth has argued, one must believe God truly to be what God appears to be in divine revelation if one is to have any basis for doing theology at all.[21] Accordingly, one must carefully consider what the New

---

[19] The prepositional phrase in the Nicene Creed is *ek tou patros* rather than *para tou patros* as in John 15:26. The same is true of the earlier baptismal creed of Epiphanius (*ek tou patros ekporeuomenon*, just as at Constantinople). The preposition was probably changed to match that used of the eternal generation of the Son (*ek tou patros gennethenta*) earlier in the creed: Schaff (1931), 33-34, 57.

[20] Calvin, *Institutes* 2.13.4; 4.17.30; Belgic Confession, Art. 19.

[21] K. Barth, *Church Dogmatics* (Edinburgh: T. & T. Clark, 1956-77), I.1:382, 479; II.1:227, 260.

Testament states about the Spirit's historical relationships to God the Father and God the Son to see what conclusions may be drawn about their eternal relationships.

In general terms, the Spirit is said to be of God, from God, given by God, and sent from heaven.[22] In relation to God the Father, the Spirit is said to be of the Father and given and sent by the Father.[23] These relationships are not reciprocal: the Father is never said to be given or sent by the Spirit (or by anyone else).[24]

In relation to Jesus Christ, the Spirit is said to be of Christ, sent by Christ, and poured out on the disciples by Christ.[25] In this respect the relationship of the Spirit to Christ parallels that of the Spirit to the Father. However, the parallel breaks down in that the Spirit's relationship to Christ is reciprocal, whereas the Spirit's relationship to the Father is not. During his earthly life Christ was begotten (in the Virgin Mary) by the Spirit, anointed and sent by the Spirit, and empowered by the Spirit to prophesy and to heal.[26] Even as the risen Savior, Christ is glorified by the Spirit, revealed as "Son of God" and "Lord" by the Spirit, empowered by the Spirit to appear to his disciples, and even empowered to pour out the Spirit on the church in his name.[27] In this respect, the relation of the Spirit to Christ parallels that of the Father to Christ.

In fact, the relationship between Christ and the Spirit in the New Testament is normally depicted as one of parity. Both Son and Spirit come directly from God the Father (each with the assistance of the other).[28]

---

22 Luke 24:49b; 1 Cor. 2:11, 12; 6:19; 1 Thess. 4:8; 1 Pet. 1:12; 1 John 4:2.
23 Matt. 10:20; Luke 11:13; John 14:16, 26; Gal. 4:6; 1 John 3:21-24; 4:12-13.
24 Calvin states that the Father is "rightly deemed the beginning and fountainhead of the whole of divinity" (*Institutes* 1.13.25) and "the beginning of all deity" (1.13.26, 29). Similar statements are found in Augustine's *On the Trinity*, IV.xx.29 and Aquinas's *Summa theologiae*, Ia. 39.5, ad 6. Barth cites the Acts of the Toletan councils (Denzinger, *Enchiridion Symbolorum*, no. 275); Barth (1975), 393.
25 Mark 1:8; Luke 24:49a; John 1:33; 4:14; 15:26; 16:7; 20:22; Acts 2:33b; 16:7; Rom. 8:9b; Gal. 4:6; Phil. 1:19; 1 Pet. 1:11.
26 Matt. 1:18, 20 (*gennethen ek pneumatos*); 3:16; 4:1; 12:15-18, 28; Luke 1:35; 4:14-19; 5:17; 6:19; John 1:32 (cf. Isa. 11:2; Wis. 7:27; Sir. 24:7, 11); 3:34; Acts 10:38.
27 John 1:33; 6:27; 16:14b; Acts 1:2; 2:33a; Rom. 1:4; 8:11; 1 Cor. 12:3; 2 Cor. 13:4; 1 Tim. 3:16; 1 Pet. 3:18, 19; 1 John 4:13-15.
28 Exactly the same Greek prepositions are used to describe the origin of both Son and Spirit. Compare John 3:2 with 1 Cor. 6:19 (*apo theou*); John 8:42 with 1 Cor. 2:12 and 1 John 4:2 (*ek tou theou*); and John 16:28 (papyri, Sinaiticus, and Alexandrinus) with John 15:26 (*para tou patros*).

Both are sent forth by God (Gal. 4:4,6). Both have direct access to and knowledge of God the Father (Matt. 11:27; John 10:15; Rom. 8:27; 1 Cor. 2:11). Both intercede for the saints (Rom. 8:26-7,34). Both are counselors or advocates (paracletes) (John 14:16; 1 John 2:1). Both are lifegiving (1 Cor. 15:45; 2 Cor. 3:6). In these and many other texts, Christ and the Spirit are placed side by side in almost interchangeable roles.[29]

The commission finds no basis in New Testament descriptions of the temporal roles of the the Son and Spirit that would suggest that only one of them had a fundamental role to play in the origin of the other as the doctrine of the biune procession of the Spirit stipulates. Any creed that followed the New Testament alone could affirm a biune procession of the Spirit—based on the Son's cooperation in sending the Spirit—only if it was balanced by a biune generation of the Son—based on the Spirit's cooperation in begetting and sending the Son.[30] No one has ever seriously suggested taking such a step. Therefore, one is left with the simpler notion that the Son is eternally begotten from the Father and the Spirit eternally proceeds from the Father as the Nicene Creed originally stated.

Here one must be careful not to miss the deeper interconnections, however. According to the New Testament, the Spirit proceeds from the Father (John 15:26). But the Father from whom the Spirit proceeds was never alone.[31] God is (and always was) the Father of our Lord Jesus Christ (John 20:17; Rom. 15:6; 2 Cor. 1:3; 11:31; Eph. 1:3). The Father from whom the Spirit proceeds is not just a father in name, but the Father of

---

29 Acts 9:31; Rom. 8:9, 10, 11; 15:30; 1 Cor. 2:12, 16; 6:11, 15, 19; 11:4, 5; Gal. 4:4, 6; Eph. 2:18, 21, 22; 4:4, 5; Phil. 2:1; Heb. 3:14; 6:4; 10:29; Rev. 2:18, 29.

30 G.S. Hendry, *The Holy Spirit in Christian Theology* (London: SCM Press, 1957), 44. Barth argues against this possibility in (1975), 485-486. As he admits, it is difficult to deal with the exegetical issue here without appealing to extraneous theological principles. In particular, Barth relies on a degree of separation between the divine and human natures of Christ that would not be regarded as normative by the church as a whole. In order to deal with the generation of the Son in the womb of Mary, for instance, he states that "Jesus has no mother as the Son of God," a statement tantamount to denying that Mary is the "mother of God" as defined by the ecumenical councils of Ephesus (431) and Chalcedon (451); cf. Barth (1956-77), I.2:138-146.

31 In reaction to the Western church's insertion of the *filioque* into the creed, Patriarch Photius of Constantinople argues in the ninth century that the Spirit proceeds "from the Father alone." Neither Photius nor anyone else suggested adding the word "alone" to the creed. However, the extremity of this statement reminds us of the fact that the Father was never alone. If God had ever been alone, God would not have been eternally Father in contradiction to the Nicene Creed itself.

a Son. In the New Testament, God is defined as Father in relationship to Jesus, the Son of God, not in relationship to the Spirit (Gal. 4:6).

Therefore, the Spirit is not just the Spirit of God in general, but specifically "the Spirit of the God who raised Jesus from the dead" and hence "the Spirit of God's Son" (Rom. 8:11). Scripture thus allows us to say that the Spirit proceeds "from the Father of the Son," if not "from the Father and the Son."[32]

To sum up these results: the New Testament clearly teaches a relationship of parity between Christ and the Spirit. Christ is begotten from the Father. The Spirit proceeds from the Father. This parity is qualified only by the condition that the Father from whom the Spirit proceeds is the Father of Jesus Christ. The Spirit is the Spirit of God the Father and hence the Spirit of God's Son. There are no biblical grounds for the doctrine that the Spirit eternally proceeds from the Father and the Son.

These findings do not allow one to conclude that the Spirit does not in fact proceed from the Son as well as from the Father. The New Testament restricts its focus to matters that are essential for salvation. Beliefs essential for salvation such as the deity of Christ and the distinct personality of the Spirit are clearly taught. So even in the absence of explicit biblical support, there might be theological grounds for concluding that the Spirit proceeds from the Son as well as from the Father. (This is considered in the next section.)

(3) What Theological Issues Are Involved?

The biblical considerations discussed above are important in a Reformed perspective because Reformed theology regards Scripture as the sole

---

32 J. Moltmann, "Theological Proposals Towards the Resolution of the Filioque Controversy" (L. Vischer, ed., 1981a), 168-69; J. Moltmann, *The Trinity and the Kingdom* (San Francisco: Harper & Row, 1981b), 184-85. Barth concludes that the Spirit is "of the Father and the Son," but the New Testament never presents us with this combination: the Spirit is only said to be "of the Father" or "of his [God's] Son" (relative form). The biblical statement about "the Spirit of his Son" (*to pneuma tou huiou autou*, Gal. 4:6) does not sustain Barth's argument for a biune procession of the Spirit any more than the biblical statement about "the Son of his love" (*ho huios tes agapes autou*, Col. 1:13) would lead Barth to the notion of a biune generation of the Son. (On Barth's equation of the Spirit with the hypostasized love of God, see section 3, "What Theological Issues are Involved?") Calvin is more reliable when he states that "he is called the 'Spirit of Christ' not only because Christ, as eternal Word of God, is joined in the same Spirit with the Father, but also from his character as the Mediator" (*Institutes*, 3.1.2).

basis of its theology. However, the development of belief in the biune procession of the Spirit and its later defense by medieval and modern theologians had more to do with overall theological concerns than with biblical exegesis in the strict sense.

Fourth-Century Fathers

Eastern theologians of the fourth century were willing to discuss the role of the Son in the origin and hypostatic existence of the Spirit. According to Athanasius, for example, the Spirit is "from the Father in the Son" and through the Son is in God.[33] According to Basil of Caesarea, the Spirit is conjoined with the Father through the Son.[34] Gregory of Nyssa said that the Son depends directly on the Father and the Spirit is derived from the Son.[35] Didymus the Blind even stated that the Spirit derives substantially and eternally from the person of the Father and from the person of the Son.[36] But the Eastern churches never settled on a definitive formula and tended to regard the matter as exceeding the limits of human language and understanding.

In the West, the idea of the eternal procession of the Spirit from the Father and the Son has sometimes been inferred from the anti-Arian treatises of Hilary of Poitiers and Marius Victorinus, both written in the late 350s. However, Hilary explicitly referred only to the sending of the Spirit upon the church.[37] Victorinus stated that the Spirit receives its being from the Son just as the Son receives his being from the Father. Further, the Spirit precedes the Son as Spirit of the Father but follows the Son as Spirit of the Son (Gal. 4:6).[38] In his hymns to the Trinity, Victorinus portrayed the Spirit as the bond that unites the Father and the Son, but he also portrayed the Son as the mediator who transmits all

---

33 Athanasius, *Letters to Serapion*, I.33 ad fin; III.5.

34 Basil, *On the Holy Spirit*, XVIII.45.

35 *That There Are Not Three Gods*, ad fin.

36 Didymus quoted in T.F. Torrance, *Theology in Reconstruction* (London: SCM Press, 1965), 324 n. 111.

37 Hilary, *On the Trinity*, II.29 (*patre et filio auctoribus confitendus est*); cf. VIII.20, 26; cf. Victorinus, *Against Arius*, I.13 (cites John 15:26). On these texts and the even less convincing ones in Ambrose, see Kelly (1964), 87-90.

38 Victorinus, *Against Arius* I.13, 16; cf. Hymn I.61-63. Origen had stated that the Spirit depends on the Son for his substance, *Commentary on John*, II.x.7576 (II.6 in *Ante-Nicene Fathers*, 10:328b).

things from the Father to the Spirit.[39] No consistent picture of the procession of the Spirit can be derived from these fourth-century fathers.

Augustine

Western theology owes the systematic formulation of its doctrine of the Trinity primarily to Augustine of Hippo, who wrote extensively on the subject in the early fifth century.[40] Like the Eastern fathers, Augustine regarded his ideas as personal speculations intended to help inquisitive Christians like himself who wished to think through their faith. As it turned out he was the last truly creative theologian to appear in the West for several hundred years. Consequently, his writings took on a greater authority than he could have imagined. A brief review of Augustine's reasons for believing in the biune procession of the Spirit are in order.

In his pre-Christian years, Augustine had been a follower of the Manicheans, a gnostic group that regarded spirits as a visible, subtle form of matter. When he became a Christian, Augustine reacted very strongly against this idea and tried to distance himself from it by stressing the immateriality, unity, and simplicity of God.[41] The Eastern notion of the Trinity as three divine "persons" related to each other by organic modes of origin and coinherence struck Augustine as being too concrete—too anthropomorphic—to be appropriate to the deity.[42]

Because be based his theology on the unity and simplicity of God, Augustine had to find a way to establish the existence of a real distinction between Father, Son, and Spirit as required by divine revelation. The distinction of Father and Son was relatively straightforward. The Father was the source of the Son, and the Son was from the Father alone (by generation). Thus the two were differentiated by a relation of opposition (source—that which is from the source) rather than by a difference of substance.[43]

But the Spirit presented a more serious problem to Augustine's way of thinking. If the Spirit were merely from the Father (by procession), then

---

39 *Hymns,* I.4, 62-63; III.242ff. Cf. Gregory of Nyssa, *On the Song of Songs* XV (bond of glory, based on John 17:22); Epiphanius, *Ancoratus,* 7, 8. On the Neoplatonism of Victorinus, see Clark (1981), 13-18, 38-40; Margerie (1982), 112-13.

40 *On the Trinity,* written c. 398-418.

41 Ibid., I.4; V.3, 5-6, 9; VI.7-9; VII.10; VIII.pref.; XV.8.

42 Ibid., V.10; VII.7-9, 11.

43 Ibid., V.6-7, 12.

there would be no way theoretically to differentiate the Spirit from the Son. In this context, the biblical facts that Father and Son were defined in relation to each other and that the Son participated in the sending of the Spirit at Pentecost took on new significance. Augustine could solve the problem of differentiating the divine persons within a simple, common divine substance by reading these relations back into eternity and supposing that the Spirit originated from both the Father and the Son (though principally from the Father), not just from the Father as the Son did. Then the simplicity of God required that Father and Son act as a single source for the Spirit. The procession of the Spirit was biune and the Godhead was shown to be triune.[44]

Augustine found supporting arguments for his construction by examining various occurrences of the image of the triune God in humanity. For example, there was an image of God in human love: Father, Son, and Spirit were like a lover, the beloved, and the love that binds them together. The procession of the Spirit from both Father and Son follows from the fact that love proceeds from both parties.[45]

A better example for Augustine was that of the human mind which exists, knows itself to exist, and loves itself (or wills itself to exist). The unity and mutual relations of Father, Son, and Spirit were thus analogous to the unity and mutual relations of memory, intelligence, and love (or will) in humans. The generation of the Son was presupposed by the procession of the Spirit as knowledge is presupposed by human love.[46]

Clearly, Augustine's theology of the Trinity was speculative, not biblical theology as understood in the Reformed tradition. Augustine's reasoning was designed to address intellectual problems associated with a particular way of conceptualizing God. Western theology has been immensely enriched by Augustine's ideas: they certainly ought to be studied in RCA theological seminaries.

---

44 Ibid., V.15; XV.29.
45 Ibid., V.12; VI.7; XV.10, 27-29. The idea of the Spirit as the bond of love between Father and Son has been advocated by Reformed theologians like Karl Barth (1975), 480; A.I.C. Heron, "Who Proceedeth from the Father and the Son: The Problem of the Filioque," *Scottish Journal of Theology*, 24 (1971), 165-66; and A. Janssen, "Thinking About God: Reflections on Filioque," *Perspectives*, 4 (October, 1989), 11-14. Heron is more critical of Augustine, however, in his more recent work—A.I.C. Heron, *The Holy Spirit* (Philadelphia: Westminster Press, 1983), 96-97, 177-78.
46 *On the Trinity*, IX.2-8; X.17-18; XIV.6-14; XV.5, 10. The same argument is used by Aquinas, *Summa contra Gentiles*, IV.24 [12]; *Summa Theologiae*, Ia. 36.2.

But Augustine can also be criticized concerning several aspects of his view of the Trinity. It has been pointed out that his emphasis on the unity and simplicity of God have introduced an undue degree of abstractness and remoteness into the Western doctrine of God.[47] His reliance on relations of opposition to define the divine persons unnecessarily limits the field of biblical language.[48] His notion of the Spirit as the bond of love between Father and Son lacks clear biblical support and raises problems for the full equality and personality of the Spirit, as Reformed theologians like George Hendry have pointed out.[49] The location of the image of God in the threefold pattern of being, knowing, and loving (or memory, intellect, and will) portrays God in terms of intra-personal mental functions, tips the theological balance towards modalism, and gives the cognitive side of life precedence over the affective.[50] Calvin himself declared it speculative and unsound.[51]

Points like these could be debated endlessly. Regardless of the outcome on specific issues, it should be clear that nothing in Augustine's use of Scripture, his theological reasoning, or the intentions he had for his readers calls for their being erected as standards of orthodoxy for the church as a whole. Augustine avoided any mention of the biune procession of the Spirit himself in his introductory manual (*Enchiridion*) for students of theology:

> It is enough for the Christian to believe that the only cause of all created things, whether heavenly or earthly, whether visible or invisible, is the goodness of the creator, the one true God...and that he is the Trinity—to wit, the Father, and the Son begotten of the Father, and the Holy Spirit proceeding from the same Father, but one and the same Spirit of Father and Son.[52]

---

47 C. Gunton, 'Augustine, the Trinity and the Theological Crisis of the West," *Scottish Journal of Theology*, 43 (1990), 38-39, 44-45.

48 The relation of Father and Son can be described as a relation of opposition. But Scripture also describes the relationship between the first two persons of the Trinity in terms that are clearly not oppositional: e.g., Lord and Lord's Christ (Acts 4:24-26); Lord and Son (Mark 12:6-11); Lord and Lord's Servant (Acts 4:27-30; God and God's Servant (Acts 3:13); God and the Word (John 1:1); God and Lord (1 Cor. 1:3, 8:6; 12:5-6; passim); Power and Son of Man (Mark 14:62).

49 Hendry (1975), 45.

50 *Confessions*, X.33; cf. Gunton (1990), 45-47.

51 Calvin, *Institutes* 1.15.4. Augustine's analogies were criticzed by Barth (1975), 475-76.

52 *Enchiridion*, 9; *Nicene and Post-Nicene Fathers*, ed. Philip Schaff (14 vols., Buffalo and New York, 1886-90), 3:240a. The *Enchiridion* was written several years after *On the Trinity*.

Within the bounds of orthodoxy, there is room for differing styles of theology and different emphases in the doctrine of God. Augustine's speculations are acceptable, but not normative.

First Ecclesiastical Use—Against the Priscillianists

Belief in the biune procession of the Spirit was not limited to speculative theology, however. It also served an important function in countering the heresies of Priscillianism and Arianism.

The errors of the Priscillianists were primarily ones of practice—they indulged in a mixture of asceticism and astrology. But the Priscillianists were also charged with the heresy of Sabellianism or modalism—the heretical view that God is a single divine person manifested successively in the modes of Father, Son, and Spirit rather than a community of three persons.[53]

The first use of the idea of biune procession against the Priscillianists apparently occurred in a creed attributed to Pope Damasus in connection with the Council of Saragossa in 380. The wording of this creed carefully stated the difference between the Spirit and the other two divine persons: "We believe...in the Holy Spirit, neither begotten nor unbegotten...but proceeding from the Father and the Son (*de patre et filio procedentem*)."[54] Even if Sabellianism was not the primary issue between the Pope and the Priscillianists, the careful differentiation of Son and Spirit in Pope Damasus' creed may have been designed as a way to discredit them on relatively secure, theological grounds.[55]

---

53 Leo I., *Letter*, XV. Pref., 1.
54 Creed of Damasus, qutoed in Kelly (1972), 360. The Latin is given in Kelly (1964), 134. In the latter (earlier) work, however, Kelly dated the *Fides Damasi* to late fifth century Gaul: (1964), 58. Even if dated to the fourth century, the wording of the Creed of Damasus has some precedent in Epiphanius, who wrote (c. 374) that the Spirit is "neither begotten nor created, neither brother...nor offspring, but out of the same substance of Father and Son," *Ancoratus*, 70-71, quoted in J.N.D. Kelly, *Early Christian Doctrines* (London: Adam & Charles Black, 1968), 263. However, Epiphanius did not include these ideas in the creeds he cited in spite of the fact that several other credal innovations were included to counter the modalism of Marcellus of Ancyra.
55 Precedent may have been found in the writing of Tertullian, who wrote against the modalists of his own time (c. 213) that the Son was "from the Father's substance" and that the Spirit was "from the Father through the Son" (*a patre per filium*), *Agaisnt Praxeas*, 4. However, Tertullian stated this in order to assure the unity of Father, Son, and Spirit, not to differentiate them.

Half a century later, in 447, Pope Leo I wrote a letter, also directed against the Priscillianists, in which-he argued that there must be a difference between one who begets, one who is begotten, and one who "proceeds from both" (*de utroque processerit*).[56] At about the same time, a creed attributed to Bishop Pastor of Gallicia (Castile) affirmed that the Spirit "proceeds from the Father and the Son."[57] This creed was approved by subsequent anti-Priscillianist meetings like the Council of Toledo (447) and the Synod of Braga (northern Portugal, 563).[58]

The theological function of the doctrine of the biune procession during the fifth century was clearly one of affirming the distinction of the divine persons, particularly the Son and the Spirit. It is significant that no biblical arguments were offered in support of the doctrine.[59] In fact, none were needed. Modalism had already been shown to be heretical on biblical grounds by Tertullian and others as early as the third century.[60] It had been condemned at the Synod of Smyrna (against Noetus, c. 180), by Pope Callistus (against Sabellius, c. 220), and at the Council of Constantinople (against Marcellus, 381). None of these had utilized the doctrine of a biune procession of the Spirit in defense of orthodoxy, however. The statements of Damasus, Leo, and Pastor only called on the idea of the biune procession as a teaching tool to reinforce established theological tradition-and thereby to call Priscillianist theology into question—not as a first line of defense for orthodox teaching.

So the original context in which ecclesiastical use was made of belief in the biune procession of the Spirit was a rather limited one—the heresy of

---

[56] Leo I, *Epistle*, 15.1. Compare the earlier statement of Epiphanius: "God is Life; the Son is Life from Life; and the Holy Spirit proceeds from Both,' *Ancoratus*, 70-71, qutoed in H.B. Swete, *The Holy Spirit in the Ancient Tradition* (London: Macmillan, 1912), 227. The biblical model here is evidently the eschatological image of tthe"water of life" flowing from the throne of God and the Lamb (Rev. 22:1).

[57] Creed attributed to Bishop Pastor: Kelly (1964), 990 (gives date as 447); Idem (1972), 360-361 (gives date as 433).

[58] Kelly (1964), 56-57; Swete (1912), 344.

[59] As expressed in the second section, "What Scripture Teaches About the Procession of the Spirit," the New Testament does not teach a biune procession of the Spirit. That does not mean that there are no texts to which appeal might be made. The eschatological vision in Rev. 22:1 forsees that the water of life will flow out to the nations from the throne of God and the Lamb. By analogy with John 7:38-39, the water of life might be interpreted as the gift of the Spirit: so H.B. Swete, *The Holy Spirit in the New Testament* (London: Macmillan, 1909), 351, 357-58. The image in Revelation 22, of course, comes from the vision of the eschatological temple in Ezek. 47:1-12; cf. Joel 3:18; Zech. 14:8.

[60] Tertullian, *Against Praxeas* (c. 213); Novatian, *On the Trinity* (c. 250); Hilary, *On the Trinity* (c. 360).

the Priscillianists of Spain. The wider popularity of the doctrine in the West is due to the diffusion of the Athanasian Creed, which originated in late fifth or early sixth-century Gaul.[61] The basic motive seems to have been the codification of the Catholic faith against heretics, particularly Sabellians, Arians, and Nestorians.[62] The Nicene Creed might have served the same purpose, but it did not come into general use in the West until after the Third Council of Toledo in 589.[63]

In the section of the Athanasian Creed dealing with the procession of the Spirit, the main target seems again to have been Priscillianist modalism. Even more than in earlier creeds the wording meticulously differentiated the divine persons of the Trinity:

> The Father is made of none, neither created nor begotten.
> > The Son is from the Father alone, not made, nor created, but begotten.
> > The Holy Spirit is from the Father and the Son (*a Patre et Filio*), neither made, nor created, nor begotten, but proceeding (*procedens*).
> > So there is one Father, not three Fathers; one Son, not three Sons; one Holy Spirit, not three Holy Spirits. (lines 21-24)

The Athanasian Creed was the first credal statement of the biune procession of the Spirit to become normative for the Western church as a whole.[64] In the early sixth century, Caesarius of Arles regarded it as an authoritative statement of the Catholic faith, the "Faith of Saint Athanasius," and recommended it for both clergy and laity.[65] It was understood to be a standard of orthodoxy by Isidore of Seville at the Fourth Synod of Toledo (633), and its memorization was required of all clergy by the Second Synod of Arles (c. 670).[66] No one at this time seems

---

61 See note 9.
62 Kelly (1964), 76-80, 94-98.
63 Kelly (1972), 351-53.
64 See note 5. At this stage, the doctrine of the biune procession had still not been introduced into the Western version of the Nicene Creed. The latter innovation occurred somewhere between the late sixth and the late eighth centuries (see section 4, "Issues Involved in the Addition of the *Filioque* to the Nicene Creed").
65 Kelly (1964), 36, 122-24.
66 Kelly (1964), 39-41.

to have realized how controversial the statement about the procession of the Spirit might be. It was simply accepted as part of established tradition and required no special rationale. In other words, the traditions and styles of Eastern and Western theology were different from the start, and the doctrine of the biune procession of the Spirit was regarded as a standard of orthodoxy in the Latin West before its divergence from the tradition of the Greek East was realized. The issue between East and West would eventually boil down to one of ecclesiastical authority.

How is one to evaluate this earliest ecclesiastical use of the doctrine of the biune procession of the Spirit? The frequency with which it was cited against the Priscillianists indicates that it was felt to be effective. A biune procession was certainly sufficient grounds for differentiating the Son and the Spirit and thereby arguing against modalism. But the great anti-modalist theologians of the third, fourth, and fifth centuries had established their case without appealing to the new doctrine. In an age when Scripture was still the primary norm of theology, it was sufficient to note the facts of the New Testament: the Father sends the Son; the Son prays to the Father; the Father glorifies the Son; the Son glorifies the Father; the Son returns to the Father; the Son sends the Spirit; the Spirit glorifies the Son. That three distinct persons are involved in the New Testament story was evident. As the Arian controversy proved in the fourth century, demonstrating the full deity of Son and Spirit and complete unity of the Trinity was a more serious challenge from a strictly biblical standpoint.

Isidore-Against the Spanish Arians

In fact, the theological focus in the West shifted from the challenge of Priscillianism to that of Arianism in the sixth and seventh centuries. Accordingly, the theological rationale for the doctrine of the biune confession shifted from one of differentiating the persons of the Trinity (particularly the Son and the Spirit) to one of uniting them (particularly the Father and the Son).

In a series of works that were to be widely influential in the later Middle Ages, Isidore of Seville appealed to the doctrine as evidence of the essential unity of the Father and the Son: "One thing which is consubstantial with two (others) could not at once proceed from them and be in them unless the two from which it proceeds were one." For Isidore, the Holy Spirit was the bond of unity that made the Father and the Son one in essence.[67] In view of the fact that Isidore's Spain was ruled by the Visigoths, one may assume that the primary heresy against which he marshalled this evidence was the local form of Arianism, which divided the Godhead into separate (if similar) substances.[68]

Like the earlier use of the doctrine of biune procession against Priscillianism, Isidore's use of it against Arianism was effective but both problematic and unnecessary. It certainly demonstrated the unity of the Godhead as required by orthodox doctrine. But, like other attempts to portray the Spirit as the bond of union between Father and Son, it raised troublesome problems regarding the status of the Spirit. Was the Spirit just an impersonal force binding the other two together? If not—that is, if the Spirit was a full person just like Father and Son—what was the agent that bound it to the other two? If it is countered that divine persons are infinitely more subtle and penetrating than humans and hence interpenetrate without need for a binding agent, then the Father and Son are seen to be perfectly one even without regard for the presence of the Spirit.

On the other hand, Arianism could be refuted without appeal to the doctrine of biune procession. In fact, the major theologians of the fourth century—Athansasius, Hilary, and Basil—who were revered in West as well as East, had done just that. The doctrine of the biune procession of the Spirit may have proved helpful in the context of Visigothic Spain, but it could hardly be required of the whole church on that basis.

With Isidore, the medieval Western constellation of theological and political ideas first comes into view. Isidore was perhaps the first Western Christian to criticize Byzantium for its caesaropapism (the authoritative role of the Emperor in ecclesiastical affairs) and to regard it as a declining force in history: the future lay with the West, particularly with Visigothic Spain. Isidore's moral contempt for the Greek East was largely due to Emperor Justinian's recent imperialistic policies towards the West and his interference in the affairs of the church. At the Fifth Ecumenical Council (Constantinople, 553), he had secured the condemnation of three popular

---

[67] Isidore, *Sentences*, I.15.2. Isidore also cited the biune procession as a way of distinguishing procession from generation: "...the Son is begotten of One, but the Spirit proceeds from Both," *Etymologies*, VII.3. Both sources qutoed in Swete (1912), 346. The idea of the Spirit as the bond of union between Father and Son goes back to Victorinus; cf. Note 38.

[68] Swete (1912), 343-47; Kelly (1964), 78-80.

Antiochene theologians, the so-called "Three Chapters," for their sharp differentiation of the two natures of Christ. Byzantine forces had finally been expelled from Spain in the 620s. Isidore particularly sympathized with two North African theologians who had labored and suffered in defense of the Three Chapters.[69]

Although the coincidence of belief in the biune procession and the strict distinction of natures in Christ may have been accidental at this stage, an inner connection between the two emphases was to be developed in the later Middle Ages. On the one hand, the Augustinian stress on the unity and simplicity of God required a differentiation of the human and divine natures in Christ (in order to avoid Docetism). Conversely, the strict distinction of natures in Christ made it possible to account for New Testament passages stressing the Spirit's role in the earthly life of Jesus in terms of the weakness of his human nature alone.[70] Such a view of the biblical evidence did not entail the biune procession, but it did neutralize one of the principal biblical arguments against it.[71]

First East-West Conflict

The unity of the divine substance and the differentiation of the two natures in Christ were apparently also the context for Pope Martin I's belief in the biune procession of the Spirit. In the mid-seventh century, the Greek Orthodox Church became aware (apparently for the first time) of the fact that the West had a different view about the procession of the Spirit. The immediate occasion was a new stage in the ongoing controversy concerning the two natures of Christ—whether along with the two natures, human and divine, there were two corresponding wills (the position later decided on as "orthodox") or just one will. At the Lateran Council of 649, Pope Martin anathematized the Monothelite ("one-will")

---

69 J. Herrin, *The Formation of Christendom* (Princeton: Princeton University Press, 1987), 124, 236, 240-42. The best known of the "Three Chapters" was Theodore of Mopsuestia. The North African theologians who served as a link between them and Isidore were Abbot Facundus of Hermiane and Bishop Victor of Tonnena: ibid., 121, 232, 241.

70 So Aquinas, *Summa contra Gentiles*, IV.24 [3]; and Barth (1975), 199-201, 485-86.

71 Antiochene theologians stressed the empowering of the Spirit for the man Jesus but still affirmed that the Spirit proceeds from the Father alone and not from or even through the Son: Swete (1912), 258-60, 269-70; G.L. Prestige, *God in Patristic Thought* (London: SPC, 1964), 250.

position and the last three Patriarchs of Constantinople who had subscribed to it.[72]

In his synodal letter to the Church of Constantinople, however, Martin stated as part of his faith the belief that the Spirit proceeds from the Son as well as from the Father.[73] It is unclear whether the pope was already aware that he was articulating a distinctively Western position on the Spirit. But the Byzantine Monothelites made the most out of this deviation from "orthodoxy" as understood in the East in an obvious effort to weaken Martin's theological credentials. Maximus the Confessor, the Eastern champion of the Dyothelite ("two-wills") cause, tried to defend the theology of his Western ally in christology. He argued that the Western view that the Spirit proceeds from the Father and the Son meant basically the same thing as the Eastern doctrine that the Spirit proceeds from the Father "through the Son." In other words, the doctrine of the biune procession of the Spirit was intended by the Western church leaders to emphasize the unity and immutability of the divine nature.[74] Presumably, Maximus based this interpretation of the biune procession on what he had learned of Pope Martin's views on the subject during his earlier stay in Rome. The doctrine that the Spirit proceeds through the Son was acceptable to Roman pontifs as an equivalent to the Western teaching (though it was not added to their creeds) as late as Pope Hadrian I in 794.[75]

So the context in which the biune procession of the Spirit took on new theological meaning in the seventh century was partly christological—the distinctively Western fear of any confusion of the two natures of Christ—and partly political—the increasing need of the West to distance itself from the Eastern Roman Empire and the Eastern Orthodox Church.

---

[72] Herrin (1987), 218. Unlike Isidore, however, Pope Martin, like his predecessors, accepted the authority of the Fifth Ecumenical Council. At this stage, Rome did not share the anti-Byzantine sentiments of the Spanish church. That did not emerge until the second iconoclast dispute of the ninth century: Herrin (1987), 472-73.

[73] M. Fahey, "Son and Spirit: Divergent Theologies Between Constantinople and the West," In Kung and Moltmann, eds. (1979), 17. The same combination of features was present at the English Synod of Hatfield (680), which followed the Lateran Council in condemning Monothelitism and affirming the biune procession of the Spirit: Kelly (1972), 362-63.

[74] Swete (1912), 279. The emphasis on unity and immutability was a traditional Augustinian emphasis: C.B. Kaiser, *The Doctrine of God* (Westchester, IL: Crossway Books, 1982), 76-81. The unitive force of the "through the Son" formula was established by Tertullian, *Against Praxeas*, 4; and Basil, *On the Holy Spirit*, 45.

[75] Hadrian I's letter to Charlemagne: Kelly (1972), 364.

What assessment is one to make of this theological rationale for the biune procession of the Spirit? Although it is one-sided, it is clearly within the bounds of orthodoxy as defined by the ecumenical councils of the church. The relations between the persons of the Trinity can never be defined exactly. Differing emphases are allowable. The same is true of the relation between the two natures of Christ. The West—since the seventh century—has typically stressed the unity and simplicity of God in the Trinity and, conversely, the distinctness of the two natures in Christ. Eastern churches allow more diversity among the persons of the Trinity and take various views on the two-natures issue.

Therefore, no one should conclude that the Western view of the Trinity (including the biune procession of the Spirit) is heretical. On the other hand, no one should take the Western view to be the faith of the whole church. One may confess the biune procession as a special viewpoint within the bounds of orthodoxy. But to make it a test of orthodoxy in the context of present awareness of the issues would be to deny the wider church beyond the West.

Thomas Aquinas

The theological arguments for the biune procession of the Spirit were summed up and sharpened by Thomas Aquinas in the thirteenth century. The ideas already stated on intuitive grounds were given clear definition and rational justification. Two of Aquinas's points deserve particular mention.

The principal objection to the doctrine of the biune procession from a biblical standpoint was that it overlooked the fact that the role of Jesus in sending the Spirit was complemented by the role of the Spirit in the sending of Jesus. Greek Orthodox opponents apparently argued this point and supported it by citing Luke 4:18: "The Spirit of the Lord is upon me, because he has anointed me to preach good news to the poor...." Aquinas deftly disposed of this text, however—and, by extension, all others that apply to the earthly Jesus—by arguing that the Son is sent by the Spirit only in relation to his human nature. Texts that refer to the risen Christ sending the Spirit, however, could be referred to his divine nature.[76]

---

[76] Aquinas, *Summa contra Gentiles*, IV.24 [2-3].

Since the New Testament witness is the only final authority in these matters, a few words on Aquinas's exegetical maneuver are in order.

It was accepted practice in the early church (and later in the Reformation) to account for certain aspects of the life of Jesus on the basis of his assumption of human nature. This was felt to be necessary in order to avoid the conclusion that aspects of his life were incompatible with his deity. The procedure assumed, however, that one knew which attributes were appropriate to which nature. Jesus' descent from David, for instance, was clearly a property of the human nature, not the divine. On the other hand, Jesus' descent from heaven applied to the divine nature, not to the human. Other texts had to be applied to the divine and human natures combined in the single theanthropic person (e.g., 1 John 1:7: "The blood of Jesus cleanses us from sin…").

The problem with Aquinas's exegesis of Luke 4:18 is that it depends on the assumption that being anointed by the Spirit is only appropriate to the human nature of Jesus and not to the divine Word itself. Unfortunately, this assumption would imply that being sent is also inappropriate to the Holy Spirit. Moreover, it overlooks the possibility that the object of the Spirit's anointing could be the divine nature or the divine and human natures combined. It might even be that only the presence of the divine Word in Christ made him a suitable resting place for the Spirit in its fullness as several early fathers said.[77] Aquinas's exegetical argument is too shaky to sustain his interpretation of the New Testament texts referring to the Spirit's sending the Son.

A second argument Aquinas gave for the doctrine of the double procession of the Spirit was based on an a priori analysis of the relations of origin among the members of the Trinity. The Father is related to the Son by reason of paternity and to the Spirit by way of breathing-forth or "spiration": Aquinas hoped everyone would agree to this much.[78] Then

---

[77] Cyril of Jerusalem, *Catechetical Lecture*, XXI.1; Gregor of Nazianzus, *Oration*, XXXIX.16: "And the Spirit bears witness to his godhead, for he descends upon one that is like him."

[78] The introduction of unbiblical terms like "paternity," "filiation," and "spiration" already raises problems for Aquinas's method. Not only do they remove the asymmetry inherent in the biblical terms, "generation" and "procession," but they make the Son more active ("filiation" from the Father) and the Spirit less active ("spiration" by the Father) than the biblical terms, "generation" (by the Father) and "procession" (from the Father) suggest.

do the two functions of paternity and spiration constitute two sources in the Godhead—one from whom the Son is begotten and another from whom the Spirit proceeds? No, because paternity and spiration are not contrary to each other. The same person can generate the Son and spirate the Spirit at the same time without contradiction. So the simplicity of God requires that there be just one source, the Father. Presumably everyone still agrees.

Aquinas applies the exact same logic to the converse relations of filiation (the converse of paternity) and procession (the converse of spiration). It is said that the Son filiates from the Father and the Spirit proceeds. But do these two functions by themselves constitute two distinct persons—one who filiates from the Father and one who proceeds? Again the answer must be no because filiation and procession are no more opposites than paternity and spiration. Theoretically, the same person could both filiate and proceed from the Father alone. Then the simplicity of God would require one to say that there is only one divine person (besides the Father) who both filiates and proceeds unless there were some other relation of origin between the one who filiates and the one who proceeds to constitute them two distinct persons. So, in order to have three persons and not just two, either the Son must filiate from the Spirit as well as from the Father or the Spirit must proceed from the Son as well as from the Father. But no one ever said that the Spirit was a co-father of the Son. It follows that the Son must be a co-spirator of the Spirit.[79]

Following Augustine, Aquinas relied heavily here on the idea of the simplicity of God. According to the Angelic Doctor, one knows that there is one source rather than two for the functions of paternity and filiation because the simplicity of God demands it. But, from a biblical standpoint, is not the reason one believes in a single source in the Godhead rather the belief that all things are ultimately referred to one source, the Father, even within the divine order itself?[80] While the non-contrariness of paternity and spiration may be a necessary condition for the existence of a single source in the Godhead, it is not a sufficient condition. Conversely, the

---

79 *Summa contra Gentiles*, IV.24 [8]; the concluding step, stating that the Spirit is not a father is implicit.
80 Rom. 11:36; 16:27; 1 Cor. 8:6; 15:28; Eph. 2:18; 4:6; 5:20; Col. 3:17; 1 Tim. 1:17; 1 Pet. 1:11; Jude 25.

existence of a relation of origin between the Son and Spirit would be a sufficient condition for their distinction as persons, but not a necessary one.

Clearly there are gaps in Aquinas's logic, but the more serious question has to do with the propriety of using this sort of a priori logic to map out the divine relations in the first place. Aquinas's conclusions follow from the mere need to demonstrate the existence of three divine persons. He also uses the traditional relations of paternity/filiation and spiration/procession, but any two non-contrary relations would do equally well. It really wouldn't make any difference what Scripture said about the divine persons in Aquinas's logic: as long as there are three of them one must proceed from the other two.

Perhaps, reasoning like this will be helpful to some believers. If so, one may be thankful to Aquinas for providing it. But there are no grounds here for making the results of such speculations binding on the consciences of all believers.

John Calvin

A far more biblical sort of reasoning about the relationships within the Trinity has been developed by the Reformed theologians, John Calvin and Karl Barth.

Prior to any mention of the procession of the Spirit in the *Institutes of the Christian Religion*, Calvin introduced the topic of trinitarian theology with a refreshing disclaimer about the imprecision of theological language. The essential truths for Calvin were that there is only one God, and that Scripture speaks of three divine "persons" with the names Father, Son, and Spirit, each of whom is truly God. Theological terms like "Trinity," "persons," and "substance" were helpful if they conformed to biblical teaching even if they were not found in the New Testament itself.[81] Calvin's fundamental concern was for the unity of the church in faithfulness to the basic biblical truths: "If, therefore, these terms were not rashly invented, we ought to beware lest by repudiating them we be accused of overweening rashness. Indeed, I could wish that they were buried, if only among all [people] this faith were agreed on: that Father and Son and Spirit are one God, yet the Son is not the Father, nor the Spirit the Son,

---

[81] Calvin, *Institutes* 1.13.3 (edition of 1536 as revised in 1539 and 1559).

but that they are differentiated by a peculiar quality."[82] By the "peculiar quality" of each divine person Calvin meant a special, distinguishing mark by which it is distinguished from the common essence of the deity and from the other two persons.[83] Calvin had in mind traditional terms like "fatherhood," "sonship," and "holiness," or, alternatively, "being unbegotten," "being only-begotten," and "proceeding," but he preferred not to burden the reader with words he felt were unnecessary for faith.

How did Calvin show that the three divine persons are distinct? Not on the basis of abstract models of binary relations, but directly from Scripture. One knows that the Son is distinct from the Father because the Word was "with God" (John 1:1; 17:5) and "went forth from the Father" (John 16:28). The Spirit is distinct from the Father because it "proceeds from the Father" (John 15:26). The Spirit is distinct from Christ because it is "another Counselor," the "Spirit of Christ," and the "Spirit of the one who raised up Christ" (John 14:16; Rom. 8:9, 11).[84]

When Calvin came to the the topic of the procession of the Spirit, he made further disclaimers. He was unsure how expedient it was to introduce analogies from human affairs. All such analogies were "quite inadequate," and Calvin wished to avoid any suggestion of rashness. But in order to illustrate the distinction of the divine persons he described them as the "wellspring of all things," the "wisdom, counsel, and ordered disposition of all things," and the "power and efficacy of that activity." To the human mind, at least, there is an order here—one similar to the order observed in human affairs except that the divine order lacks a before and an after: "...the Father is thought of as first, then from him the Son, and finally from both the Spirit. For the mind of each human being is naturally inclined to contemplate God first, then the wisdom coming forth from

---

82 Ibid., 1.13.5 (edition of 1536) as translated in McNeill, ed. (1960), 125-26.
83 Ibid., 1.13.6, 19 (edition of 1559). In the edition of 1543, Calvin briefly introduced Augustine's concept of mutual relations between the persons in order to describe the names of Father, Son, and Spirit, not their "peculiar qualities."
84 Ibid., 1.13.17 (edition of 1536 as revised in 1539 and 1559). Neither here (edition of 1536) nor in 3.1.2 (edition of 1536 as revised in 1559) did Calvin infer that the Spirit therefore proceeded from the Son: "...he is called the 'Spirit of Christ' [Rom. 8:9; 1 Pet. 1:11] not only because Christ...is joined in the same Spirit with the Father, but also from his [Christ's] character as the Mediator": J.T. McNeil, ed., Calvin: *Institutes of the Christian Religion* (Philadelphia: Westminster Press, 1960), 539. The most that Calvin ventured was to conclude that the Spirit could not be "of the Father alone": *Institutes* 1.13.23.

him, and lastly the power whereby he [God] executes the decrees of his plan. For this reason, the Son is said to come forth from the Father alone; the Spirit, from the Father and the Son at the same time."[85] So, even if the analogy of wellspring, wisdom, and power is imperfect, it may help people to see the distinction between three persons of the Trinity. Calvin saw the distinction, not the analogy, as essential to Christian faith.

But does the distinction of three persons negate the unity of God? No, Calvin answered, because the Son shares with the Father one and the same Spirit, and the latter is the Spirit of the Father and the Son.[86] The essential points again are the unity, distinctness, and equality of the three.

Calvin clearly refused to place much theological weight on the doctrine of the biune procession of the Spirit. It was part of a theological tradition dating all the way back to Augustine. But Calvin's repeated emphasis was on the basic points of the doctrine of the Trinity: one God; three persons; all equal in deity. That much could be substantiated directly from Scripture. Further speculations were helpful in so far as they illustrated the unity in distinction but were not to be pressed too far lest they give ammunition to the enemies of the faith.[87]

Karl Barth

Whereas Calvin was reacting against the tangled arguments of the medieval scholasticism, Karl Barth wanted to recover a deeper theology from the debacle of nineteenth-century liberalism. For Barth, the Spirit of God was the basis of the unmerited fellowship and love between God and humanity.[88] In order to avoid subjective idealism and romanticism, he insisted that this fellowship and love be understood as real and fully objective. Rejecting the notion that one's openness to revelation is due to an innate human capacity for God, Barth argued that the uniting function of the Spirit is grounded in the eternal Godhead. The Spirit's uniting feature as fellowship and love was associated with the doctrine of the

---

85 Ibid., 1.13.18 (edition of 1539) as translated in McNeill, ed. (1960), 143.
86 Ibid., 1.13.19 (edition of 1539).
87 Ibid., 1.13.18 (edition of 1539).
88 Barth develops these thoughts by way of commentary on the third article of the Nicene Creed. His reasoning has to do with a theology of the Spirit rather than with the formation or use of creeds or with formal exegesis of Scripture. His main concern is to avoid an outright denial of the doctrine of the biune procession.

procession of the Spirit from Father and Son and would be lost, Barth felt, if the latter were not upheld.[89]

Barth is undoubtedly the most brilliant and creative Reformed theologian of the twentieth century. Reformed scholars might not even be discussing deep theological matters like the biune procession of the Spirit if it were not for his revitalization of our doctrinal heritage. Nonetheless, Barth's theology of the Trinity is open to criticisms at several points. The fact that Barth prefers to speak of "modes of being" rather than "persons" in the Trinity has occasioned the observation that he leans in the direction of modalism. This tendency becomes particularly apparent in his treatment of the procession of the Spirit.[90] Moreover, Barth relies on the hermeneutical tactic of sharply differentiating the two natures of Christ, even going so far as to deny at one point that Jesus as the Son of God had a human mother.[91] Thus he leans about as far towards modalism and Nestorianism as is possible within the bounds of orthodoxy.

Like other theologians in the Augustinian tradition, Barth had to struggle with the paradoxes that arise from the equation of the Holy Spirit with the attribute of love in God. The New Testament clearly states that the Father loves the Son (John 5:20). However, nowhere does it equate that love with the Spirit. The closest parallel is Galatians 5:22, which lists love as the first of sevenfold "fruit of the Spirit." On the other hand, 2 Corinthians 13:14 associates fellowship with the Spirit and love with God the Father in a clearly trinitarian formula. If, for some reason, the love shared by Father and Son must be hypostatized, why not hypostatize the mutual knowledge and the mutual glory of Father and Son as well (Matt. 11:27; John 10:15; 17:1)? And then what about the mutual knowledge between the Father and the Spirit (Rom. 8:27; 1 Cor. 2:11)? Once theology is allowed to expand ideas without biblical controls, needless problems arise.

Barth's principal argument in favor of the biune procession of the Spirit is that it establishes an objective basis in the Godhead for the fellowship

89 Barth (1975), 480-84.
90 E.g.: "As God is in himself Father from all eternity, he begets himself as the Son from all eternity." This third mode of being...[results] only from their being one being as God the Father and God the Son, who are not two 'persons' either in themselves or in cooperation, but two modes of being of the one being of God." Barth (1975), 483, 486-87. On Barth's defense against the charge of modalism, see Kaiser (1982), 114.
91 Barth (1975), 486.

of God and humanity. The tendency of modern piety and theology to end in subjectivism is a real danger and must be resisted by all possible means. But can it become the basis for a theological doctrine dating back to the fourth or fifth century-long before the problems of modern theology?[92] And is it the case that Western Christians who subscribe to the doctrine of the biune procession are more objective in their piety and faith than their Eastern colleagues who deny it?

Even if these things were so, one could ask why the Holy Spirit is singled out as the basis of the fellowship of God and humanity. Is Jesus Christ not the one mediator between God and humanity (Matt. 11:27; John 14:6; 1 Tim. 2:5)? Even as an historical person, Jesus is often subjectivized by biblical criticism and evangelical piety alike. To avoid such modern tendencies, should not one, following Barth's method, think of Christ as being a mediator within the eternal order of the Godhead? Would that not lead, by the same reasoning, to a doctrine of the biune generation of the Son?

As in the cases of Augustine and Aquinas, it must be allowed that criticisms like these can be answered. Even if they can, however, it is unlikely that a theological viewpoint that is so difficult to establish on biblical grounds should be made a point of orthodoxy for all believers.

Barth's treatment of the Spirit functioned entirely within the parameters of the received form of the Nicene Creed. The only alternatives he considered were the traditional Western inclusion of the doctrine of the biune procession in the creed and its outright denial (or, alternatively, the suggestion that the Spirit proceeds "through the Son"). Since he saw valuable implications in the doctrine that would be lost if it were denied, he argued vehemently against its opponents. He did not consider the possibility, since raised by other Reformed theologians,[93] that other formulations or wordings might also provide the implications he valued. Nonetheless, Barth's biblical use of theological language suggests several

---

92 Calvin discussed the role of the Spirit as a bond between Christ and humanity without
     relating it to the idea of the Spirit as a bond between Father and Son or the doctrine
     of the procession of the Spirit, *Institutes* 3.1.1, 2.
93 Reformed theologians who agree with Barth's concern to associate the Spirit with the
     Son but not by means of the doctrine of the biune procession of the Spirit include
     Thomas Torrance (1965) and *Theology in Reconciliation* (London: Geoffrey Chapman,
     1975) and Jurgen Moltmann (1981a. 1981b).

alternatives that might prove to be helpful even though his defense of the traditional doctrine of the biune procession is found to be unconvincing.

For instance, Barth states that the Father from whom the Spirit proceeds is not an abstract father but none other than the Father of the Son.[94] In fact, the Spirit is brought forth in the Godhead, not before or after the Son, but together with the Son. "He is the Father of the Son in such a way that with the Son he brings forth the Spirit...." "...as God is the Father of the Son, and, as Father begets the Son, he also brings forth the Spirit...."[95] On the basis of the preceding article describing the eternal origin of the Son from the Father, and in view of the following phrase, "who with the Father and the Son together is worshiped and glorified," the third article of the Nicene Creed should be read to mean that the Spirit proceeds "from the Father of the Son" or "from the Father together with the Son."

George Hendry

One final theological argument for the doctrine of the biune procession of the Spirit should be mentioned. Throughout the history of the church, there have been sectarian movements described as enthusiasts or spiritualists or charismatics. In the early church there were the Montanists. The Reformers had to deal with figures like Thomas Muntzer and the Zwickau prophets.

George Hendry has argued that the real meaning of the biune procession of the Spirit is the centering of all spirituality in the person and work of Christ. Already in the New Testament, he points out, there were warnings against the influence of other spirits that do not confess that Christ is Lord and that Christ has come in the flesh (1 Cor. 12:3; 1 John 4:1-3).[96]

The difficulties with this argument are biblical and historical. For one thing, the New Testament also warns that calling Jesus "Lord" is not in itself a sufficient test of faith. The final criteria involve fruit of the Spirit

---

94 Barth (1975), 482. Moltmann develops this suggestion in (1981a), 168-69; (1981b), 184-85.
95 Barth (1975), 483.
96 Hendry (1957), 41; cf. C. Welch, *The Trinity in Contemporary Theology* (London: SCM Press, 1953), 285. Barth directs a similar argument against some forms of Russian pansophism in (1975), 481.

like obedience, love, peace, and mercy.[97]   Moreover, none of the New Testament texts that make the confession of Jesus the test of spirits raise the issue of the procession of the Holy Spirit. Conversely, none of the theologians or councils that developed the doctrine of the biune procession were concerned with Montanism or other charismatic movements. Nor is there evidence that any of the Reformers ever used the doctrine in relation to the challenge of spiritualism in their own time.[98]

So long as the Spirit is believed to proceed from the Father, no problem can arise as to the relationship of the Spirit to Christ unless Christians forget the basic meaning of the confession of God as Father. If the Father is understood in general, anthropological terms, as it often is in modern Western religious thought, then the danger of dissociation of the Spirit from the person and work will be real. But that points back to a misunderstanding (or ignorance) of the first two articles of the creed, not to a problem with the third article. In the Nicene Creed as in the New Testament, the Father from whom the Spirit proceeds is "the one who raised Jesus from the dead" (Rom. 8:11) and the one from whom the only Son of God was "begotten before all worlds."

(4) Issues Involved in the Addition of the *Filioque* to the Nicene Creed

Up to this point only the doctrine of the biune procession of the Spirit and its appearance in confessional formulas like the Athanasian Creed have been considered. In this section, the matter of its incorporation into the Nicene Creed (the *filioque*) shall be addressed as a separate issue.

Historically, the issues involved in changing the Nicene Creed were rather different from any of the theological arguments that had been offered for the doctrine of the biune procession. The *filioque* was first added to the Creed sometime between 589 and 796. One cannot be sure exactly when, but it was probably closer to the latter of these two dates. It was still absent in Latin texts of the creed as late as the tenth century.

---

[97] Matt. 7:15-23; 1 Cor. 13:1 to 14:40; Gal. 5:13 to 6:10; James 1:22 to 5:6; 1 Pet. 2:11 to 4:19.

[98] Calvin omitted any reference to the doctrine of the procession of the Spirit in his discussions on Word and Spirit; e.g. in his *Reply to Sadoleto* of 1539; H. Beveridge, ed., *Tracts of Calvin* (Edinburgh: Calvin Translation Society, 1844-51), 1:36-37; Olin, ed. (1976), 60-62. On Luther's opposition to Muntzer, see D. Ritschi, "Historical Development and Implicaitons of the *Filioque* Controversy" (L. Visher, ed., 1981), 62-63.

It used to be thought that the *filioque* was first inserted at the Third Council of Toledo in 589. The Latin Creed was formally recited by Reccared, King of the Visigoths, and recitation was henceforth mandatory in the Mozarabic rite.[99] But it is not clear that the *filioque* was present in this early version of the creed. In a separate action, Reccared pronounced his own view of the Spirit as "proceeding from the Father and the Son" (*a patre et a filio procedere*), and the Council duly anathematized anyone as an Arian who might refuse to confess the same.[100] Consistency on this point would suggest that the idea was incorporated into the recitation of the Nicene Creed as well. In fact, most copies of the Acts of the Council do include the words "proceeds from the Father and the Son" (*ex patre et filio procedentum*) in the words of the Nicene Creed as well as in Reccared's personal confession.[101] But consistency is not always a reliable guide in making inferences about one creed from another.[102] Furthermore, the next documentation of the *filioque* does not occur until the late eighth century, and present-day scholars tend to see the added phrase in the Acts of the Third Council of Toledo as a later insertion.[103]

The first indisputable evidence of inclusion of the *filioque* in the Nicene Creed dates from the Synod of Cividale del Friuli (or Frejus), held in 796 (or 797).[104] Paulinus of Aquileia proposed that memorization of the Nicene Creed was the best defense against Spanish Adoptionism, a remnant of Nestorian Christology holding that the man Jesus was only the adoptive son of God.[105] The text of the creed that he offered clearly

---

99 Kelly (1972), 351.

100 Swete (1912), 344; Kelly (1972), 361-62.

101 Ibid., (1912), 344-45.

102 For example, both the Heidelberg Catechism and the Belgic Confession teach the doctrine of creation, but only the Belgic Confession specified creation *ex nihilo* (Art. 12). Both can be confessed side by side without any sense of inconsistency.

103 "The matter still requires investigation, but the conclusion seems inescapable that, as originally recited at the Council of Toledo, the text of C [the Niceno-Constantinopolitan Creed] was the pure one without *filioque*," Kelly (1972), 362.

104 Some scholars hold that a form of the Nicene Creed that included the *filioque* was already in use in Charlemagne's realm earlier in the eighth century: R.G. Heath, "The Western Schism of the Franks and the '*Filioque*,'" *Journal of Ecclesiastical History*, 23 (1972, 99). However, the evidence cited (like that of the Synod of Gentilly in 767) only demonstrates the presence of the doctrine of the biune procession in other credal forms like the Athanasian Creed.

105 The two principal Spanish Adoptionists were Elipandus, Bishop of Toledo, and Felix of Urgel: F.L. Cross, ed., *The Oxford Dictionary of the Christian Church* (London: Oxford University Press, 1958), 18b; Pelikan (1971-89), 3:52-54; Herrin (1987), 434.

included the *filioque*. In fact, Paulinus explicitly defended the church's right to make such additions to the creed.[106] The reason for its addition had nothing to do with Spanish Adoptionism, however.[107] Rather, it was "on account of those heretics who whisper that the Holy Spirit is of the Father alone and proceeds from the Father."[108]

The heretics against whom this move was directed were the Eastern Orthodox and probably also their Western defenders. In conjunction with the Seventh Ecumenical Council (787), the Patriarch of Constantinople had circulated a letter in which he confessed that the Spirit proceeded from the Father "through the Son." Charlemagne and his court theologians rejected the proceedings of this Eastern council and, noting the absence of the doctrine of the biune procession in the Patriarch's confession of faith, petitioned Pope Hadrian to denounce it. Hadrian, however, defended the Eastern practice (794) as consonant with many of the early fathers and also with the practice of the Roman church.[109]

So the target of the actions of the Synod of Cividale may have been the Roman pontif as much as the Greek patriarch. Leo III, who became pope in 795, a year or two before the synod, continued his predecessor's policy of resisting such pressure from Charlemagne and advocated the original form of the creed (without the *filioque*). Even though he personally accepted the doctrine of the biune procession of the Spirit, Leo insisted that no one, not even the pope, might add words to the Nicene Creed.[110] Inclusion of the *filioque* in the creed of the West was not approved by a pope until 1014 when Benedict VIII did so on the occasion of the coronation of Emperor Henry II. Subsequently, the papal bull that excommunicated the Patriarch of Constantinople in 1054 accused the

---

[106] Pelikan (1971-89), 2:184-86; Kelly (1972), 355-56.

[107] Ironically, Spanish Adoptionism was reminiscent of the quasi-Nestorian theology of Isidore of Seville, the seventh-century defender of the doctrine of the biune procession of the Spirit.

[108] A.E. Burn, *An Introduction to the Creeds* (London: Methuen, 1899), 117; Kelly (1972), 364. Aquinas states the same case in *Summa Theologicae* Ia.36.2, ad 2 but then strengthens it with an appeal to "some council [unspecified] in the West on the same authority of the Roman Pontiff."

[109] Kelly (1972), 364; Heath (1972), 104.

[110] Pelikan (1971-89), 2:187; Kelly (1972), 354-55, 365-66, Heath (1972), 107-09.

Greek Orthodox Church, among other things, of omitting the *filioque* from the creed.[111]

None of these Western decisions were recognized by (or participated in) by the Eastern Orthodox. But, in the thirteenth century, at the Second Council of Lyons (1274), legates of Emperor Michael VIII Paleologus (who needed the support from Rome against the military threat of Sicily) declared their obedience to the Roman Catholic Church and subscribed to the Western form of the Nicene Creed, including the *filioque*.[112] Roman Catholics base the ecumenicity of this council (and others) not on the breadth of representation but on the presence of the pope as the principle of the visible unity of the church.[113]

In order to promote reunion, Michael VIII appointed John Beccos, Patriarch of Constantinople, in 1275, with the explicit task of promoting the Union of Lyons. Beccos failed in his appointed task, however, and Gregory of Cyprus, who succeeded as patriarch in 1283, oversaw the official rejection of the Union of Lyons by the East in 1285.[114]

The matter was taken up once again by representatives of both churches at the Council of Florence (1438-45). In exchange for a promise of military aid against the Turks, several of the attending bishops of the Eastern Orthodox churches accepted the Latin doctrines of the biune procession of the Spirit, purgatory, and the primacy of the pope. Again these actions were rejected by official synods in the East.[115]

On the basis of the Councils of Cividale del Friuli, Lyons, and Florence, it is clear that the reasons for the addition of the *filioque* to the Nicene Creed were rather different from those offered in support of the doctrine of the biune procession of the Spirit (discussed in section 3, "What

---

111 Already in the mid-860s, Pope Nicholas I had supported the introduction of the *filioque* in Frankish churches in Bulgaria against the attacks of Patriarch Photius. But this stance was reversed by the papal legates at the Council of Constantinople in 879, and Pope John VIII later returned to the position of Leo III: T. Ware, *The Orthodox Church* (Baltimore: Penguin Books, 1963), 63-67; Heath (1972), 110-12.

112 Cross, ed. (1958), 836b.

113 Aquinas, *Summa Theologicae* Ia.36.2, ad 2; B. de. Margerie, *The Christian Trinity in History* (Still River, MA: St. Bede's Publications, 1982), 176. In fact, the Second Council of Lyons is the fourteenth ecumenical council according to the Roman Catholic numbering.

114 Council of Constantinople (1285): J. Meyendorff, *Byzantine Theology* (New York: Fordham University Press, 1974), 93.

115 Mark of Ephesus was the only bishop who refused to sign the Decree of Union in 1439: Cross, ed. (1958), 510; Ware (1963), 80-81.

Theological Issues Are Involved"). The creed was not officially changed until relations with the Greek Orthodox Church became a major concern for the West.

At Friuli (796) the *filioque* was added as a way of declaring the Greek Orthodox concern for the West Church (and its Western supporters) heretical for not subscribing to the doctrine of the biune procession of the Spirit. At Lyons (1274) and Florence (1439), the addition was defended as a way of securing the submission of the Greek Orthodox to the authority of Rome (even though Rome itself had resisted the innovation until 1014). In fact, since the Council of Florence, the position of the Roman Catholic Church has been that acceptance of the procession of the Spirit from Christ legitimates the dependence of the visible church on the Vicar of Christ. In the words of a contemporary Catholic theologian:

> If it is true that the *filioque* in terms of its object is more important than the papacy, it is also true that its recognition has become in the eyes of the Roman Church, which is mother and mistress of all the Churches and of all the faithful, the sign and the manifestation of recognition of its own primacy.... Acknowledgement of the *filioque* signifies and symbolizes, at the level of critical-dogmatic realism, the full emergence of the infallible primacy of the Roman Pontiff as the dogmatically recognized guide in matters of dogmatic expression.[116]

In other words, acceptance of the *filioque* is tantamount to acceptance of the primacy of Rome. As Thomas Torrance has pointed out, the *filioque* ("and from the Son") tends in practice to reduce to an *ecclesiaque* ("and from the church").[117] No wonder the Eastern Orthodox churches have resisted the doctrine so stubbornly!

The validity of the addition of the *filioque* can be assessed in various ways. As a declaration that anyone who does not accept the doctrine of the biune procession of the Spirit (Friuli), it is no stronger than the biblical and theological grounds discussed in sections (2) and (3). As a legitimation of Roman primacy (Lyons and Florence), it can only be acceptable to those Protestants who want reunion with Rome enough to avoid any slight to the authority of the Roman pontiff. As a new point of orthodoxy

116 Margerie (1982), 176-77.
117 Torrance (1965), 227-28, 231.

that excludes the Eastern Orthodox churches, it can only be acceptable to Westerners who no longer wish to have among their creeds one that is shared by the other half of Christ's church.

(5) Should the *Filioque* Be Bracketed or Footnoted?

The Nicene Creed dates back to the fourth century. The form in which the Reformed Church in America has inherited it contains an addition that was first introduced (as far as is known) in the ninth century and was not approved by the Church of Rome until the eleventh century. This paper has concluded that the action of changing the creed was not justified on either biblical, theological, or ecclesiastical grounds.

There is certainly merit in the doctrine of the biune procession of the Spirit—Calvin himself accepted it although he only referred to it once in the entire Institutes.[118] There are grounds for confessing that doctrine in a distinctly Western (Augustinian) confession like the Athanasian Creed or a Reformed standard like the Belgic Confession (Art. 8). There are not sufficient grounds, however, to justify the addition of the *filioque* to the one creed that reflects the faith of the entire church—the Nicene Creed. The universal church with which Calvin identified himself was not intentionally limited to the Latin West. In response to a contemporary apologist for the authority of Rome, Calvin argued that the true church "...is the society of all the saints, a society which, spread over the whole world, and existing in all ages, yet bound together by the one doctrine and the one Spirit of Christ, cultivates and observes unity of faith and brotherly concord. With this church we deny that we have any disagreement."[119]

At the time of the Reformation, the amended Latin version of the Nicene Creed had been in use in the West for seven centuries—nearly half the lifetime of the church. As early as the eleventh century, Western Christians began to assume that their version was the original one. The addition was even interpolated back into earlier manuscripts, probably quite innocently. Accordingly, the Reformers accepted the authenticity of the Western version of the creed as a matter of course. Calvin, at least,

---

118 Calvin, *Institutes* 1.13.18 (first added in the 1539 edition). There is also an indirect allusion in 1.13.23 (added in 1559); cf. The Gallican Confession 6.
119 Reply to Sadoleto as trans. In Beveridge, ed. (1844-51), 1:37.

appears to have been unaware that this had been a divisive issue.[120] The Reformers' immediate challenge was to correct the abuses of the medieval Roman church. They understood themselves to be restoring the theology and practice of the church prior to the rise of papal power and scholastic theology in the twelfth and thirteenth centuries. In order to defend themselves against charges of novelty and schism, they stressed their solidarity with the early church and stressed their adherence to the three "ecumenical creeds," including the Nicene Creed in its Western form.[121]

These circumstances present anew the question of what it means to be Reformed. If it means affirming exactly the same things that the Reformers did, then Reformed Christians must retain the interpolated form of the Nicene Creed. On the other hand, if being Reformed means carrying on the reforming program of the Reformers in light of new circumstances and new information, then the possibility of revising the Reformed Church text of the Nicene Creed must be considered.

As a way of approaching this new challenge, it may be helpful to draw an analogy to a more familiar one. The problem at hand is in many ways similar to that of revising translations of the New Testament. The texts of both the New Testament and the Nicene Creed were altered in various ways over the centuries. Only a few of these alterations had been detected in Western Europe by the time of the Reformation. Accordingly, Calvin accepted the authenticity of texts such as Mark 16:9-20, which are noted as later additions in modern translations like the New Revised Standard Version and the New International Version.[122] He also accepted texts like Acts 8:37 and 1 John 5:8, which are now entirely omitted or placed in footnotes.[123] On the other hand, Calvin was already aware of the fact that John 7:53-8:11 was missing in the early Greek texts. Accordingly, he noted this fact and the possibility that it was a later insertion in his commentary on the passage and made no direct use of it in his *Institutes*.[124]

---

[120] Even though Calvin discussed terminological differences between the Greek and Latin fathers, he made no mention of differing views of the procession of the Spirit (*Institutes* 1.13.5, 18). He also quoted the Latin version of the Nicene Creed (following Augustine) as saying "I believe the church" (not "I believe in the church," as in the Greek), on the assumption that this was the universal form.

[121] E.g., *Reply to Sadoleto*, Beveridge, ed. (1844-51), 1:38.

[122] Mark 16:9-20 is cited fifteen times in the *Institutes*; see biblical references in McNeill, ed. (1960), 1571.

[123] Calvin, *Institutes* 3.1.1; 4.14.8; 16.23; *Commentary on Acts*, 7:37.

Following this model, modern editions of the Nicene Creed ought to note the fact that the *filioque* is a later addition to the Nicene Creed and that it has never been approved by an authentically ecumenical council. This may be done either by retaining the *filioque* in the text and attaching a footnote, or by bracketing it (making it optional) and explaining in a footnote, or by removing it from the text and placing it in a footnote. In view of the facts that the earliest creeds—both Greek and Latin—omit the *filioque*, that the first clear documentation of the phrase dates from the late eighth century, and that its use did not become standard liturgical practice in the Western church until the eleventh century, the option of bracketing the phrase or placing it in a footnote would seem to be most appropriate.

Conclusion

Ideally, then, the Nicene Creed should be confessed in the form ascribed to the First Council of Constantinople (381). The *filioque* should be bracketed or placed in a footnote to indicate this reform. Biblical, theological, and ecumenical considerations all point in this direction.

Eventually, an ecumenical council should be called to deal with such matters of faith and practice in a comprehensive fashion. If and when that day comes, Reformed Church in America delegates representing both sides of the issue should be allowed to participate with a view to reaching a solution acceptable to all parties. But, pending the convocation of a general council and regardless of present convictions about the matter, the Reformed Church should not hesitate to restore the version of the Nicene Creed the RCA uses to its original form. Like Calvin, Reformed Church members should identify themselves as members of the universal church who "attempt to ameliorate its condition and restore it to its pristine splendor."[125] And the Reformed Church has no more reason than Calvin did to wait for an ecumenical council to be convoked.[126] It is up to the Reformed Church to affirm its common faith with the early

---

124 *Commentary on John*, 8:1.

125 *Reply to Sadoleto* as translated in Beveridge, ed. (1844-51), 1:38. Calvin goes on to relate the "pristine splendor" of the church to the Scriptures, the early fathers, and the ancient councils. Among the latter, he normally listed Nicea, Constantinople, Ephesus, and Chalcedon: ibid., 1:260; 2:130.

church of both East and West as well as to stand by those confessions it shares with the early Roman Church and those that are distinctively Reformed standards.

Pending the decision of an ecumenical council, the Reformed Church in America should bracket the *filioque* and state in a footnote in its present-day versions of the Nicene Creed that early Greek and Latin versions of the Nicene Creed did not include the words "and from the Son."

* The literal translation of the Latin word "*filioque*" is "and from the Son." The Western form as presently confessed in the Reformed Church in America is "and the Son."

Select Bibliography

Atiya, A. S. *A History of Eastern Christianity*. London: Methuen, 1968.

Barth, K. *Church Dogmatics*. Ed. G. W. Bromiley and T. F. Torrrance. 12 part-vols. plus index vol. Edinburgh: T. & T. Clark, 1956-77.

Idem. *The Doctrine of the Word of God*. Second English ed. In idem (1956-77), Volume 1, Part 1, section 12, 2.3, pp. 466-87.

Beveridge, H., ed. *Tracts of John Calvin*. 3 vols. Edinburgh: Calvin Translation Society, 1844-51.

Bruggink, D. J. "Filioque and the Reformed Tradition." *Perspectives* 4/8:8-10, (1989).

Burn, A. E. *An Introduction to the Creeds*. London: Methuen, 1899, 114-19.

Calian, C. S. Icon and Pulpit: *The Protestant-Orthodox Encounter*. Philadelphia: Westminster Press, 1968, 145-49.

---

[126] "But those persons, whoever they be, who, under the pretext of a General Council, interposed delay, clearly have no other end in view than, by this artifice, to spin out the time and are no more to be listened to..." *The Necessity of Reforming the Church*, as translated in Beveridge, ed. (1844-51), 1:223. In his *Remarks on the Letter of Pope Paul III*, Calvin specifically rejected the need to wait for the approval of the pope before effecting reform: ibid., 1:260.

Clark, M. T. *Marius Victorinus: Theological Treatises on the Trinity. The Fathers of the Church*, 69. Washington, DC: Catholic University of America Press, 1981.

Cross, F. L., ed. *The Oxford Dictionary of the Christian Church.* London: Oxford University Press, 1958.

Cunliffe-Jones, H., ed. *A History of Christian Doctrine.* Edinburgh: T. & T. Clark, 1978.

Every, G. *Misunderstandings Between East and West.* Ecumenical Studies in History, No. 4. London: Lutterworth Press, 1965.

Fahey, M. "Son and Spirit: Divergent Theologies between Constantinople and the West." In Kung and Moltmann, eds. 1979, 15-22.

Gunton, C. "Augustine, the Trinity and the Theological Crisis of the West." *Scottish Journal of Theology,* 43:33-58 (1990).

Hanson, R. P. C. *Studies in Christian Antiquity.* Edinburgh: T. & T. Clark, 1985. Chap. 12, 279-97.

Heath, R. G. "The Western Schism of the Franks and the 'Filioque.'" *Journal of Ecclesiastical History,* 23:97-113 (1972).

Hendry, G. S. *The Holy Spirit in Christian Theology.* London: SCM Press, 1957. Chap. 2, 30-52; 42-52 is a critique of Barth (1975).

Heron, A. I. C. "'Who Proceedeth from the Father and the Son': The Problem of the Filioque." *Scottish Journal of Theology,* 24:149-166 (1971).

Idem. "The *Filioque* Clause." In *One God in Trinity.* Ed. P. Toon and J. D. Spiceland. London: Samuel Bagster, 1980. Chap. 5, 62-77. Reprinted in *Reformed World,* 39:842-52 (Dec. 1987).

Idem. "The *Filioque* in Recent Reformed Theology." In L. Vischer, ed., 110-20 (1981).

Idem. *The Holy Spirit.* Philadelphia: Westminster Press, 1983, esp. 81-86, 88-94, 176-78.

Herrin, J. *The Formation of Christendom.* Princeton: Princeton University Press, 1987.

Janssen, A. "Thinking About God: Reflections on *Filioque*." *Perspectives,* 4/8:11-14 (1989).

Jenson. R. W. *The Triune Identity*. Philadelphia: Fortress Press, 1982. Chap. 4, esp. 138-48.

Kaiser, C. B. *The Doctrine of God*. Westchester, IL: Crossway Books, 1982, esp. 41-46, 76-79.

Kelly, J. N. D. *The Athanasian Creed*. London: Adam & Charles Black, 1964, 86-90.

Idem. *Early Christian Doctrines*. Fourth ed. London: Adam & Charles Black, 1968.

Idem. *Early Christian Creeds*. Third ed. London: Longman, 1972, esp. 354-55, 358-67.

Kung, H., and J. Moltmann, eds. *Conflicts about the Holy Spirit*. Concilium 128. New York: Seabury Press, 1979. Part I, 1-30.

Leith, J. H. *Creeds of the Churches*. Third ed. Atlanta: John Knox Press, 1982.

Lossky, V. *The Mystical Theology of the Eastern Church*. Cambridge: James Clarke, 1957, 54-62.

Idem. *In the Image and Likeness of God*. Ed. J. E. Erickson and T. E. Bird. New York: St. Vladimir's Seminary Press, 1974. Ch. 4, 71-96.

McIntyre, J. "The Holy Spirit in Greek Patristic Thought." *Scottish Journal of Theology,* 7:353-75 (1954), esp. 371-75.

McNeill, J. T., ed. Calvin: *Institutes of the Christian Religion*. Trans. F. L. Battles. 2 vols. Philadelphia: Westminster Press, 1960, esp. 141-44, 537-39.

Margerie, B. de. *The Christian Trinity in History*. Trans. E. J. Fortman. Still River, MA: St. Bede's Publications, 1982, 110-21, 160-78, 315-22.

Meyendorff, J. *Byzantine Theology*. New York: Fordham University Press, 1974, esp. 60-61, 91-94.

Moltmann, J. "Theological Proposals Towards the Resolution of the *Filioque* Controversy." In L. Vischer, ed., 164-73 (1981a).

Idem. *The Trinity and the Kingdom*. San Francisco: Harper & Row, 1981b, 178-87; 180-90 are a different translation of a slightly condensed version of 1981a.

Pelikan, J. *The Christian Tradition: A History of the Development of Doctrine*. 5 vols. Chicago: University of Chicago Press. 2:183-98, 275-77; 3:19-22, 229-31, 279-80; 4:78-79; 5:21-22, 197, 258 (1971-89).

Prestige, G. L. *God in Patristic Thought*. London: SPCK, 1964, 249-55.

Ritschl, D. "The History of the Filioque Controversy." In H. Kung and J. Moltmann, eds. 3-14 (1979).

Idem. "Historical Development and Implications of the Filioque Controversy." In L. Vischer, ed. 46-68 (1981).

Runciman, S. *The Eastern Schism: A Study of the Papacy and the Eastern Churches During the XIth and XIIth Centuries*. Oxford: Clarendon Press, 1955, esp. 29-34, which are marred by the confusion of terminologies stemming from the trinitarian and christological controversies.

Schaff, P. *Creeds of Christendom*. 3 vols. 6th ed. New York: Harper and Row, 1931.

Swete, H. B. *On the History of the Doctrine of the Procession of the Holy Spirit. From the Apostolic Age to the Death of Charlemagne*. Cambridge: Deighton Bell, 1876.

Idem. *The Holy Spirit in the New Testament*. London: Macmillan, 1909.

Idem. *The Holy Spirit in the Ancient Tradition*. London: Macmillan, 1912, esp. 222-29, 251-252, 258-60, 279-80, 284-85, 298, 304, 322, 328-33, 340-51, 367-72.

Torrance, T. F. *Theology in Reconstruction*. London: SCM Press, 1965, 217-19, 229-39.

Idem. *Theology in Reconciliation*. London: Geoffrey Chapman, 1975, 35-36, 231-239.

Idem. *The Trinitarian Faith*. Edinburgh: T. & T. Clark, 1988.

Vischer, L. *Spirit of God, Spirit of Christ: Ecumenical Reflections on the "Filioque" Controversy*. London: SPCK; Geneva: WCC, 1981.

Ware, T. *The Orthodox Church.* Baltimore: Penguin Books, 1963, esp. 58-60, 62-66, 218-223.

Idem. "Christian Theology in the East, 600-1453." In H. Cunliffe-Jones, ed., 207-12 (1978).

Watkin-Jones, H. *The Holy Spirit in the Medieval Church.* London: Epworth Press, 1922, esp. 41-54, 161-69, 324-28.

Welch, C. "The Holy Spirit and the Trinity." *Theology Today,* 8/1:29-40 (1951).

Idem. *The Trinity in Contemporary Theology.* London, SCM Press, 1953, 200-03, 281-90.

4
Confirmation and the Reformed Church

Definition

"Confirmation" is difficult to define. It has meant different things to different Christian traditions. This is an attempt at a definition that is as inclusive as possible:

Confirmation is a rite or public ceremony of the church, having to do with initiation, supplementary to baptism and somehow completing it, in which the candidate receives the laying on of hands, usually with the promise of the gift of the Holy Spirit, and sometimes also with "chrismation" (anointing with consecrated oil), or "signation" (the sign of the cross), or both.

Since the late Middle Ages confirmation has also been seen as admittance to communion, and this has been maintained by some Protestant churches. Confirmation belongs only to the Western tradition of Christianity; the Eastern Orthodox churches baptize, anoint, and communicate infants in a single rite.

Three Stages of Development of Confirmation in the Reformed Church in America

Does the Reformed Church in America practice confirmation? The answer is a qualified "yes." The Commission on Worship's proposed liturgical form for "Confirmation of Baptismal Vows" was approved for provisional use by the 1991 General Synod (*MGS,* 1991: 214, R-2). A decision to include this service in the *Liturgy* will not be made until 1994. However, the *Book of Church Order* has already been revised to reflect the practice of confirmation, with the use of the term "active-confirmed member" (*MGS,* 1990: 230-38; *MGS,* 1991: 48-9).

The practice of confirmation is a recent development in the Reformed Church. As late as 1906 Corwin's *Digest* noted: "the word 'confirmation' did not occur in the *Formularies of the RCA* in an ecclesiastical sense."[1] However, in that same year, the denomination published an important revision of its *Liturgy,* which included for the first time a liturgical office

---

1   Edward T. Corwin, *Digest of Constitutional and Synodical Legislation of the Reformed Church in America* (New York: Board of Publications of the RCA, 1906), 157.

for the public reception of church members. This was not confirmation per se, but it began the development that has culminated in confirmation.

The three stages in the development of confirmation in the Reformed Church are:

1. 1906 *Liturgy*, "The Office for the Reception into Full Communion of Those who have been Baptized in Infancy" (24).
2. 1968 *Liturgy and Psalms*, "The Order for Admission to the Lord's Table of Those Baptized in Infancy" (53).
3. *MGS*, 1990: 200 (proposed but not adopted) and *MGS*, 1991:203 (revised and adopted for provisional use), "Confirmation of Baptismal Vows."

Confirmation officially came into practice in the Reformed Church only in 1991. Unofficially, however, some Reformed Church congregations have been practicing it for a long time. Also, liturgically speaking, although the 1968 *Liturgy and Psalms* order is not actually called "confirmation," it satisfies enough of the definition given above to be taken as such. Though it lacks chrismation and the gift of the Holy Spirit, it is manifestly a public initiatory rite which is understood to complete baptism and which includes the laying on of hands.

Furthermore, the word "confirmation" does show up in the public reception portion of the 1968 *Liturgy and Psalms* "Order for the Admission to the Lord's Table of Those Baptized in Infancy: "You stand here for the deliberate and public confirmation in your own person of that covenant of God of which your Baptism is the sign and seal" (55). Now, "confirmation" here is wholly a later, post-Reformation use of the word, signifying that the candidate does the confirming by what he/she says. The original use of the word referred to what the church did to the relatively passive candidate. Protestantism, characteristically, turned the objective act of the church into the subjective act of the candidate. Objective or subjective, the point was the same: the candidate's baptism needed somehow to be completed; it was not enough. That this was at variance with the Belgic Confession (Art. 34), the official doctrine of the church, seems not to have been noticed; hence the Reformed Church in America *Constitution*, which included both the Belgic Confession and the 1968 *Liturgy and Psalms* "Order for Admission to the Lord's Table of Those Baptized in Infancy," was at odds with itself.

At the General Synod of 1990 two proposals reflected the fact that confirmation was settling into the Reformed Church. First, it was proposed to bring the idea of confirmation into the *Book of Church Order* by the creation of two new membership categories: "active-confirmed" members and "unconfirmed-baptized" members. Neither the Scriptures nor the Doctrinal Standards know what these unwieldy categories are, but they are now part of the *Book of Church Order*. Remarkably, these terms suggest an "objective" notion of confirmation.

The second proposal (not approved at the 1990 General Synod but approved with revisions by the 1991 General Synod for provisional use) was the aforementioned rite of "Confirmation of Baptismal Vows," prepared to succeed the 1968 *Liturgy and Psalms* order. This rite includes both subjective and objective notions of confirmation. The whole first part of the public ceremony is a subjective repetition of the baptismal covenant. The second part, the "Confirmation: Blessing, Charge, Declaration," is an objective act by the church, including the laying on of hands, a blessing, and the promise of the increase of the Holy Spirit (*MGS*, 1991: 203-14).

The 1991 rite differs from the 1968 *Liturgy and Psalms* order in one small item that has significant implications. Like the 1968 *Liturgy and Psalms* order, the new order opens with a private meeting with the elders. Until now in the Reformed Church, it was this meeting with the elders that actually effected the candidate's admittance to the Lord's Table, and the public ceremony—heretofore always optional—was considered a liturgical witness to what had already been done. With the 1991 rite, the private meeting ends with the elders setting a date for the public liturgical confirmation, which is no longer optional. The effect of this is that for Reformed Church congregations which do not practice the communion of children, a new liturgical act of initiation has been inserted between baptism and communion, and admission to the Lord's Table is now no longer a simple, pastoral act of the eldership.

Ironically, this new 1991 order was proposed to the denomination at the same time that elders were encouraged to admit children to the Lord's Table. These were two absolutely contradictory developments. The first was that baptism itself was recognized as sufficient qualification for church membership, which included participation at the Lord's Table at an age elders deemed appropriate. This was wholly in keeping with the

Belgic Confession. The second development was the feeling that the Reformed Church ought to practice confirmation, by adding a rite of confirmation to its *Liturgy*, and revising the *Book of Church Order* to incorporate the terminology of confirmation. The fact that the new membership terminology was trying to satisfy both of these contrary developments made them unwieldy. No wonder the 1990 General Synod instructed the Commission on Theology to study the whole issue of confirmation (*MGS*, 1990:212).

It is commonplace in liturgical circles to say confirmation is a ceremony that is looking for a theology. There is no doubt that the Reformed Church has been looking outside of its own doctrinal tradition to find not only the rite but also the theology behind it.

The Reformed Church has never made the theological decision, "we will now practice confirmation." However, liturgical practices of other traditions have piece by piece been borrowed into it. This is not necessarily bad in itself, except that, ironically, just as the Reformed Church is importing confirmation from the outside, those denominations that have long practiced it—like the Lutherans and the Anglicans—are trying to get rid of it. It is the position of this paper that the Reformed Church should back out of confirmation altogether, go back to 1906, and start over down a different path: the path that, with the admittance of children to the Lord's Table, it has been trying to move to. Indeed, if the *Church Order of 1874* were still in effect, modern boards of elders would have no problem in admitting children to the Lord's Table![2]

History of Confirmation

In order to understand the pre-1906 position of the Reformed Church in America, some history is in order. The *Constitution* was reflecting its Calvinistic heritage, and its *Liturgy* had not been changed since the Synod of Dort. The Calvinistic churches had scrapped confirmation altogether

---

2 *Church Order of 1874*, Art. 47: "None can be received as members in full communion unless they first shall have made a confession of their faith before the Minister (if any) and the Elders." The article gives complete authority to the local elders to determine the sufficiency of the confession of faith. The elders would have been quite free to admit young children to the table after an age-appropriate confession, though it is doubtful that any would have done so. This right of the elders is what the General Synod of 1990 reinforced with suggested procedural guidelines for children at the Lord's Supper (*MGS*, 1990: 221, R-8).

because they believed it not to be a practice of the early church.[3] They found no specific biblical warrant for confirmation, nor any New Testament example of it.

There are plenty of scriptural examples of the laying on of hands and of anointing with oil, but in no case are these connected with a distinctly identifiable event that might be considered an apostolic antecedent for the rite. If anything, the laying on of hands is directly connected with baptism, although there are New Testament baptisms in which that act is not mentioned. Neither can it be defended from the Book of Acts that the gift of the Spirit is meant to be something identifiably different from water baptism. Sometimes these occur together, sometimes not. There is no evidence that anything like confirmation was practiced in the sub-apostolic age.

The earliest attestation of the ceremony which ultimately came to be called "confirmation" is to be found in the baptismal rites of Hippolytus' *Apostolic Tradition* (AD 215) and Tertullian's treatise *De Baptismo* (AD 198). Both works attest a ceremony after baptism consisting of a prayer said by the bishop with his hands extended over the candidates, the anointing of the candidates on the forehead, the imposition of the hand on the head of each, and the sign of the cross on the forehead. The precise manner and order in which these elements were combined varied in the subsequent development and they did not always appear in their entirety.[4] Clearly, although the multiplication of signs and ceremonies was beginning, these were not yet separated from baptism. Infants and adults received them equally,[5] and baptism was regarded as granting admission to the Lord's Table.

In the primitive church, the bishop, as the representative of the apostles, performed the entire baptismal rite. In those days each congregation had its own bishop, who was the local pastor. With the growth of the church, however, things began to change. The church of each city came to be divided into smaller worshiping parishes, served by "presbyters" (translated either as "elders" or as "priests," depending on

---

3 Modern liturgical scholarship has vindicated this judgment.
4 "Confirmation," *The Westminster Dictionary of Worship*, J. G. Davies, ed. (Philadelphia: Westminster Press, 1972).
5 Originally no distinction was made between infants and adults in the use of this post-baptismal ceremony. When infants were baptized they were also anointed and hands were laid on them ("Confirmation," *Westminster Dictionary of Worship*, 1972).

one's theology) on behalf of the bishop, who remained the head pastor of the whole body of Christians in the city.

When it became impossible for the bishop to be present at every baptism in person, one of two adjustments was made. Almost everywhere the parish presbyter replaced the bishop as the minister of the entire rite, as he had earlier replaced him as the usual celebrant of the Eucharist. However, in Rome and those parts of Italy under the pope, the final anointing and laying on of hands were reserved to the bishop alone, and so became separated from the rest of the rite on those occasions when no bishop was present at the administration of baptism. During the Middle Ages, this local Roman usage spread throughout Western Europe. This separated episcopal action has developed into what we know as confirmation.[6] Eventually, the Roman rite of confirmation developed into a separate sacrament, one of seven, independent of baptism and equal to it; and it also became, in baptism's place, admission to Holy Communion.[7]

With the Reformation's greater appreciation for the two scriptural sacraments of baptism and communion, there was a devaluation of the other five sacraments, confirmation included. Luther rejected "confirmation" as "mumbo-jumbo" which could add nothing to baptism, and instead devised catechisms which explained the significance of baptism and then gave explications of the Apostles' Creed, the Ten Commandments, the Lord's Prayer, and the sacraments. He stated that children should give an account of these before being admitted to communion, but devised no rite to be associated with such graduation from catechetical instruction. He did state that he found no fault if a pastor examined the faith of the children and "confirmed" them by laying on of hands.[8] Luther also proposed something entirely different from confirmation. It was a private pastoral act connected with education. It was subjective, done by the child, and not objective, done by the church

---

6 *Holy Baptism with the Laying-on-of-Hands*, Prayer Book Studies 18: On Baptism and Confirmation (New York: The Custodian of the Standard Book of Common Prayer, 1970), 16. This is one of the best short studies on the subject. It proposed a thorough reform of the practice of the Episcopal Church. It ultimately proved too radical, and the 1979 Prayer Book is a retreat from it.

7 Prayer Book Studies 18, 16.

8 Marion J. Hatchett, *Commentary on the American Prayer Book* (New York: The Seabury Press, 1980), 259.

to the child. The only similarities lay in the age of the subjects and in the use of the laying on of hands.

Calvin took almost exactly the same position as Luther. He wanted a similar instruction in catechism and a profession of faith, and the age he suggested for this was ten![9] At the same time Calvin provided no specific public rite or ceremony for it because he no doubt feared confirmation as the "devaluation of baptism."[10] Calvin emphasized that children should profess their faith publicly before being able to take communion. This profession should not be understood by people today as some kind of discrete step within the process of initiation or "faith development," but rather as a symptom of the Calvinist conviction that all Christians, children no less than adults, should be ready to give clear testimony to their faith.[11]

This is the origin of the act of "Profession of Faith," which the Reformed Church has historically practiced, not as a *kind* of confirmation, but *instead* of confirmation. The *Palatinate Church Order* maintained the practice in connection with the Heidelberg Catechism, and thus it entered into the Dutch Reformed Church.[12] The *Church Order of Dort* specifically required that "no person be admitted to the Lord's Supper but those who make a profession of their faith in the Reformed religion, agreeably to the practice of the churches to which they are joined."[13] This profession would take place before the consistory, and there was never any liturgical form provided for it. It can be concluded, then, that profession was understood as a pastoral or even juridical matter rather than a liturgical event. There was a public act before the congregation, but this happened at the (afternoon) catechetical service when all the students were publicly examined; this was hardly a liturgical act. So here again, profession is not

---

9   *Institutes*, 4.19.13 (cf. Hatchett, *Commentary*, 260).

10 Ibid., 4.19.8.

11 "Articles concerning the Organization of the Church and of Worship at Geneva 1537," "Draft Ecclesiastical Ordinances, September and October 1541," and "Ordinances for the Supervision of Churches in the Country," February 3, 1547, in *Calvin: Theological Treatises*, The Library of Christian Classics, Ichthus Edition, J.K.S. Reid, ed. and trans. (Philadelphia: Westminster, 1954), 53, 67, 79.

12 For the *Palatinate Church Order*, see Wilhelm Niesel, ed., *Kirchenordnungen der Kurpfalz, 1563*, in *Bekenntnisschriften und Kirchenordnungen der nach Gottes Word reformierten Kirche*, 3rd ed. (Zurich, 1938), 148. For the Dutch Reformed Church see Daniel Meeter, "The North American Liturgy: A Criticl Edition of the Liturgy of the Reformed Dutch Church in North America, 1793" (Ph. D. dissertation, Drew University, 1989), 45-46.

13 *Church Order of Dort*, Art. 61.

so much a step in initiation or faith development as it is a sign that, in Dort's words, "no person," adult or child, should be unable to "make a profession of their faith."

So far then, it can be seen that confirmation was rejected by both Luther and Calvin for its lack of apostolic and patristic authenticity. The Reformed churches emphasized catechesis and profession of faith, and these were connected with admittance to the Lord's Table, from the motive that such testimonies were expected of all communicants. Thus— and this is a critical point—in the Dutch Reformed tradition, there was nothing liturgical per se between baptism and communion. What was in between was catechism. When one had learned his/her catechism and could knowledgeably "profess his/her faith" before the elders—and maybe also before the congregation—one was granted admittance to the Lord's Table.

Church membership was very simple, and of only one sort. It was active, adult, confessing, communicant membership; and the *Church Order of Dort* reflected this. Profession of faith was not originally regarded as "becoming a church member"—that happened in baptism, as both the Belgic Confession and the historic Form for Baptism clearly stated. Baptized non-communicants were simply members-in-waiting, and hardly thought of in the manner as today, with the use of such a term as "baptized non-communicants," as a separate and identifiable class of members. It was just like citizenship is today: an infant is regarded as a full citizen by the *Constitution of the United States* and is entitled to all the privileges of citizenship. The United States recognizes no such category as "non-voting citizen," but the full responsibilities of citizenship, such as voting, military service, and eligibility for office, are held off by statutory laws until the appropriate age. (It is important to remember that for centuries the Western church regarded participation in communion as more of a responsibility than as a privilege.)

Change in the Reformed Church in America

In the Reformed Church in America things began to change in 1873 when, for the first time, a committee of General Synod prepared a new "Form for the Admission of Baptized Members to Full Communion." In 1876 this was approved as a "specimen" form, meaning that it was optional and not part of the *Constitution.* In 1906, the whole *Liturgy* was thoroughly revised, and it included, no longer as only a specimen form, the "Office for the Reception into Full Communion of Those who have been Baptized in Infancy." The office was a "public ratification" of the "covenant of...your Baptism." The heart of the office was the asking of the candidate the three parts of the Apostles' Creed, followed by two vows. After this the minister made a formal welcome to full communion, gave a scriptural blessing, and prayed. It did not even hint at any rite of confirmation or the laying on of hands. Yet the Reformed Church had taken its first steps down the path toward confirmation, since there was now something in the *Liturgy* that suggested that baptism was not enough, that it required some sort of public act of subjective ratification.

The order in the 1968 *Liturgy and Psalms* was a substantially expanded version of the 1906 office. The first alteration was the provision of an excellent model for the private interrogation of the candidates before the elders. Second, in the public ceremony, the congregation was included in the recitation of the Apostles' Creed, and the candidates' vows were expanded. Third, for the first time, the laying on of hands was rubricated, with a declaration to be said by the pastor. Though the word "confirmation" was never used, the act was unmistakable.

As if to prove that Calvin was right in his fear that confirmation would devalue baptism, the 1968 *Liturgy and Psalms* (57) did just that with these unfortunate declaratory words: "I declare that N. , received into the visible membership of the holy catholic Church through Baptism, is now admitted to the Lord's Table."[14] Baptism was now the sign of "visible" membership only, and in this context "visible" was hardly a positive word. The 1968 order backed away from the Belgic Confession's straightforward teaching that baptism is the trustworthy sign of membership in the church: "By it [baptism] we are received into God's Church and set apart from all other people and alien religions, that we may be dedicated entirely to the one whose mark and sign we bear. It also witnesses to us that God, being our gracious Father, will be our God forever (Art. 34). The Belgic Confession does not recognize the distinction between the "invisible" and "visible" church. It knows only the true and false church, both of which are visible and "easily discerned."

---

14 It is not that the new order itself devalued baptism, but rather that it only reflected the larger devaluation of baptism that had already infected the Reformed Church in America.

So although the first part of the 1968 *Liturgy and Psalms* order (the section "Before the Elders," 53-55), introduced some good material into the *Constitution*, the second part ("Before the Congregation," 55-58), unfortunately introduced material which put the *Liturgy* of the Reformed Church out of accord with its doctrine. This material has continued to grow and has now produced the three proposals which were considered by the 1990 General Synod (*MGS*, 1990: 197-212). The Reformed Church now finds itself in the same predicament that the Episcopal church was in 1970, when a prayer book study said: "Confirmation as currently practiced disrupts the connection between Baptism and the Holy Communion."[15]

Influences

If confirmation does not arise out of its native theological and liturgical tradition, then where did the Reformed Church in America get it? Of course the rite was living on in other Protestant churches which the Reformed Church was watching, and it was therefore ready for the borrowing. However, it hardly had to be imported from the outside when, in the nineteenth century, there were many German evangelical congregations joining the denomination. These congregations practiced confirmation and called it such. It was not too difficult to correlate this practice with the Dutch Reformed profession of faith. Confirmation was in the Reformed Church, unofficially at least, long before the preliminary steps of 1906.

The rite undoubtedly is attractive to those groups in the Reformed Church who, in the name of "liturgical renewal," have favored the general multiplication of ceremonies in recent years. What is salutary in confirmation is its liturgical involvement of the body (kneeling, laying on of hands) and the inclusion of young people. These elements are certainly welcome in a liturgical tradition that tends towards intellectualism. At the same time, one wonders whether the elaboration of the confirmation ritual has come as a substitute for the much more difficult task of extended catechetical training of the confirmands. A confirmation class of only eight or ten weeks instead of two or three years is hardly redeemed by a memorable ceremony.

---

15 Prayer Book Studies 18, 18.

Influence of Revivalism

There was certainly, however, another motivation at work behind the development of confirmation in the Reformed Church. This was the influence of American revivalism. This brand of Christianity also devalues baptism, for different reasons, perhaps, but no less strongly than medieval Catholicism did. Indeed, when taken to the full, revivalism has a difficult time with the baptism of infants.[16] It assumes that children cannot be born again, that they must first reach the age of discretion. If there is any liturgical ceremony at all that can fit in with revivalism, it is confirmation.

Revivalism is a much more powerful theological influence in the Reformed Church than its own doctrinal standards. The result is that there are views of baptism widespread in the denomination which are contradictory to the official doctrine. Traditional baptism is still practiced, but, as often as not, it is understood in a less than fully sacramental sense. It is not to baptism that this kind of Protestantism looks as the sign and seal of ingrafting into Christ, but to the thoroughly subjective act of "personal conversion." Confirmation can be taken as a tolerable liturgical substitute for the conversion event, complete with public testimony, even though that testimony might have to be programmed. It should come as no surprise, therefore, when, in spite of the Belgic Confession, there are still strong voices out of the influence of revivalism calling for the retention of confirmation.

Eight Theological Benchmarks

If confirmation is not in keeping with the Reformed Church in America's Doctrinal Standards, what should the denomination put in its place? It can hardly go back to the *status quo ante* 1906. Also, there are some good items that should be salvaged from the current forms. To guide future developments, some theological benchmarks are in order.

---

16 The writings of John W. Nevin fully explore these problems. It can be argued that the revivalist churches which continue to practice infant baptism are juggling mutually exclusive conceptions of salvation. Many historic denominations which maintain infant baptism have succumbed to revivalism by teaching baptismal doctrines which are more or less at variance with the primitive Reformation heritage. One example is the RCA's own John Henry Livingston, educated at (Puritan) Yale, who, in 1814 without synodical authorization, deleted Luther's "Flood Prayer" from the Form for Baptism in his editions of the *Liturgy*.

First, baptism itself must be protected from devaluation. The Reformed Church's Doctrinal Standards teach that baptism is the sole rite of initiation into the Reformed Church in America. Baptism, not confirmation, is the ordination to the priesthood of all believers. Baptism, not confirmation, is the liturgical sign and seal of the gift of the Holy Spirit. Baptismal water is itself the anointing. No chrismation with oil is needed. Chrismation in itself is good and scriptural, but it is a pastoral act which may be done repeatedly. It is not a sacramental act, and it should not be allowed to detract from the baptism per se. Likewise, baptismal water is itself the sign of Jesus' poured-out blood, not the sign of the cross, so no signation is needed. The acts of anointing and laying on of hands are good and scriptural, and they may well be given as blessings. However, they are not sacramental acts, and their use should not be allowed to detract from the water of baptism, as has happened in many traditions.[17] They are pastoral acts which may be done repeatedly and on different occasions, and they ought to be practiced more in the church.

Second, baptism is the sufficient sacramental and liturgical qualification for Holy Communion—although in admitting someone to the Lord's Table, the board of elders is called always to take account of pastoral and disciplinary considerations (such as relative maturity or evidence of repentance after gross sin). Holy Communion is not just a ceremony, but an actual communion in and union with Christ. Baptism is the trustworthy sign and seal of one's ingrafting into the person of Christ, and this is true for infants. There is an important connection to be made between ingrafting into Christ and being a "member" of Christ's body (1 Cor. 12.12-27). If the church is the body of Christ (Eph. 4.1-16), then it is only reasonable to teach, as the Belgic Confession does, that a baptized infant is a member of the church. The question of the church "membership" of baptized children is wholly a function of the reality of their having been ingrafted into the body of Christ. To say that infants are members of Christ but not of the church is contradictory.

Of course it is true that many people, even though they are baptized, give no evidence in their lives of being ingrafted into Christ. Baptism is

---

[17] "It seems...probable that the early Syrian church recognized no sign other than water by which the Spirit was imparted in Christian initiation. If this is correct, it carries with it the important implication that a second sign other than water in Christian initiation was not a matter of universal observance in the early church" ("Confirmation," *The Westminster Dictionary of Worship*, 1972).

not some automatic guarantee of salvation. (This is why the Reformed Church gives weighty authority to the elders to supervise the Lord's Table.) Why God has allowed so many of the baptized to be unfaithful is a mystery. However, the Reformed Church should not let this be a cause for retreat from the full promise of baptism. Such a retreat is reflected in the modification of the baptismal declaration to state that baptism means membership only in the "visible" church. This is foreign to the pre-1968 *Liturgy and Psalms* and to the Reformed confessions. The Belgic Confession distinguishes, as mentioned above, not between the visible and the invisible church, but only between the true church and the false church. Indeed, the whole point of the sacraments, according to the Doctrinal Standards, is the trustworthy unity of things visible and invisible in the Holy Spirit.

The third benchmark is that, in the Reformed Church in America, admittance to the Lord's Table belongs properly to the board of elders (with the pastor), and not to the congregation assembled. This act of admittance was originally meant to be an act of pastoral supervision, not of liturgical initiation. Before 1906, admission to the Lord's Table was not dependent on a public confession before the whole congregation, and it should not be so now. It is entirely in keeping with the Reformed Church's disciplinary tradition, therefore, for elders to regulate the admission of young children to communion after an intimate interview.

Both confirmation and profession of faith have often been regarded as the act of joining a particular congregation. However this, too, happens at baptism. One cannot be a member of the church catholic without being a member of a particular congregation. The Reformed Church has seen a decline from its high Calvinistic ecclesiology toward a mix of congregationalism and American voluntarism. The church is not a voluntary organization like the Veterans of Foreign Wars; it is a (divinely) governed society, more like a city. When one moves to another city, one does not "join" that city; one comes under its jurisdiction. For most of the Reformed Church's history, one did not join a congregation; one came under the care of a particular consistory. Transfer of membership was one consistory transferring a member of the church catholic to the care of another consistory. This is technically still the case in the Reformed Church, and the public reception of a transferred member in a worship service is simply a celebration of what has already been done by the consistory. At the same time there would seem to be some value in making a public statement of commitment to a local congregation, within a liturgical ceremony that includes a welcome from the congregation. This is most fittingly done in connection with communion, perhaps by making particular mention of new names from the Lord's Table.

Fourth, "conversion," which is an extremely important word for many Christians, must be understood in the full Reformation sense. Reformed theology sees conversion as both subjective and objective. Subjective conversion is the necessary decision for Christ as Lord and Savior. This decision, as the Reformation understood it, is never something once-for-all, but a process, something that is always continuing—the daily dying of the old self (Adam in us) and the daily coming to life of the new self (Christ in us) (HCat., Q 88). There will be as many different experiences of this conversion as there are individuals, but it must include a conscious turning away from sin and hatred of it (Q 89), and a joyful turning toward Christ and the will of God (Q 90). Subjective conversion is a never-ending calling, or as Luther wrote, "the whole life of Christians is penance," meaning repentance.

However Luther, when plagued by his subjective doubts and the survival of the old man in him, also said, "I am baptized." In this case he was referring to the objective side of conversion, which is once-for-all. This, too, is being born-again, but it is signified and sealed by baptism, since it depends not on our decision for God but on God's decision for us. The Canons of Dort beautifully describe this work of God in us: "And this [conversion] is the regeneration, the new creation, the raising from the dead, and the making alive so clearly proclaimed in the Scriptures, which God works in us without our help....it is an entirely supernatural work, one that is at the same time most powerful and most pleasing, a marvelous, hidden, and inexpressible work, which is not less than or inferior in power to that of creation or of raising the dead" (III/IV, Art. 12).

This is the objective side to conversion, of which baptism is the trustworthy sign and seal, of great comfort to the believer. As the Belgic Confession says, "Yet this baptism is profitable not only when the water is on us and when we receive it but throughout our entire lives." Baptism is the hearty promise that we may daily be born again (subjectively) because we have been born again (objectively) "without ourselves" (as the unabridged Baptismal Form of 1906 said).

So, like any revivalist, a Reformed believer should have good reason to say, "I have been saved, I have been born again," as a once-for-all event. But this Reformed believer will not presume to assign a date to when this once-for-all rebirth happened, such as, "I was born again on such-and-such a day at such-and-such a rally." This is more than one can know. As the Canons of Dort point out, the timeline of one's personal regeneration is a mystery even to one's self. The only certain date that anyone can point to is his or her baptism, which is the event in their lives when they receive a sure sign and seal that the Holy Spirit incorporates them into Christ's death and resurrection. Since Holy Baptism so powerfully signs and seals the objective side of conversion, then, the Reformed Church really has no interest in the objective elements in confirmation.

However, because of the subjective side of conversion, the Reformed Church is quite interested in the subjective act of publicly confessing faith and the remembering of baptismal vows. This should not be something "once-for-all," as confirmation tends to make it, nor should it be regarded as part of one's "Christian initiation." Rather, this remembering of the baptismal covenant bears repeating time and again through life, and this may be done corporately with the whole congregation, or individually before the congregation. Every time the congregation participates in a baptism, this remembering happens corporately. There is nothing to prevent groups or individuals from engaging in such renewal many times after having taken first communion, so long as no new rights or privileges of membership are added besides those stemming from baptism. Such an event could include the laying on of hands as a pastoral act.

Fifth, the Reformed Church continues to value public profession of faith, especially of young people when they have reached the age of discretion and have been prepared through serious catechism. Admittance to the Lord's Table should not exempt children from preparing for this purely subjective act of identifying with the confession of the church. At what age should this happen, and after how much catechism? Calvin suggested age ten, the Hungarian tradition was age twelve, and the Dutch tradition was age eighteen or older. Age eighteen would seem to allow for a much more informed confession of faith. Yet Christ reminds us that we best come like little children. Perhaps the Reformed Church could devise an educational system that is directed toward a series of public professions of faith, keyed to the successive stages of faith development, continuing into adulthood.

Sixth, the baptismal covenant does not require people to renew it. Ceremonies of profession of faith in the Reformed Church should be careful of language which suggests this. For this reason the Reformed Church should be careful in what it borrows from the recently developed rites for the "renewal of the baptismal covenant" developed by the Anglicans, the Methodists, and the Consultation on Common Texts. These rites are powerfully moving and contain a great deal of value. At the same time, these too threaten to devalue baptism, suggesting that its virtue can break down over time. Yes, baptism is covenantal; but its only covenant is that "new testament in my blood" ratified upon the cross, to which God will always be faithful. Baptism is the sign and seal that God keeps us in that covenant, and not the other way around, as if we should have to keep renewing the covenant in order to maintain our baptisms. People do not need to renew their baptisms any more than they need to complete them; what they need is daily to live out of them. People do this by "remembering," in the fullest sense of the word. Just as, in communion, the church "remembers" Jesus' passion without ever renewing that once-for-all sacrifice, so people can find ways to "remember" their baptismal covenant and recommit themselves to it without presuming to renew it.

Seventh, the reality of baptism, as well as communion, is meant to be a part of every Sunday service, whether or not the sacraments are celebrated. Every service that includes confession of sin, assurance of pardon, the call to new obedience by means of the Law, and the confession of the Apostles' Creed is a corporate echo of Luther: "We are baptized." Congregations might celebrate heightened services of preparation for communion in the form of a baptismal service, whether there are individual candidates or not, in which the congregation "remembers" its baptism. This is not "covenant renewal," but a periodic renewal of commitment, as African-American churches do by means of their revivals.

Eighth, the Reformed Church in America historically understood serious catechesis as essential to Christian formation, but this has been in decline. Catechesis is the particular educational obligation of the church to the believer. Catechesis may include, but is not limited to, teaching the catechism. It is through catechesis that the theological doctrines of the church are applied to the life of the believer. It is a kind of education that is distinct from the educational roles of the family and of the school, even a Christian school. Catechesis is even distinct from Sunday school. The elimination of confirmation ought not to be an excuse to do less catechesis, but an opportunity to do more of it in better ways.[18] This will require the Reformed Church to make a renewed commitment to catechesis as the heart of its educational ministry.

Conclusion

In summary, the supplementary rite of initiation called "confirmation," which has recently come to be practiced in the Reformed Church in America, is a mistaken direction which the denomination ought to reverse. At the same time, the Reformed Church should take advantage of a tremendous opportunity to renovate its doctrine of baptism, to open up catechism to whole-life education, to encourage professions of faith in new patterns, and to reappropriate the Lord's Supper as the weekly diet that strengthens one's life of confession rather than the reward for having made one's confession once and for all.

---

[18] A good example of creative catechesis currently in use in the RCA is Sonja M. Stewart and Jerome W. Berryman, *Young Children and Worship* (Louisville: Westminster/John Knox Press, 1989).

5
Book of Church Order Conscience Clauses

Background

The 1980 General Synod discussed and approved "A Proposal to Maintain Peace in Diversity in the RCA Concerning Women as Church Officers" (*MGS*, 1980:276). The 1980 General Synod adopted with recommendation for approval by classes four amendments to the *Book of Church Order.*

The above four *Book of Church Order* sections amended in 1980 state:

1. Ministers are those men and women who have been inducted into that office by ordination in accordance with the Word of God and the order established or recognized by the Reformed Church in America (*BCO*, chap. 1, part I, art. 1, sec. 2).

2. If individual members of the classis find that their consciences, as illuminated by Scripture, would not permit them to participate in the licensure, ordination, or installation of women as ministers, they shall not be required to participate in decisions or actions contrary to their consciences, but may not obstruct the classis in fulfilling its responsibility to arrange for the care, ordination, and installation of women candidates and ministers by means mutually agreed on by such women and the classis (*BCO*, chap. 1, part II, art. 2, sec. 7).

3. Ministers shall not be pressured in such a way as to lead either one who supports or one who opposes, on scriptural grounds, the ordination of women to church offices to offend against one's conscience; nor shall any minister be penalized for conscientious objection to or support of the ordination of women to church offices; nor shall any minister obstruct by unconstitutional means the election, ordination, or installation of a woman to church offices (*BCO*, chap. 1, part II, art. 13, sec. 14).

4. It [board of elders] shall not permit or penalize any member for conscientious objection to or support of the ordination of women to church offices; nor shall it permit any member to obstruct by unconstitutional means the election, ordination, or installation of a woman to church offices (*BCO*, chap. 1, part I, art. 5, sec. 2h).

Numbers 2-4 above are commonly known in the Reformed Church as the "conscience clauses."

Analysis of the Conscience Clauses

1. The understanding of conscience in the clauses is a Reformed one.

On two occasions the Reformed Church in America dealt with the role of conscience in its belief and polity:

a. The Commission on Theology submitted to the 1976 General Synod a report, "Authority and Conscience in the Church" (*MGS,* 1976:231-35). This report was submitted in response to the 1974 "Report of the Special Committee to Review RCA Participation in the NCC" (*MGS,* 1974:135, R-2).

b. The Commission on Theology submitted to the 1984 General Synod a report, "The Role of Conscience in the Belief, Practice, and Polity of the Reformed Church in America" (*MGS,* 1984:256). This report was submitted in response to an overture from the Classis of New Brunswick, requesting the commission to study the role of conscience in the belief, practice, and polity of the Reformed Church (*MGS,* 1981:122-23).

Both of the above reports and the conscience clauses themselves are clear that Scripture must inform the individual conscience. Conscience is not a pure or privileged source of moral and religious authority. A person's conscience is shaped by many forces in the course of living, and without the influence of the Scriptures and the authority of the church, the conscience can and does err. Of course, sorting out the many forces, both good and evil, that shape a person's conscience in the case of women's ordination is difficult—especially difficult in an American culture that is saturated with pornography and that encourages men to view women merely as objects of sexual desire.

2. The conscience clauses strictly limit the nature and scope of objection, and this limit is necessary to preserve the Reformed understanding of the authority of officeholders.

The conscience clauses limit objection to "the licensure, ordination, or installation of women as ministers" and to "the election, ordination, or installation of a woman to church offices." The conscience clauses do not allow for objection to women officeholders once they are ordained and installed. Once ordained and installed, women officeholders exercise the authority of the Lord of the church as described in the preamble of the *Book of Church Order.*

The conscience clauses also limit the nature and scope of objection. Objectors may not obstruct. The assumption here is that they remain loyal to the Reformed Church, respect its decision to ordain women, and in no way seek to undermine them.

3. The conscience clauses assume a process for determining whether an objector's conscience has been biblically informed, but the conscience clauses do not provide such a process.

Given the fact that an individual conscience may or may not be biblically informed, the appeal to conscience in the Reformed tradition requires a process of discernment. The conscientious objector needs to appear before the church body to whom he or she is accountable. In some form, the objector needs to share his or her process of spiritual formation, to explain his or her understanding of Scripture, and to explain why participation in the process of ordaining women will do him or her spiritual harm.

In the present arrangement for dissent on women's ordination, there is no accountability in dissent and therefore little possibility for people within the Reformed Church in America to constructively engage one another and to grow together spiritually. The failure to delineate a process of dissent is one of the reasons for the high degree of anger and tension surrounding the conscience clauses. It is also one of the reasons why the hope of the original framers of "A Proposal to Maintain Peace in Diversity in the RCA Concerning Women as Church Officers" has not been fully realized.

4. The conscience clauses are closely tied to a particular moment in the life and history of the Reformed Church in America.

In the late 1970s and early 1980s the Reformed Church was threatening to split over the issue of women officeholders. The conscience clauses were formulated "to bring peace in diversity in the RCA over the issue of women in church offices" (*MGS,* 1980:275). The main reason for the writing of conscience clause *Book of Church Order* amendments in the early 1980s was the ordination of women, and appeals to conscience were entirely focused on the ordination process. Also, in the early 1980s, there were very few Reformed Church in America ordained women ministers and it was not anticipated that there would be significant numbers of ordained Reformed Church women ministers in the future. The conscience clauses approved in the 1980s do not address what conscientious objection to women officeholders means when there are a substantial number of Reformed Church women ministers.

This failure to address the longer-term issues reflects a more fundamental problem with the historical particularity of the conscience clauses. These conscience clauses did not anticipate the long-term consequences of bringing the concerns of a *particular* situation into the *Book of Church Order* when the *Book of Church Order* is a book of *general* rules and procedures. The conscience clauses set a precedent of settling specific theological disputes by amending the *Book of Church Order*. If this precedent were followed consistently, it threatens undermining the *Book of Church Order* as a constitution. The commission believes that particular theological issues of this sort should not be legislated in the rules of governance but should instead be addressed through more appropriate processes of confession, discernment, and mutual accountability.

Deeper Theological Issues

The struggle, tension, and anxiety around the conscience clauses are a sign of theological ferment in the life of the Reformed Church in America. At the same time these struggles call the denomination to a process of self-examination and theological reflection. Behind the ferment are at least three issues.

1. The authority of officeholders

The preamble of the *Book of Church Order* lays the groundwork for a Reformed understanding of office. In the preamble section, "The Nature of the Church's Authority," the authority of officeholders is defined as follows:

> The authority exercised by those holding office in the church is delegated authority. Their appointment to their special tasks is by the Spirit of the Lord, and they are responsible first of all to the Lord of the church. Their authority is of three kinds: ministerial, declarative, and spiritual. Ministerial authority is the right to act

as Christ's servants. Declarative authority is the right to speak in his name within the limits set by Scripture. The church shall declare what is in the Word and act upon it, and may not properly go beyond this. Spiritual authority is the right to govern the life and activity of the church and administer its affairs.

In the Preamble section, "The Equality of the Ministry," the issue of authority is expanded on as follows:

> The principle of the equality of the ministry, conceived now in its broadest sense as including the functions of the elder and the deacon, is based upon the fact that the entire ministerial or pastoral office is summed up in Jesus Christ himself in such a way that he is, in a sense, the only one holding that office. Every ministerial function is found preeminently in him. By his Holy Spirit he distributes these functions among those whom he calls to serve in his name.

Jesus Christ, through the Spirit, calls people to office and delegates authority. Respect for this authority is essential for unity and good order in the church. Respect for this authority is one way Christ is honored as the only source of salvation. The Reformed understanding of the authority of officeholders makes no distinction between men and women officeholders. The Reformed Church in America needs to face honestly and forthrightly the question whether the conscientious objection to "the licensure, ordination, or installation of women as ministers" undermines the historic, Reformed understanding of Christ's delegated authority and respect for officeholders functioning in the name of Christ. Is it possible to object, based on a biblically informed conscience, to the licensure, ordination, and installation of women as ministers of Word and sacrament, and still to recognize and accept the authority that Christ has delegated to them? The commission finds it hard to imagine how such a position is possible. And if it is not possible, is not such a failure to accept this authority consequently a failure to accept the authority of Christ himself? More and more in the Reformed Church, the central problem is not the *ordination* of women but the *recognition of the authority that Christ delegates to women officeholders*. This is an issue the conscience clauses do not address.

Consequently, the commission concludes that the conscience clauses are internally contradictory. The two essential phrases in the conscience clauses stipulate that objectors "shall not be required to participate in" and yet "may not obstruct" the ordination of women. But the refusal to participate in the ordination of a woman is a refusal to recognize the authority that Christ delegates to a woman in that office. Such refusal, however passive, must itself be construed as a form of obstruction to the mutual recognition and respect that is essential among officeholders if they are to be effective servants and representatives of Christ. It is shortsighted and inadequate for the *Book of Church Order* to address only the obstruction of the ordination service without ever considering how objectors to the ordination of women must almost inevitably be forced to obstruct women officeholders in the exercise of their ministry. An unpublished study of the experience of women officeholders in the Reformed Church in America recently completed by the Commission for Women contains a disturbingly large number of cases where such obstruction has indeed taken place.

2. The role of dissent in the church

The commission believes that the conscience clauses as currently written in the *Book of Church Order* place both women and objectors to the ordination of women in contradictory positions. Yet this does not mean that the Reformed Church in America can ignore the issue of conscientious objection; rather, the denomination needs to address the problem more holistically. In the course of its history, the Reformed Church has faced a number of difficult situations in which a minority dissented from the majority on a given issue. The issue of women officeholders is just a recent example. The minority made an appeal to the right of conscience, and the majority recognized this right. How the Reformed Church handles dissent is crucial to the health of the body. The dissent of the minority can lead to anxiety and divisiveness in the church, but it can also keep important issues before the church and contribute to its theological development and health.

The Reformed Church needs to build on the Reformed understanding of conscience and devise a process of dissent whereby the right of conscience is legitimately exercised on a given issue and leads to the upbuilding of the church. The present conscience clauses lack the breadth and clarity adequately to address even the question of women officeholders, and the conscience clauses provide no guidance for dealing with other issues of conscience. Broader guidance and more general principles are needed in the *Book of Church Order*.

3. *The nature of the* Book of Church Order

This need for broader guidance and more general principles raises a third basic problem. The *Book of Church Order* contains the "rules of church government." In 1566 the Reformed Church in the Netherlands was formally organized and formulated some preliminary rules. These rules were revised numerous times over the years, which led to the current *Book of Church Order.* "Rules" by definition are "a prescribed guide for conduct and action." Such a guide functions best when it establishes general regulations and procedures that are applied to many different situations over time. The *Book of Church Order* cannot be encumbered with the particulars of every specific situation. The historical particularity of the conscience clauses is inconsistent with the spirit of the *Book of Church Order.*

Conclusion

The commission recognizes that there are sectors in the Reformed Church in America who do not believe it is the right time to delete the conscience clauses from the *Book of Church Order.* But the commission also believes that the present wording of these conscience clauses in the *Book of Church Order* is very problematic and that their interpretation requires clarification.

6
"The Crucified One is Lord":
Confessing the Uniqueness of Christ
in a Pluralist Society

In 1996 the General Synod of the Reformed Church in America addressed several overtures dealing with the question of salvation through Christ alone. In response to these overtures, the synod adopted the following resolution:

> BE IT RESOLVED that the one hundred ninetieth regular session of the General Synod of the Reformed Church in America, meeting in Orange City, Iowa, on the thirteenth day of June, 1996, joyfully and gladly reaffirms its confession that God's unique, unrepeatable, and decisive activity in Jesus Christ is the only sure hope for this world. God's work in Christ alone reveals the deepest truths about God, our life, and our world. God's work in Christ alone saves all who believe. Indeed, there is salvation in no one else, as the Old and New Testaments themselves teach.
>
> Further, this position marks not the end, but the beginning of the church's attempts faithfully to witness to the gospel. In our culture, there is an increasing tendency to view religious issues merely as matters of personal preference. Such an attitude renders the church's confession more difficult for many to understand and to embrace. Increasing contact with adherents of other religious traditions and those outside the Christian faith also stretches the boundaries of Christian understanding, as Christians recognize truth and value in religions and perspectives other than their own, even while challenging them with Christ's unique claims about himself.
>
> Therefore, in light of these changes in our world, the Reformed Church in America seeks fresh guidance on how to interpret and to live out its faith in the uniqueness of Christ in the midst of a pluralistic world with diverse religious perspectives; and further,

The 1996 General Synod directs the Commission on Theology to engage in a study on "Christian Witness to the Uniqueness of Christ among People of Other Faiths" which will both interpret the nature and character of Christian claims regarding the uniqueness of Christ and also guide Christians in understanding and assessing the religious experience and claims of those outside the Christian faith (*MGS*, 1996:402-3, R-3).

In response to this directive from the General Synod, the Commission on Theology presents this paper. In accordance with the directive from General Synod, this paper attempts to address three basic concerns: What do we believe about Jesus Christ? How do we interpret and live out these beliefs in a pluralistic world? How are we to understand the implications of these beliefs for adherents of other religions? In response to all three of these questions, this paper can only touch broadly upon the most major concerns, since comprehensiveness is impossible.

What Do We Believe About Jesus Christ?

The earliest and most basic of all Christian confessions is the acclamation, "Jesus is Lord" (e.g., Rom. 10:9; Phil. 2:11; 1 Cor. 12:3; 2 Cor. 4:5). To confess "Jesus is Lord" expresses a number of important understandings and commitments. It is first of all a recognition of God's unique activity and presence in Jesus of Nazareth. The term Lord, although it is used in many different ways in the Bible, is used throughout the Bible in distinctive ways to refer to God's own being. The Hebrew equivalent adon, "Lord," is the regular word used in normal speech to speak of God in the Old Testament. When the full scope of New Testament usages are carefully analyzed, it becomes clear that to say that Jesus is Lord is to attribute to Jesus the same sovereign power and authority that we attribute to God.[1] Therefore to say "Jesus is Lord" is to point to what we believe about who Jesus is, that he is not only "fully human," but also that

---

[1] For example, Phil. 2:10-11 states, "at the name of Jesus every knee should bend, in heaven and on earth and under the earth, and every tongue should confess that Jesus Christ is Lord, to the glory of God the Father." When compared with Isaiah 45:23, where God is speaking, the similarity of the language is striking: "By myself I have sworn, from my mouth has gone forth in righteousness a word that shall not return: 'To me every knee shall bow, every tongue shall swear.'"

he is "true God from true God," to use the more developed language of the Nicene Creed.

But to say that Jesus is Lord is not merely to affirm his deity; it is also to make the claim that every human authority is finally subject to Jesus. Even though the world may not acknowledge it yet, every governing official, every religious leader, indeed every human claim to authority must finally acknowledge the authority of Christ (Phil. 2:10-11; 2 Cor. 5:10; Rev. 11:15, 19:16). This confession has throughout the ages been the backbone of Christian resistance to evil and the hope that has sustained the church through its darkest hours.

This means that the statement "Jesus is Lord" not only conveys certain information about Jesus; it also expresses a whole range of commitments, values, and intentions of the community that gathers under this confession. To make this statement is like reciting a pledge of allegiance. It acknowledges Jesus as our Lord, and expresses the hope that Christians will see Jesus' lordship extend and be acknowledged over the whole earth.

Moreover, the confession "Jesus is Lord" is the response evoked from us when we experience the power of God made available to us in the name of Jesus. As we experience healing, forgiveness, release from the power of evil, and new life breaking into our lives, our hearts cry out in praise and adoration, "Jesus is Lord!" For Christians, the confession "Jesus is Lord" is an expression of the Spirit's work in our lives, as the power of God awakens in us the awareness of where our help really comes from. This is why the Bible declares that no one can say "Jesus is Lord" apart from the work of the Holy Spirit (1 Cor. 12:3).

This confession of the lordship of Christ is thus a response to the saving work that Christ accomplished on our behalf. We acclaim Jesus as Lord not only because of who he is, but also because of what he has done. Indeed, we discover fully who he is only when we realize all that he has done: he has revealed God's love and purpose for humanity in his life and teachings; he has redeemed us through his sacrificial death; he has triumphed over the power of sin and death in the resurrection; he has ascended to the right hand of the Father, where he continues to enliven the church through the Holy Spirit given in his name; and he will come again in judgment to blot out evil and restore the whole creation. Revelation 5:9 points powerfully to this celebration of Christ's work: "You are worthy to take the scroll and to open its seals, for you were slaughtered and by your blood you ransomed for God saints from every tribe and language and people and nation." Jesus is Lord because it is his life, death, resurrection, ascension, and final return that restores creation, providing salvation for all those whom God has chosen to redeem.

Moreover, the churches of the Reformation have consistently emphasized that Christ is both necessary and entirely sufficient for salvation. The Reformed emphasis on solus Christus ("Christ alone") reminds us that there is no other mediator between God and humankind. This focus upon Christ alone is closely related to Reformed emphases on sola gratiae ("grace alone") and sola fide ("faith alone"), which underscore the necessity and sufficiency of Christ's sacrifice on our behalf and the necessity and sufficiency of faith in Christ, without reliance on human works. Even the doctrine of sola scriptura ("Scripture alone") draws its basic rationale from the unique role of Scripture in its witness to Christ.

How Do We Interpret and Live Out These Beliefs in a Pluralistic World?

While almost all Christians continue to celebrate this confession as their personal belief, some Christians have become uncomfortable asserting it in the "public square." Some are not so sure any more whether this confession can be held as true, not just for oneself, but with the whole world in view. There are a variety of reasons for this unease. Changes in our culture have called into question whether anyone can claim to know any truth that transcends one's own context and experience. Past abuses committed by the church ostensibly in the name of the lordship of Jesus—from the Crusades to the Inquisition to slavery to a silent acquiescence in the Holocaust—have given some Christians pause about the way this confession should be used in the public arena. In addition, we find ourselves encountering adherents of other religions with increasing frequency in North America. Such contacts often raise questions about the uniqueness of Jesus and the exclusive claims made by Christians. It is important to explore these reasons for discomfort, and to discern how the church can constructively address them. How can we open up fresh perspectives on this ancient confession, which may enable the church to confess it with new conviction, sensitivity, and clarity? In our exploration, we shall pay particular attention to the function of confessing "Jesus is Lord" in addition to the content of that confession. That is, we shall be concerned with those assumptions and practices that surround our confession and bring its implications into engagement with the world around us. We want to concern ourselves with the concrete differences it makes in our lives and in our culture when we rightly confess that Jesus is Lord.

Fears about the Use and Abuse of Authority

To speak about Christ's lordship is to speak about authority. In our culture, however, this is a subject of great controversy. People from a variety of theological perspectives have questioned the language of lordship and authority in its application to God or to Christ. It has been argued that such terms are outmoded, reflecting a patriarchal and hierarchical society very different from the democratic egalitarianism of contemporary life. When the church honestly examines itself, it must acknowledge that this language has at times been used, even in the church, to condone oppressive relationships that reflect nothing of the Spirit of Christ.

Yet to reject this language entirely on the basis of these abuses is to confuse a distorted reflection with the true reality. It is also a failure to understand the distinctive way in which the confession of the lordship of Jesus functioned in the ancient church. Far from being used to legitimate human hierarchies and patriarchies, the confession of Jesus' lordship was used to relativize and critique all such human structures of authority. For example, Matthew 23:9 states, "And call no one your father on earth, for you have one Father—the one in heaven." In Acts 5:29, when the disciples are ordered by the religious authorities to be silent, Peter responds, "We must obey God rather than any human authority." In both of these examples, God's authority supersedes and relativizes all human authority.[2] The same is true in the Book of Revelation, where the lordship of Jesus is the starting point for resistance to a cruel and oppressive Roman Empire claiming power and lordship for itself. To confess that Jesus is Lord is not to give sanction to human authority, but to subject it

---

2   Cf. Calvin's *Institutes*, 4.20.30-31, and the contemporary discussion in Richard Mouw's study, *The God Who Commands* (Notre Dame, IN: University of Notre Dame Press, 1990).

to a penetrating critique that challenges any claim to authority apart from or different from the authority of the Christ who gave himself for the life of the world. Jesus turns the authoritarian and patriarchal world of his day on its head by declaring "The greatest among you will be your servant. All who exalt themselves will be humbled, and all who humble themselves will be exalted" (Matt. 23:11-12). To confess the lordship of Jesus is radically to redefine what lordship and authority mean in the first place! It is to embrace as our rule and guide the distinctive way in which Jesus embodies authority.

At the core of the Bible's understanding of authority is its affirmation of divine grace. Even the creation itself is expressive of God's gracious authority; God speaks, and the things that are not must respond and come into existence (Rom. 4:17). The world is sustained by the gracious decrees that proceed from the throne of God (Isa. 55:10-11). Yet this authority never expresses itself in domination, but rather in service (Luke 22:25-27). It is difficult to underestimate the significance of the graciousness of divine authority. God's authority gives life, it forgives and renews, it encourages diversity while binding people to each other.

Throughout human history, authority and power have usually been won by shedding the blood of others. But Jesus is acclaimed as Lord precisely because he has shed his own blood on behalf of the world. To say that Jesus is Lord without recognizing this distinctive understanding of gracious divine lordship is gravely to misunderstand the Christian confession.

This combination of authority, power, and self-giving is seen most clearly at those points where Jesus' claim to authority appears strongest. Consider John 14:6, where Jesus states, "I am the way, and the truth, and the life. No one comes to the Father except through me." One can scarcely imagine a more exclusive claim to authority. Yet the "way" of which Jesus speaks in this text is precisely the "way" of suffering and death (cf. 13:36, 14:3). It is because Jesus establishes and models this "way" of self-offering that he is also "truth" and "life." In other words, Jesus' claim to be the sole mediator of salvation derives from the uniqueness of his self-offering in death. Self-offering, power, and authority always come wrapped up in each other.[3]

---

[3]   It is striking how many of the "I am" sayings of Jesus in the Gospel according to John combine an exclusive claim about Jesus' status and authority with a pointer to his

This is not to say that divine authority never challenges, confronts, or judges. The same Jesus who gave himself for his enemies also challenged them, rebuked them, and warned them of God's judgment. But the judgment that Scripture speaks of is always in the service of grace. It is carried out by a God who loves this world more deeply than we can imagine, and whose wrath therefore will not allow anything in all creation finally to deny, demean, or destroy the love of God revealed in Christ, the love that energizes the whole creation and holds the universe together.

When we recognize this distinctive function of the confession "Jesus is Lord" in the early church, it raises some important issues surrounding how we make our confession of the lordship of Jesus. It is possible for us today to be entirely "orthodox," saying all the right words, but to do so in a way that attempts to establish the privilege and superiority of the church rather than to call the church and the world to discipleship in Jesus' way. It is not enough to be clear on what we should say; we need also to be clear on how we should make use of that confession in the life of the church.

The Challenge of Religious Pluralism in a Post-Christian Context

This leads to another challenge that is often heard today to the confession "Jesus is Lord." Some have argued that to confess that Jesus is Lord is arrogantly to presume that Christians have a monopoly on the truth. Here the complaint centers not on the notion of lordship or authority; it focuses upon the way in which Christians attribute final authority only to Jesus of Nazareth, not just for themselves, but for the whole world. The same complaint is heard in many variations: "It's OK for you to believe in Jesus, but you have no right to impose your beliefs upon others." "It doesn't matter what you believe, as long as you are sincere." "Every religion has important truth in it, and you can't say one is better than another." "There are many paths up the same mountain, but they all reach the same top. There are many religions, but they all are saying

gracious self-offering. Jesus is the bread of life (6:35), and that bread is his flesh, offered up in death (6:51). When he claims to be the light of the world (9:5), he demonstrates that claim by giving sight to the blind man. When he claims to be the gate (10:9), and the good shepherd (10:11), he goes on to speak of laying his life down for the sheep. When he identifies himself as the vine in whom the disciples must abide (15:1), he goes on in that same context to call them to lay down their lives for each other, just as he did for them (15:12-14).

basically the same thing." "How can you claim to know more about God than anyone else?"

All these comments, diverse as they are, share a common resistance to the confession "Jesus is Lord." In each case, the final and public allegiance to Jesus' lordship grates against the pluralism and individualism so deeply embedded in North American religious consciousness. Most people prefer that religion be kept private—out of the public sphere—and that it be kept humble and subservient, never claiming access to any truth or authority that might impinge upon others.

In one sense, the resistance of the dominant culture to the confession "Jesus is Lord" is as old as Christian faith itself. The early Christian martyrs were not put to death simply for believing in Jesus; they were put to death because they would not take part in the imperial cult of Rome. That is, they were not willing to regard their own religious beliefs and practices as part of an eclectic smorgasbord in the way most religions did. Rome was remarkably tolerant of a wide range of religions, as long as they made no claims to ultimate authority nor demanded final allegiance. But the early Christians would not go along with that. For them, to say that Jesus is Lord was to say that Jesus represented both the rule by which all other religions should be assessed (including the imperial cult), and the allegiance that superseded every other loyalty (including loyalty to the emperor). That allegiance cost many of them their lives.

Although resistance to the claim that Jesus is Lord is not new, our own culture has distinctive reasons for resisting this confession—reasons that we must try to understand. To do so, we must first go back to the period following the Reformation, when the so-called "wars of religion" tore Europe apart in the late sixteenth and early seventeenth centuries. By the time the Peace of Westphalia was concluded and these wars brought to a close in 1648, much of Europe was physically, economically, and culturally devastated. This anguish over religious conflict paved the way in the seventeenth and eighteenth centuries for approaches to the relationship between religion and public life which increasingly moved religion out of the public sphere and into the realm of subjectivity and private life. The implicit assumption driving much of this change was the belief that religion, when it acquires too much power, becomes explosive and divisive. Europe had come to that conclusion through the hard knocks of experience.

This disenchantment with a public role for religion was furthered by developments in the Enlightenment during the eighteenth century. Not only did political thought during the Enlightenment increasingly separate the role of church and state, but the empiricism and rationalism of the Enlightenment drew an increasingly sharp opposition between religion and science. Empiricism stated that our only access to truth is through the five senses; rationalism insisted that truth must be based upon reason alone, rather than faith. Because religion could not be empirically or rationally proven, it was relegated even more decisively to the realm of private opinion and feeling rather than to public truth. In this context, to say that Jesus is Lord might be meaningful as an expression of one's own feeling or belief. Yet since such a statement could not be empirically or rationally proven, it would be meaningless as an affirmation of public, objective truth that might make a claim on others or on the world as a whole. Ironically, the intensely inward and subjective character of the pietistic heritage of much American Christianity has often played directly into the hands of this public-private split in the function of religion.

The twentieth century, however, brought about a weakening in the Enlightenment's confidence in empiricism and rationality. The most scientifically advanced societies in the world almost brought themselves to extinction in two world wars, horrible beyond belief. In the late twentieth century our own postmodern context is suspicious, not only of religion, but of reason as well. More and more our culture is coming to the belief that all knowledge, both religious and scientific, is partial and provisional. We have come to recognize the ways in which reason itself is often merely a tool driven by the deeper and darker forces of ethnocentrism, greed, and the will to power.

And so in our own culture we are beginning to extend the same suspicions toward other social institutions that have long been directed toward the church. Our culture increasingly is suspicious of all claims to objective truth and all final allegiances. On almost any subject, people are encouraged to keep their opinions to themselves and to avoid the mortal sin of imposing their beliefs on anyone else. We are a deeply suspicious people.

This emphasis on the provisional and tentative character of our knowledge is further intensified by our increasingly pluralistic society. Economic developments, immigration, and changes in communications and travel technologies cause us to be exposed to many different kinds of people, more so than ever before. We work and go to school with Muslims, Buddhists, Jews, and adherents of many other religions. We are confronted almost daily by people who believe differently from us, and these people are often decent and respectable. Sometimes they may even strike us as admirable, embracing societal values we share or even religious ideals to which we may also aspire.

This loss of a public role for the church, combined with increasing contact with adherents of other religions, places the church in a new social position that often feels uncomfortable for us. In the past, Christian faith appeared to have influence in the society as a whole. We still have long-established memories of a European Christendom where the church played a central role in society. Now North American Christians ironically are finding themselves increasingly in the same position as Christians in many other parts of the world: they are a minority faith, often with little respect or status in the dominant culture, competing in a wide-open marketplace of diverse religions. Christendom—that mutually reinforcing alliance of religious institutions and public, secular power—is dead.

These changes in our world and in our own experience pose fresh challenges to the church. The deepest challenge, however, is not from outside, but from within. These social and cultural changes have affected us as Christians. We are not always as confident as we once were. Our privileged place in society as religious leaders is increasingly questioned. Our own patterns of thinking have been deeply influenced by the culture around us. There are many who are willing to acknowledge Jesus as their "personal Lord and Savior" but are not sure whether this confession has public significance for their neighbors and the world as a whole as well. They are hesitant to "impose" their beliefs on others. They are reluctant to suggest that their own beliefs might be superior to or more true than the beliefs of others, especially when they suspect that their own moral behavior and that of their fellow Christians is not always superior to the morality of adherents of other religions.

Public Witness in a Pluralistic World

How then do we bear witness to the lordship of Christ from this new social location? We are increasingly a minority faith, relegated to the sidelines of many public debates. Our confession of the universal lordship of Christ seems to many quaint at best, and at worst a threat to the pluralistic fabric of our society. Some Christians, particularly in the United States, respond to this situation by longing for and working for a reassertion of Christendom, where the church works hand in hand with government to influence public life. If we can only again seize the reins of power, they argue, we can reassert our nation's historic Christian identity and reestablish the credibility of the church's witness to the lordship of Christ.

Yet thoughtful Christians are increasingly questioning this approach. The rise of religious pluralism and the peripheral position of the church in our culture as a whole need not be seen only as a failure and a loss. In many respects, it can be seen as a fresh opportunity for the church. We may be in a situation today that is closer to that of the New Testament church than ever before. As we are freed from the false security of being an established religion and forced to compete in an open marketplace of ideas and perspectives, the Holy Spirit may be opening an opportunity for renewal and transformation in the church, leading us into a fresh and deeper witness to the world, a witness undergirded not by the status and prestige of the institutional church, not by smarter politics, better marketing, or more money, but by the quality and character of our lives. Christians all over the world have been living and thriving as minority faiths in such pluralistic contexts, and they have much to teach us.

Even in a pluralistic world, the reality that no one can deny is the transformation of human lives into the image of Christ. Perhaps more than ever before, the church is called to witness to the gracious and transforming lordship of Christ through a blended witness of word and deed. If our faith does not transform our lives to reflect Jesus Christ, no one will listen to us. If we do not find creative ways both to point to and to exhibit the radical, shocking, and subversive love of Christ, no one will pay any attention to us at all. But once we gain their attention, if we do not tell them the story of Jesus and challenge them to faith and discipleship, our witness will not bear fruit.

In the middle of this century, when the church still had a certain measure of public prestige, the style of evangelism was built around large crusades and the invitation to "come and listen." In our day the challenge must be "come, see, and learn." In our pluralistic world, people must often first see the transforming power of Jesus' lordship, and then they will learn the way of faith—often not in a onetime decision, but gradually, over a period of time. This process of conversion is no less a work of the Holy Spirit. It is the same Spirit who energizes our witness in word and deed. It is the same Spirit who speaks both through the words of the preacher and through the life of the church.[4]

This means as well that the church must pay very careful attention to the formation of Christian identity and maturity in its members. We live in a society where the supports for Christian faith and life are crumbling. To choose to live as a Christian requires intentional commitment. We must learn to recognize the powers in our world that continually undermine and subvert Christian faith and commitment. We must find fresh ways of encouraging each other to stand as lights in a dark world, of picking each other up when we fall, of supporting each other in the radical and subversive act of confessing Jesus as Lord.

How Are We to Understand the Implications of the Lordship of Christ for Adherents of Other Religions?

The challenges of pluralism come to a particular focus when the question of salvation is raised, particularly with reference to adherents of other religions. In the context of a pluralistic culture in which the provisionality of all knowledge is assumed, it becomes harder for many Christians to affirm that Jesus is Lord of the whole world and that salvation is found in Jesus alone. In our time it is becoming increasingly popular to adopt a general approval of all religions, a view that assumes that all religions are expressions of the same basic human quest for God. By this view, all religions that are sincerely followed are capable of mediating salvation to their adherents.

Yet such a perspective, as gracious and magnanimous as it may appear, is both highly questionable on its own grounds and incompatible with the central affirmations of Christian faith. It must first be asked, "How do we know that all religions are capable of mediating salvation to their adherents? What kind of evidence or arguments might be advanced to support such a position?" When pressed, it becomes clear that this position is in reality little more than wishful assertion, and it has little if any clear evidence or argumentation to support it.

---

4   Cf. Acts 2:37-47.

When examined closely, it is not at all clear that all religions are trying to achieve the same sort of salvation. Indeed, many careful scholars of comparative religion have emphasized the degree to which different religions conceive of salvation itself in very different ways. Only by the most reductionistic and simplistic analysis can it be said that all religions express the same quest for God or offer the same salvation. It is by no means certain that all religions are even attempting to mediate salvation in the way that Christians think of the concept.

But from a Christian perspective, there is an even deeper problem. Such a general approval of all religions cannot be reconciled with the message of Jesus. Jesus came proclaiming, "the reign (or kingdom) of God has come near."[5] In so doing, Jesus was not simply stating that something interesting or unusual was in the offing. That phrase "the reign of God" evokes all the hopes and dreams of the people of God for God's final redemption of Israel and the whole world. When Jesus declared that the reign of God was coming in his ministry, he meant that all of God's saving purposes for the whole world were coming to their climax and fruition in his ministry. Jesus never claimed to be opening one new path to God amid many others; he claimed that in his ministry, God's saving purpose for the whole world was coming to its culmination (cf. Matt. 24:14).

This emphasis on the reign of God points to an even more fundamental challenge to the assumption that all religions lead to the same goal. The most basic metaphor for the popular view of religions is the image of paths up the mountain. This view assumes that there are many paths to God and that each of us must find the path that is best for us. But note two important features of this metaphor. First, God is passive, waiting to be found at the top of the mountain. Secondly, human beings are the active ones, climbing up the mountain, struggling as best they can to find God, in an enterprise that requires a great expenditure of effort. The great drama of history, in this view, is this: how and when will humans ever make it to the top of the mountain to find God?

The biblical view, summarized in the message of Jesus, is quite the opposite. The great drama of history is not how humans will find God;

---

5   Biblical scholars have recognized for some time that the kingdom of God is not conceived in the New Testament primarily in spatial terms, but in terms of divine *activity*. The kingdom of God is preeminently associated with God's royal action to save and to restore. Hence the translation "reign of God."

it is rather when and how an active, seeking God will finally get through to a resistant humanity. When Jesus declared that the reign of God was at hand, he was not claiming to open a new path to God; he was claiming that God was blazing a new path to us in him. Christian faith is, in the final analysis, not about our going to God, but about God's coming to us in Christ. Christian faith is not about discovering God; it is the experience of having been found, despite our resistance and rebellion, by a God in search of us: "For the Son of Man came to seek out and to save the lost" (Luke 19:10). Christian faith is incompatible with a general affirmation of all religions because of a fundamental difference in understanding what religion is.[6] For Christians, it is not our quest for God, but our response to God's quest for us in Christ.

Nowhere is this more clearly seen than in the cross of Christ. Here is the moment where God meets us in all our rebellion, resistance, idolatry, and violence. At precisely the point where humanity is most resistant to God, the love of God shines most brightly, overcoming our rebellion, forgiving our violence, and inviting us into a new way of living. Christianity's distinguishing mark is not that we are seekers who have found God; we are sinners—enemies of God whom God has loved and forgiven. Christianity is about grace, from beginning to end.

Consequently, Christians do not so much claim to have discovered the truth as to have been apprehended by the truth. Their great joy comes not so much from what they have found, but from the fact that they have been found by God. Their concern is not so much with the wisdom they have acquired, but with the wise One who has drawn them to himself. If all Christians had to offer was another spirituality, another ethic, another path to fulfillment, Christianity would indeed be just one of many religions. But this is not the heart of the gospel. The gospel affirms that at the center of reality is the living, resurrected Jesus Christ, at work in the world through the Holy Spirit; everything else flows from this living person who has gripped the hearts and minds of those who call themselves Christian.

---

6   Cf. the technical discussion of the idea that different religions envision the nature of religion in dramatically different terms in S. Mark Heim, *Salvations: Truth and Difference in Religion* (Orbis: Maryknoll, NY, 1995).

Can Christians Learn from Other Religions?

Because the gospel is centrally concerned with God's grace in the midst of human failure, Christian faith manifests a distinctive combination of confidence and humility. True faith is confident enough of God's gift in Christ to commend Jesus Christ to the whole world and to risk all in trusting Jesus. But Christian confidence is based, not on our grasp upon God, but on God's grasp upon us. We do not understand or know everything—far from it! But we are known by the One who does. Our only comfort (and confidence) is that "we are not our own." This combination of humility and confidence means that Christians expect humbly to learn from others, even non-Christians. Christians acknowledge every week their own sinfulness, limitations, and shortcomings before God and the world in the confession of their sins in public worship. But everything that Christians learn is set in the context of the central confidence that defines Christian life at its core: We are not our own, but belong, body and soul, in life and in death, to our faithful savior, Jesus Christ.[7]

Christians look at other religions from this dual perspective. Because other religions do not recognize the unique way in which God has come to us in Christ, they participate in the bondage of all humanity that can only be broken through God's mercy revealed in Christ. Paul speaks of those apart from God's gracious covenant as "having no hope and without God in the world" (Eph. 2:12). These words are in keeping with a long biblical tradition that exposes the futility of idolatry and the diverse ways in which human religious activity is not so much a seeking after God as an avoidance of the true God who comes to us in promise and judgment (e.g., Isa. 44:6-20). Insofar as other religions do not recognize who Jesus is and what he has done, they lack the joyful assurance of reconciliation with God that stands at the heart of the gospel. This they need to hear, and all the church's evangelistic efforts are rightly directed to that end. Without this discovery, no other form of religious life can bring assurance of salvation. We have something vitally important to share with other religions.

But that does not mean that other religions have nothing to share with us. There is another perspective that Scripture and the Reformed

7   HCat, Q/A 1.

tradition provide as well. Reformed theology has always acknowledged that something of God's truth can be known through the natural world. Article 2 of the Belgic Confession states:

> We know God by two means: First, through the creation, preservation, and government of the universe, since that universe is before our eyes like a beautiful book in which all creatures, great and small, are as letters to make us ponder the invisible things of God: God's eternal power and divinity, as the apostle, Saint Paul, says in Romans 1:20. All these things are enough to convict humans and to leave them without excuse.

Reformed theology denies that God's self-revelation available in creation and culture is sufficient to bring us to salvation because it takes seriously the depths of human resistance to God. We do not respond appropriately to God's self-revelation in the world around us. We twist and distort it to our own idolatrous purposes. But the knowledge of God is nonetheless available in the natural world and is reflected in many religious traditions, partial and distorted though it may be.

A good example of this is found in Acts 17:16ff., where Paul identifies the altar "to an unknown god" as a groping after God, and says, "What therefore you worship as unknown, this I proclaim to you" (vs. 23). Paul goes on to cite several Greek poets as pointers to the truth found in the gospel. Of course, Paul never suggested that the religious perspectives he found in Athens were sufficient to bring about the true and complete knowledge of God. They are pointers to the truth, not the truth itself. Their value for Paul lies in their capacity to point people to the gospel of Christ. Yet in this capacity, they have real value. Paul's sermon illustrates a broad theme found throughout Scripture. Melchizedek and Jethro, the father of Moses, stand outside the covenant community and yet are channels through whom God instructs his people. Much of the wisdom in Proverbs 22:17 to 24:34 bears close affinities to Egyptian wisdom documented from other sources. Isaiah declares that Cyrus of Persia is God's anointed who has been raised up to do God's will (Isa. 45:1).

The same understanding has repeated itself frequently in the history of the church. Many of our cherished Christian practices were originally borrowed and adapted from non-Christian religions. Christmas trees find their origin in northern European pagan practice. Even the date of

Christmas coincides closely with a pagan Roman festival devoted to the sun god. Rather than denying any truth or value in such practices, the church saw them as early pointers to the gospel and incorporated them under the banner of the lordship of Christ, always making sure that they pointed clearly to Christ. Christians do not deny that there is truth or value in other religions or that God works through other cultures. Rather, Christian faith simply declares that all religions (including the Christian church in a continual way) must respond to what God has done, in sending his Son into the world and in calling all to respond in faith to him.

This means that Christians should always expect, not only to teach, but also to learn in their encounters with adherents of other religions. Yet we often find it very difficult both to teach and to learn. Sometimes we become so driven to challenge people with the gospel and to call them to repentance that we fail to see the remarkable ways in which the Holy Spirit is already at work in their lives and even in aspects of their religious heritage. The result is a self-righteous posture that does little to commend the gospel winsomely. Others become so captivated by the pluralist spirit of the age that they lose sight of the transforming power of Christ and the urgency and necessity of challenging people with the gospel at all. The result is a veneer of tolerance that conceals a callused indifference to the suffering and spiritual confusion of many. Neither extreme is faithful to Scripture. We have a wonderful gift to offer in the life-giving power of the gospel. But we can also learn from other religions. The artistry of faithful witness is to learn how to do both together.

What does it mean for Christians to learn from other religions? There are several ways in which that learning takes place. Sometimes other religions challenge us to embrace more deeply the implications of our own faith. The regularity of the prayer life of our Muslim neighbors may confront us with the infrequency of prayer in our own lives. The interest in the spiritual world among Native Americans may confront us with our own materialism and indifference to the Spirit of God. The celebrative affirmation of the law in Judaism may challenge our own cheap grace that fails to see God's law as a gracious gift. In all these ways and many others, dialogue with other religions may help us to become more truly and deeply Christian.

Other religions may also teach us fresh wisdom that is entirely in keeping with the gospel of Christ. In acknowledging this, the church must also acknowledge the danger of diluting or distorting Christian faith with practices or beliefs incompatible with the gospel. All things must be tested by the Scriptures and by the Spirit at work in the Christian community. Yet Christians around the world are finding architectural forms, meditative techniques, rituals, and patterns of worship in other religious and cultural traditions that are not only compatible with the gospel of Christ, but enable the gospel to be expressed more beautifully and powerfully in the lives of people.

There is also a third way—perhaps the most important of all—in which Christians can learn from adherents of other religions. This is not a learning of concepts, or beliefs, or practices, or values. It is rather the learning of persons, motivated by the love of God. We rarely encounter religions in the abstract. We encounter people, with their own culture, history, relationships, and values. We encounter people deeply loved by God, whom God also calls us to love. And love is always hospitable and open to the other. Love not only gives the gift of the gospel, but receives the gift of the other in turn, with care and gratitude. In the mystery of the work of the gospel, our capacity deeply to listen to and to learn from others will be directly related to their capacity to hear from us and accept the truth of Christ.

Learning from other religions and witnessing to the uniqueness of Christ are therefore not competing or incompatible options. Rather, they must be understood as complementary and mutually reinforcing activities. Christians who will not learn from other religions will easily become arrogant and will find it increasingly difficult to gain a hearing with adherents of other religions. Christians who fail to witness to Christ's uniqueness will easily become indifferent to the plight of those "having no hope and without God in the world" (Eph. 2:12). But those who can listen as well as teach, who can affirm as well as challenge in their encounters with other religions, are often used by God in remarkable ways to heal religious strife, to bring some justice and wholeness to a pluralistic world, and to lead many people to the good news of God's remarkable love in Jesus Christ.

Salvation and Other Religions

But what of salvation? Should Christians claim that there is no salvation apart from those who explicitly confess Jesus as Lord and Savior? In order fully to answer that question, a number of preliminary comments are necessary. First, Reformed theology has always taught that salvation is ultimately in God's hands, beyond the pale of human understanding. Calvin states that "we must leave to God alone the knowledge of his church, whose foundation is his secret election" (Institutes, 4.1.2).

A basic posture of humility should characterize all discussions of the scope of salvation. Christians claim not to have mastered the truth, but to have been mastered by it, and thus should be cautious about claiming to know too much of God's saving ways. God is greater than we, and we ought not to claim to know all of God's saving plan. While the Scriptures call us to discern between good and evil and between truth and falsehood, they also repeatedly caution against judging—that is, against attempting to determine the ultimate destiny of any person (Matt. 7:1; Luke 6:37; Rom. 2:1, 14:10; 1 Cor. 4:5; James 4:12). It is sufficient for us to be guided by the Scriptures which led us to Christ, affirming what seems clear and remaining silent where Scripture itself speaks with less clarity or finality. To probe too deeply into these matters is to subject oneself to grave spiritual danger, assuming knowledge and authority that rightly belong to God alone.

Secondly, it is important that we think of salvation in the broad biblical sense and not simply as a ticket to heaven. According to the Bible, salvation is, in the deepest sense, our covenantal response to God's initiative. God comes to us to restore our relationship with God and with the creation, beginning here and now and extending into eternity (2 Cor. 5:18-19). Hence, for Christians it is meaningless to suggest that people will be saved unless this salvation actually begins to be experienced concretely in their lives in the present. To speak of salvation without also speaking of repentance, the freedom of the Spirit, the forgiveness of sins, participation in the redeemed community, and the transformation toward a new and holy life is to speak of a meaningless salvation, abstract and devoid of content. To claim that salvation is present where these realities are not experienced is for Christians to strip salvation of most of its content. If Christians' discussions of salvation tend to become otherworldly at times, it may reflect the loss of a firm grip on what it means to be a redeemed community in the here and now.

Thirdly, we must remember that salvation has to do ultimately not only with individuals, but with the restoration of the whole creation. The salvation won in Christ comes to its culmination at the judgment seat of Christ, when there will be a new heaven and a new earth, when swords will be beaten into plowshares, when the wolf will lie down with the lamb, and when justice will cover the earth as the waters cover the sea. Hence when we think about the salvation for which we hope, we must not only consider how individuals will stand at that great and terrible day. We must also consider how and where the Spirit of God is already bringing to light the seeds of justice and peace that will come to flower when Jesus Christ restores all of creation to God's intention.

Finally, it is important to remember that the Bible always links salvation (in its full scope, present and future, personal and corporate) with faith in God's gift and promise. Without faith there is no knowledge of God and no salvation (Heb. 11:6; Eph. 2:8). But faith must not be construed as a "work," as something we do that wins God's favor. Faith is not a precondition for God's grace; it is a work of God's grace. The whole process by which faith emerges is under God's gracious providence.[8] Faith is the other side of the coin of salvation. It is not only the grateful receiving of God's salvation, but also the fruit of that salvation. To discover God's surprising mercy in Christ and to place one's trust in that mercy that reconciles us to God and to one another is, in itself, the experience of salvation (cf. Luke 19:9). Christians say that there is no salvation apart from faith because faith is itself our grateful receiving of salvation and our joyful entry into the redeemed community. A salvation that is not so received is no salvation at all.

Salvation in the Name of Jesus

With these preliminary considerations, we turn to the question of the place of Jesus Christ in the salvation of persons. Is explicit faith in Jesus as Lord necessary for salvation, or is it possible that adherents of other religions will also be saved? What does the Bible say about this, and can the Bible's perspective make sense for us today?

---

8 The HCat Q/A 61 states, "It is not because of any value my faith has that God is pleased with me. Only Christ's satisfaction, righteousness, and holiness make me right with God." Q/A 65 goes on to state, "Where does that faith come from? The Holy Spirit produces it in our hearts by the preaching of the holy gospel, and confirms it by the use of the holy sacraments." Ephesians 2:8 makes it clear that the entire process of being saved by grace through faith is *all* "the gift of God."

The Bible makes some very strong statements about the centrality of faith in Christ for salvation. Jesus declares in John 14:6, "I am the way, and the truth, and the life. No one comes to the Father except through me." In Acts 4:12, Peter says, "There is salvation in no one else, for there is no other name under heaven given among mortals by which we must be saved." In Romans 10:9, Paul affirms, "if you confess with your lips that Jesus is Lord and believe in your heart that God raised him from the dead, you will be saved."

Clearly, the central affirmation of the New Testament is that God extends his salvation to the world through Christ. The Bible does not say that God comes to us in many ways to save; it affirms that God's salvation has come to us in "the fullness of time" in Christ. Hebrews 1:1-2 speaks of how God long ago spoke "in many and various ways," but that "in these last days he has spoken to us by a Son, whom he appointed heir of all things, through whom he also created the worlds." One can scarcely imagine a more central role for Jesus in God's saving purpose for the world. Christian faith is absolutely clear: Jesus is God's definitive word— the only Savior.

But what if the name of Jesus is not known? Must Jesus be explicitly named in order for salvation to be experienced? On this subject, the Bible speaks with a clear central message. The central message and emphasis of Scripture falls upon the centrality and significance of the name of Jesus and the hearing of the gospel. Paul summarizes this theme in Romans 10:14: "But how are they to call on one in whom they have not believed? And how are they to believe in one of whom they have never heard? And how are they to hear without someone to proclaim him?"

Paul bears witness here to the passion that drives the whole New Testament church: the passion to make Christ known. Such passion is incomprehensible apart from the conviction that the name of Jesus is critical to the experience of salvation. Paul believed that God intends people to find salvation through the name of Jesus. He believed that Jesus was God's Messiah, the one appointed to bring salvation to the world. Along with the entire New Testament church, Paul believed that the means by which God has chosen to bring salvation to the world is the proclamation of the gospel of Jesus Christ.

This is the mandate given to the church, to be the agents through whom God extends his salvation to the world, through witness to Jesus Christ in word and deed. There is no assurance of salvation revealed to us apart from confessing Christ and trusting in him alone. Yet the church also must confess that it does not know the limits of God's grace. We cannot be certain that God will not impart saving faith in Christ, even perhaps where his name is not explicitly known. Throughout Christian history the great confessions of the church have affirmed with clarity that our salvation is found in Christ alone, while at the same time exercising restraint in determining too sharply the extent of that salvation or how God may bring people to a saving relationship with Christ.

The Second Helvetic Confession (1566), an important and widely used Reformed confession, allows that God can save in ways other than through the preaching of the Word. After arguing that "the preaching of the Word of God is the Word of God" (no low doctrine of preaching here), the confession goes on to state, "We know, in the meantime, that God can illuminate whom and when he will, even without the external ministry, which is a thing appertaining to his power; but we speak of the usual way of instructing men, delivered unto us from God, both by commandment and examples" (Chap. 1).[9]

In an analogous move, the Westminster Confession (1646), states, "Elect infants, dying in infancy, are regenerated and saved by Christ through the Spirit, who worketh when, and where, and how he pleaseth. So also are all other elect persons, who are incapable of being outwardly called by the ministry of the Word" (Chap. 10, Sec. 3, italics added).[10] The confession goes on immediately to rule out the notion that such a belief might be used to argue for the salvation of all non-Christians: "much less can men, not professing the Christian religion, be saved in any other way whatsoever, be they never so diligent to frame their lives according to the light of nature and the law of that religion they do profess" (Chap. 10, Sec. 4)"[11] The Westminster Confession thus walks a middle road, rejecting both the idea that other religions can mediate salvation and the notion that only those who are capable of being outwardly called by the ministry of the Word" can be elect. It is also worth noting that the confession walks this middle road specifically out of a desire to preserve both the necessity

---

9   Trans. by Philip Schaff, reprinted in *Creeds of the Churches*, rev. ed., ed. John H. Leith (Richmond, VA: John Knox Press, 1973), 134.
10 Ibid., 206.
11 Idem.

of the gospel of Christ for salvation, and also the freedom of God to work "when, and where, and how he pleaseth."

Calvin emphasizes primarily the necessity for explicit faith in Christ and rejects any idea that salvation is mediated through means other than the gospel of Christ. Yet even Calvin held that though preaching is the "normal mode which the Lord has appointed for imparting His Word," God's saving ways cannot be restricted only to preaching. Commenting on Romans 10:14, Calvin writes, "If it is contended from this that God can instil a knowledge of Himself among men only by means of preaching, we shall deny that this was the meaning of the apostle. Paul was referring only to the ordinary dispensation of God, and had no desire to prescribe a law to His grace."[12] At the same time, Calvin observes, "It is enough to bear this fact alone in mind, that the Gospel does not fall from the clouds like rain, by accident, but is brought by the hands of men to where God has sent it."[13]

These two streams that flow from the Reformation are both important. We must never lose sight of the centrality and necessity of the preaching of the gospel of Christ. On the other hand, the affirmation of divine freedom in passages like that found in the Second Helvetic Confession rightly cautions the church against arrogating to itself human control or complete knowledge of God's saving work. In the face of a corrupt Roman church that had insisted on its own mastery over the mediation of salvation, the reformers insisted on the freedom of God and the freedom of the Word of God. The Reformed emphasis on the freedom of God provides an important caution, lest the church again be tempted to claim for itself control over God's saving ways or too deep a knowledge of the extent of God's salvation.

The relationship between divine freedom and God's use of human agency is a mystery. It is wise for us to confess with conviction what God has revealed—that the only assurance of salvation revealed to us is found through explicit faith in Jesus Christ. At the same time it is also wise for us to avoid saying what we do not know—exactly how God will deal with all those who have not heard or responded to the gospel. We do know that God is both completely gracious and completely just. That is enough for

---

12 *The Epistles of Paul the Apostle to the Romans and to the Thessalonians,* trans. By Ross Mackenzie (Grand Rapids: Eerdmans, 1960), 231.
13 Ibid.

us. With Abraham we confess in hope, "Shall not the Judge of all the earth do what is just?" (Gen. 18:25).

When the church confesses that it does not know the limits of God's grace, however, this in no way weakens the urgency of its mandate to evangelism, its joyful responsibility to be heralds of the gospel to all the nations. The church can never smugly sit back and declare "God will somehow make it all right" when billions of people live and die in hopelessness, poverty, oppression, and despair, without the transforming and life-giving power of the gospel of Christ. We live in the hope that God will finally set all things right, but we also believe that the means God has chosen for this end is the preaching of the gospel of Christ in word and deed.

To be a Christian is to be entrusted with the gospel, with the commission of bringing God's light to the whole world. And yet it is finally God's gospel and God's mission, not ours. As a saint once quipped, we are to preach as if everything depended upon our proclamation, and to pray as if everything depended upon God. To follow that advice is to preserve the Bible's emphasis on the necessity and centrality of the proclamation of the name of Jesus, while also recognizing that salvation is finally in God's hands and not in ours. And in any case, it is always Jesus who is the Savior. He is God's Messiah; it is his sacrifice that has atoned for the sins of the world and reconciled believers to God.

The Ongoing Challenge

But simply knowing this truth and believing it is not enough. In our society the Christian claims regarding the uniqueness of Christ and the necessity of salvation in Christ will immediately raise suspicions of arrogance and a fear of domination. In other parts of the world they raise painful memories of colonialism, forced conversion, and oppression. The church's history of confessing the lordship of Christ has not been without its failures. In subtle and powerful ways the church can be tempted to want to reign with Christ without following the path of Christ, the path of humble service. There is simply no place for self-congratulatory superiority in our pointing to the uniqueness of Jesus Christ. At the same time there is no place for hesitancy, lack of confidence, or lack of conviction as the church points to Christ's uniqueness. If Christians really believe that the love of God revealed in Christ is the only hope for this world, if they really believe that Jesus is "King of kings and Lord of lords," then they cannot be silent about the claim of the gospel on the life of every person, every community, every culture. Christians who claim to have been transformed by the surprising love of Christ cannot and must not keep that love to themselves. If Jesus really is Lord, then his gracious lordship must be made known to all. No task is more central to the church's mission.

But there is a world of difference between efforts to impose or coerce Christian faith and the gracious commending of Christian faith by words and lives that are empowered by the Spirit. The church will be able to point credibly to Jesus as the only Savior of the whole world only if it makes that claim as a community that assumes a posture of humble service, if it seeks out the lowest places of service, and loves where no one else is willing to love. Only then will Christians be able to persuade the world that Jesus comes, not to destroy our cultures, but to renew them; not to reinforce patterns of domination, but to give life to all; not to negate our religious searching, but to show us the reality for which we have been longing; not to impose uniformity, but to bring many diverse gifts to full expression. If this is the Savior whom we have come to follow, we will indeed have good news not just for ourselves but for the whole world.

3
Church and Sacraments

Introduction

The Commission on Theology paper, "Children at the Lord's Table," presented to the General Synod of 1988, is in two parts. Part I summarizes in chronological order the fifteen-year (1972-1986) history of the issue in the Reformed Church in America. The major components of this history are the two commission studies, "Baptized Non-communicants and the Celebration of the Lord's Supper," brought to the General Synods of 1977 and 1984. The circulation of these papers with the specific request for response produced minimal response from the church.

The 1988 paper's second part expresses the commission's agreement with the positions of past commissions, offers a list of salient biblical, historical, and theological data for the synod's consideration, and urges it to adopt the commission's central recommendation, "To encourage boards of elders of RCA congregations to include baptized children at the Lord's Table using the specific suggestions for implementation found in the 1977 and 1984 papers until such time as revisions are made and materials prepared by the appropriate agencies" (*MGS*, 1988:385).

Although the advisory committee advised the synod to vote against this recommendation, it was adopted. A motion to substitute language that spelled out more precisely the requirements for children lost. Later, a

154

point of order was raised as to whether the action taken on the recommendation was in violation of the *Book of Church Order* and therefore out of order. Following discussion with the committee of reference, the president ruled that the action taken on the recommendation was not in violation of the *Book of Church Order* and was therefore in order. When that ruling was challenged, the synod voted to uphold its president.

The Paper

Children at the Lord's Table

Introduction and History of the Issue in the Reformed Church in America

In 1972 the Classis of Albany submitted an overture to the General Synod:

> To instruct the Theological Commission to study the possibility of allowing baptized members of the church to partake of the Sacrament of the Lord's Supper before making a public profession of faith (*MGS*, 1972:86).

Since this overture, issues surrounding admission of children to the Lord's Supper have been addressed in the Reformed Church in America. The actions of the General Synod and the studies of the Commission on Theology follow:

1972

> The Classis of Albany overture to General Synod (*MGS*, 1972:86) was denied on grounds that the commission was already studying the matter.

1973

> The Classis of Mid-Hudson overture to General Synod received the identical response (*MGS*, 1973:108).

General Synod received from its advisory committee recommendations (1) "that all persons may participate in the supper who understand that they belong to Jesus Christ, and who share in the ongoing life of his people. This means that covenant children who have this understanding may participate in the sacrament," and (2) "that there be retained in the church a program of Christian education, the purpose of which is to prepare young people for confirmation of their faith ('communicant class')." The former was not adopted, the latter was (*MGS,* 1973:193).

1974, 1975, 1976

Work-in-progress reports were made to the General Synod from the Commission on Theology.

1977

The paper, "Baptized Non-Communicants and the Celebration of the Lord's Supper," addressed seven areas of concern: (1) baptism in the life of the church, (2) the meaning of baptized non-communicant members, (3) the Lord's Supper in the life of the church, (4) the place of children at the Lord's Table, (5) biblical and theological grounds for requiring baptized children who have been participating in the Lord's Supper to confirm their faith publicly, (6) a procedure for the local church to admit baptized children to the Lord's Supper, and (7) the exercise of care in the discipline of baptism and the provision of continuing instruction, nurturing, and pastoral care to foster the obedience of faith which baptism requires.

The General Synod approved the paper for distribution to churches and classes, which were requested to respond to the Commission on Theology by May, 1978.

1978

The commission made no report on the issue to the General Synod.

1979

At General Synod the Advisory Committee on Theology debated the issue and recommended that the General Synod not approve the commission's recommendation to adopt the 1977 theological basis for having children at the Lord's Supper and the suggested implementation of the paper. The General Synod agreed not to adopt by a very narrow margin.

1981

The Classis of California submitted an overture "to allow our children of the covenant participation in the Lord's Supper (*MGS*, 1981:120).

The Advisory Committee on Christian Faith recommended deferring action on the basis of insufficient information. The General Synod adopted the following: (1) to defer action until the General Synod in 1982, (2) to redistribute the 1977 paper to the churches, and (3) to reprint the 1977 paper in the General Synod Workbook for 1982 (*MGS*, 1981:121).

1982

The General Synod took up the deferred issue, adopting the recommendation of the advisory committee to deny the 1981 overture of the Classis of Central California and to refer the 1977 paper to the Commission on Theology for revision.

1984

The Commission on Theology presented to the General Synod, "Baptized Non-Communicants and The Celebration of the Lord's Supper," which built on the 1977 paper and added two dimensions: (1) insights from historical theology and (2) aid in understanding the issue from the behavioral sciences (*MGS*, 1984:248-255).

The General Synod did not adopt the paper (*MGS*, 1984:256). The reasons given were that the paper (1) overemphasized the efficacy of infant baptism and (2) did not give sufficient emphasis to a personal commitment to Christ and to a confession of faith before partaking of Holy Communion.

The recommendations of the Commission on Theology to instruct the commissions on worship and church order to consider and recommend changes in the *Liturgy* and the *Book of Church Order* were not considered since the paper was not adopted.

1985

The Particular Synod of New York submitted an overture "to instruct the Commission on Theology to restudy the 1984 paper in light of the 1984 General Synod discussions and to present its findings to the 1986 General Synod.

The General Synod adopted the following:

(1) to instruct the Commission on Theology to restudy the 1984 report and to address several matters: (a) practice of confirmation and profession of faith; (b) baptism and regeneration; (c) pastoral supervision of parental responsibility; (d) baptized children of baptized non-communicants; and (3) any other substantive issues arising from the study.

(2) to present progress reports in 1986 and 1987 and a final report in 1988, and

(3) to distribute the annual reports and the 1977 and 1984 studies to all RCA consistories for study and comment to the commission (*MGS*, 1985:266).

1986

The General Synod received an interim report on "The Practice of Confirmation and Profession of Faith" (*MGS*, 1986:322-23).

The General Synod voted "to invite written response to the interim report."

1987

The Commission on Theology reported its continuance of discussion of the issue.

Despite this fifteen-year history of the issue in the church, the circulation of both the 1977 and 1984 Commission on Theology papers on the topic, and the specific request for response from all consistories by the 1986 General Synod, the Commission on Theology received only six responses from congregations (three positive letters and three negative letters), one negative response from an individual, and one letter from a classis which took up the question but could not conclude its views and did not forward further discussion as it had promised.

The Commission on Theology Report to the 1988 General Synod of the Reformed Church in America

The Commission on Theology has studied the 1977 and 1984 papers and the issues referred to it by subsequent actions of the General Synod. The present Commission on Theology agrees with past commissions and concludes that the proposal to include baptized children at the Lord's Table is fully consonant with the Reformed doctrines of baptism and the Lord's Supper and the work of the Holy Spirit, and that no serious impediments to the proposal emerge from biblical, historical, or theological grounds.[1] Further, the present commission urges the General Synod this year to consider the selected salient biblical, historical, and theological data as itemized below; and to adopt the appended recommendations.

1. The decision to include baptized children at the Lord's Table is grounded in the Reformed view of baptism, which has its roots in the biblical concepts of the covenant and church, and is also grounded in the nature of the Lord's Table and in the work of the Holy Spirit. Baptism is the sign and seal of a continuing life in Christ through the Holy Spirit within the body of Christ. Children

---

[1] The indebtedness of the present commission to the past commission papers for research, some of the language, reference to historical and biblical passages, is hereby acknowledged.

of believers as well as individual adult believers are heirs of the kingdom and members of the body of Christ (Gen. 18:19; Deut. 6:7; Mark 10:13f.; Acts 2:39; 1 Cor. 7:14).

2. The covenant—initiated by God with Abraham, maintained with faithfulness to Israel, and envisaged by the prophets to be renewed to include all the families of the earth—provides the key to the understanding of the church as the covenant people of God today (Gen. 12:1-3; 13:15; 15:13; 17:7-14; Jer. 31:31-34; Matt. 26:28; Rom. 11:17-24; Gal. 3:7-14, 26-29; Eph. 2:11-12; Heb. 8:8-13; HCat, Q 74).

3. Baptism is a means of grace whereby God is pleased to incorporate us into the covenant of grace with God's people. To be introduced into the covenant is to be introduced into Christ and the blessing of the Holy Spirit (1 Cor. 6:17; 12:13; 2 Cor. 3:17-18).

4. Based on the foregoing Scriptures, the baptized gain a growing sense of identity as children of God, an increasing awareness of their privileges and responsibilities, as well as an increasing assurance that grounds their hope of eternal life. This growing life in Christ is the work of the Holy Spirit who nurtures us through Word and sacrament in communion with God's people.

5. The Belgic Confession, Article 34, and the Heidelberg Catechism, Question 74 (cf. Q 69, 70, 73) affirm with strong statements that children are through baptism members of the church because they are included in God's covenant of grace and all its benefits.

6. This affirmation recognizes God's active presence in a baptized child's life. The complementary affirmation is that personal faith, expressed increasingly in a person's developing life, demonstrates trust in God. Both must be affirmed. Taken alone, the latter leads to works of righteousness, which Reformed theology has also consistently rejected. Taken together, however, baptism and profession of faith jointly recognize the grace of God throughout the Christian life.

7. Baptized children, like all of us, have begun a journey. Along the way and at the journey's end, they and we require the blessing of

the Holy Spirit in the hearing of the Word of God, the sacrament of the Lord's Table, and the affection and nurture of the Christian community. In baptism, God wills that baptized children shall be led by the Holy Spirit to appropriate all of God's promises and to affirm the knowledge of God's grace in their own public confessions of faith. Such is the faith expressed by the Apostle Paul: "I press on, to make it my own, because Jesus Christ has made me his own" (Phil. 3:12). Indeed the church must provide the most sound and comprehensive program of nurture and education possible in order that the church's children will make public profession of faith in Jesus Christ as Savior and Lord.

8. However, nothing in the Scriptures, in Reformed theology, or in the early history of the church requires such a confession of faith to be a prerequisite to participation in the Lord's Supper. Rather, the Lord's Supper is understood as a *means of grace* for nourishing and strengthening us to eternal life, righteousness, and glory. God grants to covenant children in the Supper the infinite goodness of our Savior and makes us all to be partakers of all God's blessings (cf. *Liturgy and Psalms*, 64). As such, the Supper must surely not be considered as the *goal* for baptized children. It is not a reward for making confession of faith. Rather, the sacrament is a means of grace that properly leads one to public confession of faith. We do not withhold food and drink from our children until they are old enough to say they need it. On the contrary, the food and drink provided for them are among the means by which our children grow to maturity. The Belgic Confession, Article 35 (cf. the Canons of Dort, v. 14) clearly presents this nurturing and covenantal view of the Lord's Supper:

> We believe and confess that our Savior Jesus Christ has ordained and instituted the Sacrament of the Holy Supper, to nourish and strengthen those whom he has already made alive and members of his family, which is the Church.... Now, as it is sure and beyond doubt that Jesus Christ did not enjoin us the use of his Sacraments in vain, he works in us all that through these holy signs he presents to our eyes, although the manner surpasses our understanding, and is

beyond our grasp, even as the working of the Holy Spirit is invisible and beyond our grasp.

9. Throughout the early history of the church, the Holy Supper was understood as a means of grace to nurture the children of the church.[2] After 1,200 years, and then only in the Latin West, the Roman Catholic Church excluded children from the Table. This was done for two reasons. First, the bishop alone, it was believed, could "confirm" a person making a profession of faith, and the practice was declared to be a sacrament. Thus, a step-by-step sacramental sequence was established: baptism, confirmation, then the Lord's Table, and the other sacraments. Even after this action children were not immediately excluded. A second action combined with the first to change the practice gradually. The Fourth Lateran Council, A.D. 1215, defined the doctrine of transubstantiation in which the elements of the Holy Supper were regarded as too holy to be handled by any except a consecrated brother, priest, or bishop. So, children were excluded lest they "slaver" and desecrate the holy elements. For the same reason, the cup was withheld from lay Christians.

Reformed Christians do not believe in transubstantiation, but in the spiritual presence of Christ in the sacrament of the Table. Neither do we believe in confirmation as a sacrament. Nor is there any necessity for the individual's public confession of faith, essential though it be, to be a precondition for participation in the Lord's Supper.

10. Some object that the nature of the Supper and the caution not to eat unworthily in 1 Corinthians 11:27-29 require a more mature discernment than young children can attain. This view is based on the idea that "discerning the body" means an intellectual, rational grasp of the doctrines of salvation and the symbols of the Table. But Paul's argument in I Corinthians 11 offers a different understanding of the phrase. When the Corinthians gathered to

---

2   The church history material of this report is from Donald J. Bruggink, "The Lord's Supper for All God's Covenant Community," a lecture given at the 1979 Fall Institute, Western Theological Seminary, Holland, Michigan.

eat, "each one goes ahead with his own meal, and one is hungry and another is drunk" (1 Cor. 11:21). The context is divisiveness in the church. What was not being discerned through insensitive and exclusive behavior was the corporate character of the "body of Christ," the church. What was being broken was the communal nature of the Supper. Participation of baptized children at the Lord's Table is another effort not to eat unworthily. By including baptized children we are properly "discerning the body of Christ": the church in its fullness.

The participation of children at the Lord's Table before public confession of their faith was a standard practice in the early church. Our own theological tradition nearly a hundred years ago demonstrates a congruence with the practice in the Children's Catechism approved by the General Synod of 1889:

What is the duty of the child?

It is the duty of a baptized child to worship God and to come to the Lord's Supper as soon as he is drawn to it by love for the Savior.

11. The Reformed Church in America should not understand Paul's cautionary words of "discerning the body" (1 Cor. 11:29) to mean the disqualifying of anyone of any age, even and perhaps especially a child, who believes in or loves the Savior and trusts the Lord alone for salvation. One need not be perfect morally, spiritually, or intellectually in order to benefit from the Supper. Indeed, as Calvin's Geneva Catechism makes clear, precisely because we are not perfect, all believers need to come to the Table:

But is it necessary to have perfect faith and charity?

Both should be entire and unfeigned, but to have such a perfection, from which nothing is wanting, will not be found among man. Moreover, the Supper would have been instituted in vain if no one could receive it unless he were entirely perfect... It is an aid and support for our weakness....

12. What is required of anyone to partake of the Lord's Supper is faith in and love for the Savior, ability to experience the Savior's love expressed in the bread and the cup, and the sense of belonging to the covenant community. The believing and discerning of the child can be as fully authentic as that of the adult, but the believing and discerning will be at the level appropriate to the child's age. Children can show the kind of love, trust, and thankfulness appropriate to their place in the family of God. They can love Jesus and experience Jesus' love in return. We are reminded of Jesus' words, "Let the children come to me, and do not hinder them; for to such belongs the kingdom of heaven" (Matt. 19:14). They can be loved by parents, friends, and other members of the body of Christ who have taken responsibility for their nurture as children in the church. They can commit themselves meaningfully to Christ and obey and serve their Lord. Indeed, current research in cognitive development affirms the importance of the church's sacramental life for nurturing children in the faith.

13. Where does responsibility rest for the nurture and instruction of baptized children as they participate in the Lord's Supper? It rests on the believing parent(s), on the Christian education program of the local church, and with the board of elders of each congregation. Pastors serve as an important resource for constructing and implementing a program of pastoral care and fostering a congregational climate that encourages appropriate spiritual life for all members of the body of Christ.

14. Grounded thus in the nature of baptism and of the Lord's Supper, and in reliance on the work of the Holy Spirit who makes alive and leads to fullness of life in Christ, the commission commends the practice of including baptized children at the Lord's Table.

4
Church and Ministry

Introduction

The Role and Authority of Women in Ministry

In response to a 1988 General Synod recommendation to undertake a comprehensive study of "The Role and Authority of Women in Ministry" (*MGS,* 1988:387, R-9), the commission in concert with the Commission on Women, presented this paper to the General Synod of 1991. The paper celebrates the service of women past and present, provides a framework for understanding the nature and authority of the church's ministry, and urges new roles for both women and men as co-laborers with Jesus Christ for the sake of the whole creation.

Individuals and church groups who seek a systematic treatment of the biblical texts relating to ministry of women are referred to the paper's bibliography. Included there are the *Reports of the Committee on the Ordination of Women to the General Synods of 1957 and 1958.* These reports include a comprehensive survey and discussion of pertinent biblical texts and conclude with a recommendation that the General Synod make the following declarative statement: "Scripture nowhere excludes women from eligibility to the offices but always emphasizes their inclusion, prominence, and equal status with men in the Church of Jesus Christ" (*MGS,* 1958:328).

The General Synod voted to make this paper available on request, together with the 1957 and 1958 General Synod reports of the Committee on the Ordination of Women, to Reformed Church pastors and consistories for study and use in their congregations.

Concerning the Practice of the Laying on of Hands in the Ordination Services of the Reformed Church in America

An inquiry regarding the participation of elders in ordination services prompted the commission to initiate this study for the benefit of the denomination as a whole. The paper explores the place and purpose of ordination to office in the Reformed tradition; the meaning of the laying on of hands in ordination; the relationship between the offices of deacon, minister, and elder; and relationship of these offices to the ministry of the whole people of God.

With regard to the laying on of hands, the commission finds both constancy and change in the practice of the Reformed Church in America. Its liturgy for the ordination of minister of Word and sacrament has always included it although there have been changes concerning who should participate in this liturgical gesture. The commission concludes that both elders and ministers should lay hands on those being ordained to the office of minister of Word and sacrament. Regarding elders and deacons, all members of the consistory of the church in which these officers are being ordained should be invited to participate in the laying on of hands. Further, the commission concludes that classes and consistories should be encouraged to invite other persons both ordained and non-ordained, both within and beyond the Reformed Church in America, to participate with all the members of the consistory or classis in the service of ordination, including the laying on of hands.

The synod adopted the commissions' recommendation to commend the paper for study and use in the denomination and to instruct the Commission on Worship to examine the *Liturgy of the Reformed Church of America* in light of this paper and to recommend appropriate changes.

The Commissioning of Preaching Elders

In 1994 the Classis of Mid-Hudson overtured the General Synod to appoint a committee to study the feasibility of setting up a process to certify qualified laity for ministry as preachers and pastors. Although that synod referred the overture to the Commission on Church Order, the General Synod of 1995 referred it to the Task Force on Standards for the Preparation for the Professional Ministry in the Reformed Church in America; and further, to the Commission on Theology for study and report to the 1996 General Synod. In response, the commission brought to that synod the paper, "The Commissioning of Preaching Elders."

The substance of the paper has a three-fold focus. First, it rehearses the variety of issues that have kept the concern of the overture before the church since at least 1984. Second, the paper argues for the use of the terminology reflected in its title. The term "preaching elder" is deemed more appropriate within the Reformed tradition than the term "lay preacher" because, for example, the elder already bears special responsibility, along with the minister of Word and sacrament, for evangelization, catechesis, discipline, and the proper interpretation of Scripture. The term "commissioning" is preferable to either "licensure" or "certification" because the latter pair is currently used with respect to the Office of Minister of Word and Sacrament. Thus, "commissioning" not only avoids confusing the distinction between preaching elders and ministers of Word and sacrament, but also emphasizes that the authorization of elders to preach is for a particular time and place. Third, from a theological perspective, the paper addresses the question of the relationship of elder to minister of Word and sacrament in more detail than has been done in the past, and seeks to clarify the church's understanding of ordination and its relationship to lay ministers. The paper concludes with nine suggestions for the implementation of any policy for the commissioning of preaching elders.

The General Synod voted to distribute the paper for study, comment, and response to the commission by January 31, 1997; to direct the commission, in consultation with the Commission on Church Order and the Task Force on Standards for the Preparation for the Professional Ministry in the Reformed Church in America, to determine from congregational responses if it is appropriate to propose revisions in the

Book of Church Order which would incorporate the principles of the paper; and to instruct the commission to report to the 1997 General Synod its findings from congregational responses, any revisions of its paper, as well as any proposed revisions of the *Book of Church Order.*

Moral Standards for Holders of Church Offices

This paper was presented to the General Synod of 1998, which directed that it be distributed to the church for study and comment to the Commission on Theology by April 1, 1999; and that the commission present a final report with recommendations to the 1999 General Synod. However, to allow more time for responses, the commission decided to delay a final recommendation until the General Synod of 2000. After reviewing all responses received during the additional time period, the commission concluded that the points raised were not sufficiently persuasive to warrant a rewriting of the paper. Thus the commission sent the paper to the General Synod of 2000 for a vote on the recommendations it contains for changes in the *Book of Church Order.* This history explains why the text of the paper appears in the *Minutes of the General Synod* of both 1998 and 2000.

The paper itself welcomes the opportunity to reaffirm the concern with godly or holy living on the part of office holders, a concern present in the liturgy of 1968, 1908, and 1882, but lacking in the 1987 "Order for the Ordination and Installation of a Minister of the Word." In a time of moral relativism and confusion, the church's office holders need to have a clear standard to which they may aspire and by which their behavior can be measured. Scripture teaches that at the most basic and important level, this standard is Jesus Christ himself. Beyond that assertion, we must be clear on how that standard actually shapes the way we live. The commission focuses on money, sex, and power as three central areas of life where we need to describe the moral implications of our life in Christ. This trio, represented in the early church by poverty, chastity, and obedience, and in our day by generosity, chastity, and humility, offers a middle ground between asceticism and laxity. Therefore, the paper proposes the addition of one sentence to the solemn promises made by elders, deacons, licensed candidates, ministers, and professors of theology: "I promise to live a holy and exemplary life, guided by the Holy Scriptures as interpreted by the Standards of the Reformed Church in America, in generosity, chastity, and humility."

The General Synod of 2000 voted to adopt the commission's recommendations to revise the *Book of Church Order, Formularies of the Reformed Church in America*, to include this promise, and to recommend the revision to the classes for approval.

The Constitutional Inquiries

This brief paper responds to an overture the Classis of Illinois addressed to the General Synod of 1998. In it, the classis requested the synod to direct the Commission on Theology to study and prepare recommendations concerning the purpose, appropriateness, and wording of the constitutional inquiries.

The commission's response begins with a brief history of these inquiries that includes their origin in the Netherlands and their evolution in America. For more than 150 years there were seven inquiries whose essential content remained unchanged. An eighth inquiry was added in 1986, a ninth in 1989 (amended in 1991), and a tenth in 1995. The paper's second section explains that the purpose of the constitutional inquiries is to provide a means by which classes can provide pastoral oversight of their congregations and to provide guidelines for congregations in the developments and maintenance of their wellbeing, both spiritually and materially. The paper's concluding section chronicles the failed attempt to add to the first inquiry a subsection containing confessional language.

The Papers

1
The Role and Authority of Women in Ministry

Introduction

The roles which may be filled by women in the ministry of Jesus Christ are as unlimited as the scope of God's faithful activity in creating a new heaven and a new earth. But women's participation in these roles is limited by the church's understanding of the proper role of women in the context of God's creative activity. On the one hand, from the moment God first created until this moment, God commissions women and men, created in God's image, to be partners in service to one another, to all people, and to the whole creation. On the other hand, there are still questions for the church concerning the role and authority of women in ministry. These questions cannot be addressed apart from a broad discussion of the nature of the church's ministry and the authority by which all Christians, male and female, engage in ministry.

The Roles of Women

In the Beginning

The church's ministry is commissioned by Jesus Christ whose own work began in the creation of the world. In his earthly ministry Jesus enfleshed and encouraged the full potential of humankind as first set forth in creation. By God's design, Adam and Eve would know the fullness of God's image and likeness in them when, together, they claimed their mutual role as partners with God in the keeping of creation. God created, invited, and commanded Adam and Eve to be God's image on earth through their life in relationship, their tilling and planting, their fruitful and faithful caring for one another and their children, their delight in the birds of the air, their protection of the beasts of the fields, their careful use of the flowing waters, and their obedient consumption of the abundant fruits of God's earth. Human beings, male and female, were created by God for a life of service in "unity, solidarity, mutuality, and equality."[1]

But they thought equality with God a thing to be grasped, and in grasping, lost sight of the equality and unity in which they were created to serve. In their isolation from God and one another, their differences as male and female were no longer perceived to be complementary, together reflecting the richness of the One who made them. Instead, they became opposites whose cooperative service for God in the world would be undermined by their opposition and separation.

As the author of creation, God authorized human beings, created in God's image, to exercise a derived authority in the universe which is God's domain. The authority which Adam and Eve received was an authority to serve in God's domain—they were given dominion over and for the sake of creation. But the practice of dominion as service in partnership was replaced by dominion as domination—male over female, this race over that race, rich over poor, humans over all beasts and birds and soil.

In order to understand the role and authority of women in ministry, one must first recall that God's intent for females and males is clearly expressed through their creation in God's image for partnership in service to creation. The loss of this partnership to destructive patterns of domination obscures God's will for women and men.

In Israel

God called the people of Israel and labored to shape them into a community built on love, mercy, and justice, reflecting God's image. Through them God continued the work begun in creation, commanding them to love God and serve their neighbors—the orphan, the widow, the stranger, and the alien. Women and men served God in Israel.

The women filled their primary roles in Israel as wives, concubines, mothers, and grandmothers. The wombs of the women held the promise of the nation. In bearing and caring for their children, they were faithful to the work of creation, and they patterned their lives on the life of the One who in the beginning labored to bring forth the world, and who later brought forth the nation of Israel and patiently taught it to walk.

[1]   Walter Brueggeman, "Of the Same Flesh and Bone," *Catholic Biblical Quarterly* 32 (1970), 532-42.

Women also served as the special agents of God's liberation (Exod. 1). The Hebrew midwives Shiphrah and Puah trusted God and refused to obey Pharaoh's orders. When instructed by Pharaoh to kill the male children, but to let the daughters live, these daughters of Israel preserved the lives of all the newborn. They risked their own lives in order to serve God's purpose in setting the Israelites free from their slavery in Egypt.

In the midwives' story begins the whole story of Exodus, the paradigm of God's liberating activity in the world. Pharaoh let the daughters of Israel live because he believed they were powerless, a non-threat to his own power. What Pharaoh did not realize is that in God's scheme, both women and men can be agents of liberation. So God called the midwives and empowered them to serve in new ways.

God empowered the widow of Zarephath to offer lodging and food to the prophet Elijah (1 Kings 17:7-16). Her ministry of hospitality came at a critical time for Elijah, and this poor widow placed herself and her child at risk by offering her only food to the prophet. Through her acts of service to Elijah, the widow of Zarephath advanced God's work in the world and was sustained by God because of her service.

Through their prophecies, Miriam (Exod. 15:20ff.) and Huldah (2 Kings 22:12ff.; 2 Chron. 34:20ff.) revealed the divine will. They were spokeswomen for God. Deborah was both a prophet and a judge in Israel, dispensing God's justice in the hill country of Ephraim. She also directed Barak in a battle against the Canaanites. All of these daughters of Israel were called by God to serve in surprising ways, in roles which were usually filled by men.

In their totality, these stories cannot and do not define the limit of the ways in which women can serve. Although there are only a few stories which recall the special roles which women played in the history of Israel, there are enough such stories to remind God's people that God is always doing a new thing in the world. If these stories were the only stories in the Bible about women who served God in special roles, one might conclude that they present exceptions to the rules about the proper roles of men and women, and therefore should not be considered normative. But taking clues from the creation story, these stories reaffirm that women and men are equally able to be partners with God in the never-ending work of creation and re-creation. They do not show exceptions to God's order and purpose in creation, rather, they illustrate God's true intent for the roles of women and men in the world.

If one takes seriously the roles of women and men articulated in the creation story, then exceptions to God's purpose will be found not in the stories of the women who are empowered to serve, but in the stories of the women who are powerless, and who become victims of violence and abuse. It is in the stories of Hagar, Dinah, Tamar, and Lot's and Jephthah's daughters that one finds abhorrent exceptions to God's creation design. These stories of men overpowering women through rape, broken covenants, and murder, blaspheme both the Creator and the human creature.

If one seeks to discern God's intent for the lives of women and men today, the creation story must be heard anew. One must also hear the stories of women's leadership and service in Israel as testimony to God's intent that women and men should be co-laborers with God in the work of creation. In these stories God's good purposes erupt, pointing people toward, and drawing people to, the place where God is restlessly moving and doing a new thing now.

In the Ministry of Jesus Christ

Jesus of Nazareth was doing a new thing in Israel. Born of a woman, Jesus was the perfect image and likeness of the almighty Creator whose divinity he shared. In Jesus, God's intent for the human race was reasserted and finally sealed. Jesus came to serve and to call women and men to God's service.

At a time when the participation of Jewish women in the religious life of the community was largely restricted to their domestic roles as wife and mother; at a time when few women were instructed in the Torah, and few were allowed to teach it; at a time when women were frequently cut off from temple service because they were ritually unclean; Jesus offered new roles for women.

Jesus did not require women to give up their domestic roles in order to embrace new roles. Rather, he presented an expanded view of family relations which created additional possibilities for the service and participation of women. Women, children, and men gathered around Jesus to constitute a different kind of family, biologically unrelated, but joined together by their decision to embrace the good news of the reign of God. It was a family joined by faith, learning, and service in which both women and men could freely, fully, and equally participate. It was a community whose kinship transcended and transformed all other types of kinship (Mark 3:31-35).

While calling together a new family, Jesus also called for changes in traditional family patterns. Under Deuteronomic law, a woman could not divorce her husband. However, there were laws in the first century which allowed a husband to divorce his wife if she was barren, or in the extreme, if she burned dinner. But, Jesus taught that a husband could divorce his wife only if she committed adultery (Matt. 19:3-9). His teaching was designed to protect a woman from the losses she might suffer because of her husband's whim or fleeting anger. Jesus preached against the very notion that wives could be tossed away by unsatisfied husbands.

Unconcerned about their status as ritually clean or unclean, Jesus taught, touched, and healed women. He welcomed them into lives of discipleship. Through his life and with his words, Jesus asserted that women could no longer be regarded as the objects of male sexual satisfaction—either in fact or fantasy. In forbidding men even to lust after a woman, Jesus bid women to come and stand with him as whole persons in the community of disciples. In offering new roles to women, Jesus positively transformed the traditional male role which he filled, thereby offering new roles to men as well. One can become so accustomed to the life and ministry of Jesus that one tends to lose sight of its revolutionary character. Jesus was not chastised for maintaining the status quo. He was killed for disturbing it.

For Jesus, the lives of men and women served equally well as examples of God's activity in the world. In order to communicate that both women and men are equally objects of God's salvific activity, Jesus told the good news using parables which both could understand. Jesus pictured God's love for humankind using the parables of the shepherd who searches the hillside for the lost sheep, and of the housewife who searches her house for a precious coin (Luke 15).

It was not always easy for women to embrace the new roles which Jesus held out to them. The story of Mary and Martha illustrates this fact beautifully (Luke 10:38-42). Martha complains that while she labors to prepare a meal for their guest, Mary sits at the feet of Jesus listening to his teachings. Martha plays the role of a proper Jewish women while Mary plays the role of a male disciple. Jesus declares that Mary has chosen the better part. Martha's appeals for support of the traditional role which she has chosen, do not prevail against the fact that women, like men, are called first to be hearers and doers of Jesus' words. The coming of God's reign demands it. But becoming Jesus' disciples did not require these women to abandon their traditional domestic roles. Instead, "it gave these roles new significance and importance, for now they could be used to serve the Master and the family of faith" of which they had become a part.[2]

When Jesus gratefully received the anointing of the woman whose gender and lifestyle made her action a scandal to many, Jesus transformed the meaning of priesthood and kingship forever. Jesus' anointing by this woman was an action-parable for professing that his own identity as priest would be most evident in the priestly sacrifice of his own self, and that his own identity as kingly ruler would be achieved not in the taking of power, but only in giving it up.

The women who followed Jesus day by day followed him all the way to the cross where the meaning of the parable played itself out. These women, who came in their traditional role to anoint his body in the tomb, were the very first to fill the role of those who bear witness to Christ's resurrection. In following Jesus these women discovered their calling to be his disciples. In bearing witness to Christ's resurrection, they discovered the purpose and fullness of their own freedom in discipleship, and they began to claim their responsibility as priests and rulers with Christ forever.

In the Early Church

By the teaching and example of Christ and by the preaching and power of Pentecost, the early church was firmly founded as a community of equals enjoying new freedom in Christ. On Pentecost, over the din of the rushing wind, the apostle Peter preached what Joel had prophesied long before him. Peter proclaimed that a new day—the last days—had dawned on the world. The Holy Spirit was poured out on God's people, without discrimination. Young and old, men and women, slave and free, Jew and Gentile, by the Spirit's power would prophesy, dream dreams, and see visions (Acts 2:16-18). God's Spirit came on Pentecost burning through

2   Ben Witherington, *Women in the Ministry of Jesus* (Cambridge: Cambridge University Press, 1980), 118.

barriers of age, sex, class, and race. Indeed, these last days would be radically new days for God's people on earth.

People were welcomed into the early church through this baptismal affirmation: As many of you as were baptized into Christ have clothed yourselves with Christ. There is no longer Jew or Greek, there is no longer slave or free, there is no longer male and female; for all of you are one in Christ Jesus (Gal. 3:27-28).[3]

Through its baptismal liturgy the church proclaimed that all who were joined to Christ enjoyed a new status altogether. They were freed from the curse of the law, sin, and death, and were joined together through Christ as a community of equals. This freedom and equality was not limited to spiritual status. It was not simply a matter of saying "now everyone can receive God's salvation"—this was true for women and slaves before Christ came. But after Christ's coming, all who are joined to the body of Christ are set free to live and serve and bear witness to the resurrection according to the gifts given them by the Holy Spirit.

Thus women in the early church enjoyed not only spiritual freedom, but also the freedom to claim new social and religious roles in keeping with their spiritual gifts. The writings of the New Testament bear witness to the activity of women in the early church. Paul commends the work of sister Phoebe, who was "a deacon of the church at Cenchreae" and "a benefactor of many and of myself as well" (Rom. 16:1). The Apostle refers to Prisca and her husband Aquila as co-workers "who risked their necks for my life" (Rom. 16:3). Also mentioned as diligent co-workers in Romans 16 are Mary (v.6), Tryphaena and Tryphosa (v.12), and "the beloved Persis" (v.12). The women in Corinth prayed and prophesied in the assemblies of the congregation. The female deacons mentioned in 1 Timothy held an official status in the church.[4]

In time, the church's enthusiasm for the freedom of the Christian life, and the egalitarian impulse which it nurtured, became something of a mixed blessing. Both the writings of Paul and the pastoral epistles contain instructions aimed at the restraint of Christian freedom in the lives of women. In all likelihood, these instructions were given out of concern for public opinion which was, in that time and place, "profoundly conservative

---

[3] All scripture references are from the New Revised Standard Version.
[4] Jane Dempsey Douglas, *Women, Freedom, and Calvin* (Philadelphia: Westminster Press, 1985), 62.

with regard to female equality."[5] Roman household codes articulated the proper roles of slaves, women, and children in relation to the master or father of the house. The experience of the church at Corinth suggests that external pressures to conform were joined by internal pressures to bring some order out of the chaos created by the shifting roles of women in the church. It seems that, at least potentially, the freedom enjoyed by Christian women placed the continuing life of the whole community in jeopardy. It was better for women to practice a bit of restraint in freedom than to risk losing every opportunity to proclaim the gospel.

The record of the early church bears witness to the culturally conditioned reality of the church's understanding and proclamation of the gospel. Each generation of believers must evaluate the ways in which its own understanding and proclamation of the gospel are conditioned by cultural realities past and present. Convinced of Christ's freedom for men and women, John Calvin placed Paul's instructions for the conduct of women in the church among those teachings which are historically and culturally conditioned—like questions concerning whether one should stand or kneel when praying in public. Calvin concluded that they were not important to the gospel and therefore could lay no claim to permanence in the practice of the church. Although it did not happen in his day, Calvin foresaw the day when it would be absolutely necessary for women to speak and lead in the church.[6]

One is not required to reach the same conclusions that the Pauline or Johannine or Genevan churches reached concerning the roles of women in the community of faith. One is required to hear at the very core of the gospel the proclamation that in Jesus Christ all people are made free and equal. Whenever the church concludes that it must restrict the practice of full Christian freedom for women, the church must ask who will benefit from such restrictions. If, for example, the restriction of some Christians is effected for the benefit of a few who are anxious about their own position in the church, then such restriction is a sin.

Jesus invites both women and men into full freedom as his disciples. For Jesus the question of who can teach or preach or heal is simply a question of who can be a faithful follower. Who can be a reliable witness

---

5 Joulette M. Bassler, "The Widow's Tale," *Journal of Biblical Literature* 103 (1984), 30.
6 John Calvin, *Institutes* (1536), 6.33. For further reading on this subject see: Douglas, op cit.

to the resurrection? Who can, by the power of the Holy Spirit, embody the servant ministry of Jesus Christ?

In the Reformed Church in America

This paper has identified in the story of creation, the life of Israel, the ministry of Jesus, and the experience of the early church, clear patterns for the roles and service of women in God's world. These patterns were repeated and even expanded throughout the history of the church. At times these patterns were restricted and at other times new roles for women in the church emerged. For example, during the middle ages celibate women served as spiritual guides to male priests. They engaged in works of charity and wrote some of the greatest spiritual treatises of the Christian tradition.[7]

Recognizing the richness of the lives of women throughout the church's long history, the commission regrets that it is not possible to detail women's religious history in this paper. However, in this section of the paper the focus is on the ministries of women in the Reformed Church in America, remembering the patterns of women's service set forth in creation, Israel, the ministry of Jesus, and the early church. Remember too that the ministries of women in the Reformed Church stand on the shoulders of many generations of faithful Christian women.

Throughout the years, women in the Reformed Church have offered a variety of gifts and filled many roles as they engaged in the church's ministry. Their many works can be called a ministry because they have been given for the edification of the whole body of Christ and for the glory of God.

Women have faithfully provided nursery care for the little ones. Women have nurtured the faith of children through their work in church school and vacation Bible school, as well as in their homes. Women have sewn thousands of costumes for angels and shepherds and warm-blooded beasts. For generations women have joined together in the middle of the week to pray and offer praise to God. Women have planted and plucked up gardens whose colors made the sanctuary sing on Easter morn. Women have sung and played instruments. Women have prepared

---

[7] See for example: Catherine of Siena, *The Dialogue* (New York: Paulist Press, 1980); Julian of Norwich, *Showings* (New York: Paulist Press, 1978); Teresa of Avila, *The Interior Castle* (New York: Paulist Press, 1979).

a million feasts, from soup suppers to the Lord's Supper. Carrying food and comfort, women have entered their neighbors' sickrooms; women have come to those who mourn; women have visited the lonely. There are times when men share in these many ministries, but they have been, for the most part, women's work in the church.

Women played a key role in the Reformed Church in America's early mission work. They organized the Women's Board of Domestic Missions to raise money for the support of missionaries at home and abroad. In 1895, the Women's Board accepted under its care a missionary to the American Indians. They gathered clothes and furniture for the missionaries and for those among whom they labored. In order to raise consciousness and support from the churches, women gathered the stories of people in China, India, and Arabia, and published them on the pages of the *Missionary Gleaner.*

Women themselves went out to be missionaries. Sometimes they went alone, such as pioneer missionaries Ida Scudder and Mary Kidder, with special training as doctors, nurses, and teachers. Many women, such as Harriet Scudder and Amy Zwemer, were pioneers with their husbands who were trained as doctors or ministers. Many of these women missionaries, whether they went alone or with their families, engaged in evangelistic work, taught and preached, and provided leadership in the church overseas.

In their ministry, one discovers a curious contradiction in the church's theology. These women were not allowed to teach and preach at home because they were to be submissive and were not allowed to have authority over men. Yet they were praised for their teaching and preaching to men (and women) overseas. Quite probably, a shortage of male missionary personnel made it necessary for women to assume leadership roles in the mission church which they were not permitted to assume at home. However, this practical reality does not change the fact that the church was, theologically speaking, sending a mixed message to its women missionaries whose ecclesiastical authority shifted depending on the male audience in question. Nevertheless, in their role as missionaries, and in spite of certain theological ambiguities attending the role, these women have always returned home to tell their stories, thereby providing important models for young girls in the Reformed Church.

In their roles as ministers' wives, women have made tremendous contributions to the life and ministry of the denomination. When the Commission on Women put out a request for stories of Reformed Church women which should be collected and published, a large number of the stories received were about minister's wives. Their contributions need to be recognized and celebrated. For generations women have ministered full-time with their spouses—visiting the sick, coordinating the religious education programs, directing the choir, leading the women's groups, and playing piano or organ for church functions, among other things. To this day, some still fill this role, although one recognizes that the church can no longer assume that the spouse of the minister will also commit herself or himself to full-time ministry in the church. By 1918 the Holy Spirit had led some in the Reformed Church to conclude that women should be welcomed into new roles in the church, and two overtures came to the General Synod requesting changes in the language of the *Book of Church Order* which would allow women to be ordained as elders and deacons. Fearing friction and factions in the church, the General Synod refused to entertain the request. The same request came to the General Synod in 1921, 1932, 1941, 1945, and 1951—each time from a single classis. But, in 1952, there were thirteen overtures concerning the ordination of women, six asking for a constitutional amendment to permit it, and seven opposing such change. At this time it was argued that,

> in recognition of the full share of the work of our Reformed Church in America which has been done by women, and in accord with the action of our country in civil matters, and with the teachings of democracy, justice, and equal opportunity by our Lord when on earth,

there should be no limit on the ways in which women could serve in the body of Christ.[8] The synod agreed to submit a request for amendment of the *Book of Church Order* to all classes for a vote. The classes voted against the proposed amendment. It was then decided that the Commission on Theology should prepare a report concerning the ordination of women as elders, deacons, and ministers of the Word.

---

8   RCA, "Reports of the Committee on the Ordination of Women to the General Synods of 1957 and 1958," 42.

In 1958 the General Synod approved the report of the Commission on Theology which recommended that General Synod make the following declarative statement: "Scripture nowhere excludes women from eligibility to the offices but always emphasizes their inclusion, prominence, and equal status with men in the Church of Jesus Christ."[9] In the same report, the commission recognized that,

> even in the Church of Jesus Christ, sociological and practical difficulties make themselves felt and may for a time restrain Christians from translating what is considered right on the basis of Scripture into new forms of communal action, fearful of accepting the clearly-indicated responsibility of moving forward in response to the Spirit's leading."[10]

The report also cautioned, "Tradition…which is important in the life of the Church, must not be the determining factor in deciding the issue."[11]

Since 1972, women in the Reformed Church have been entering new roles as ordained deacons and elders, and since 1978, as ministers of the Word and sacrament. Nevertheless sociological and practical difficulties, as well as tradition, still restrain the church on questions regarding the leadership of women in the church. The women who now serve in these roles recall their struggle to serve. Some tell of their confusion and sense of betrayal in a church which welcomed them into full membership through their baptism, nurtured them in the faith, blessed them when they made a public confession of their love for Jesus Christ, invited them to sit at the Lord's Table, encouraged in them the gifts of the Spirit, but then said "no" when these young women wished to dedicate themselves to certain forms of service and ministry in the church.

Through their ministry as deacons, elders, and ministers women are able to offer more of their gifts and experiences to the church. Very often women bring to their ministries, by their nature and nurture, a unique set of experiences and expectations.[12] Most little girls grow up playing games

---

9 Idem.
10 Ibid., 43.
11 Ibid., 75.
12 For further reading on this subject see for example: Carol Gilligan, *In a Different Voice* (Cambridge, Mass.: Harvard U., 1982); Mary F. Belenky, et al., *Women's Ways of Knowing* (New York: Basic Books, 1988); Mary Stewart Van Leeuwen, *Gender and Grace* (Downers Grove, IL: InterVarsity Press, 1990).

which are more cooperative than competitive. They learn that their own success depends on the success of the whole group, so it is in their best interest to care for the group as much as, if not more than, they care for themselves. As the primary caretakers of children and aging parents, women have attended to the physical, emotional, psychological, and spiritual growth of others. In many cases, women's socialization has allowed them to express their emotions, and to encourage such expression in others. Even women who have not chosen for themselves roles as nurturers and caretakers have inherited models from their mothers and grandmothers.

Furthermore, although they have not chosen it, many women carry with them an experience as victims of violence and abuse. Even Christian women raised in the church and/or married to Christian men share this experience.[13] The abuse of women takes many forms.[14] North Americans are quite aware that women are physically and sexually abused, both as children and adults. A less obvious form of abuse—emotional abuse— occurs when a woman or child is verbally degraded, threatened, denied basic feelings and abilities, or blamed for the suffering which is inflicted upon her by someone else. Environmental abuse isolates a woman from family and friends, and from the possibility of work, thereby forcing her into relational and economic dependencies on the very person who actively deprives her. Finally, social abuse is the form of abuse which reinforces all others. Social abuse occurs where "rigid life roles are imposed on men and women, limiting the expression of feelings to anger and depression, teaching that women are not as capable as men."[15]

The church must own its part in perpetuating social abuse through its teaching that women must submit and be subject to the authority of their fathers and husbands, and, by extension, to the authority of all men. Both implicitly and explicitly, the image of God the Father often serves in the church to explain and sanction male authority over females. In exchange for their submission to men, women are promised care and protection in their roles as wives and mothers. This cycle of submission to men in

---

[13] For further reading on this subject see, for example: James Alsdurf and Phyliss Alsdurf, *Battered into Submission: the Tragedy of Wife Abuse in the Christian Home* (Downers Grove, IL: InterVarsity Press, 1989); Marie H. Fortune, *Sexual Violence: the Unmentionable Sin* (New York: Pilgrim Press, 1983).

[14] "Domestic Violence," *MGS*, 1986:94ff., and "Child Sexual Abuse," *MGS*, 1987:50-58.

[15] *MGS*, 1986: 95.

exchange for protection by men makes women prime targets of male violence and abuse, and it is the same cycle which makes it difficult for women to assume positions of leadership in the church.

Having articulated the roles of women as nurturers, caretakers, and as victims of violence and abuse, it must be said that none of these experiences or ways of being are true for every woman, nor are they absolutely unique to women—men also share in them. Still, they are at present more typical for women than for men, and so they shape the ways in which women carry out the ministry which has been given them.

Finally, whether these experiences are claimed by women or men, in and of themselves none of them can be considered the Spirit's gifts for the church. They become gifts of the Spirit when through them the people of God are able to know, hear, see, feel, and believe the gospel of Jesus Christ more fully. The experience of caring for children or aged parents becomes a gift for the church when it shapes a holistic ministry of caring and teaching and discipling. The experience of abuse becomes a gift for the church when its telling breaks the cycle of submission, shame, and silence, and when it demands God's justice and mercy for men, women, and children.

Today there are nearly 1,800 women serving the Reformed Church in America as deacons, elders, and ministers of the Word and sacrament.[16] Their ministry with the whole people of God is changing the shape of the church. The church is gathering in the middle of the week, with the minister, to hear the text for Sunday's sermon and to give voice to their own hearing of it. The church is gathering on Sunday mornings around tables in the fellowship hall to share in the Word and Sacrament. Through their traditional roles and their new roles in ministry, women are offering fresh insights, urgent concerns, and new understandings of what it means to be Christ's servants in the church and in the world.

God's people know God's call and the Spirit's power in the lives of the women who minister to them through the womens' caring, discipling, teaching, preaching, healing, and sacramental service. So the church has never been able to conclude in the abstract whether this one or that one has been called to a certain form of ministry and service in the church. Rather, the church faithfully, honestly watches and listens in order to

16 Edwin Mulder, "Full Participation—A Long Time in Coming!," *Reformed Review* 42, No. 3 (Spring, 1989), 238-441.

affirm God's call to particular persons, regardless of their gender, race, or class. To watch and listen in any other way is to quench the Spirit.

The Authority of Women in Ministry

As the sole author of creation, God is the One who authorizes all human beings to become partners together with God. Created in the image of God, men and women are authorized to reflect in their living the character of the One who authored them. God's character shines forth in God's authorship of the universe. God builds up and makes new. God seeks goodness and delight, wholeness and harmony, equality and productivity. God welcomes and persuades partnership. God exercises dominion not through domination, but through faithful, loving care and service. God, the author of creation, opposes those who misunderstand and abuse the authority given to them as persons created in God's image. In the beginning God authorized women and men to exercise a creating, partnering, servant authority on earth.

The proper exercise of this servant authority is demonstrated most clearly in the life of Jesus Christ. Jesus Christ came to preach good news to the poor, to proclaim release to the captives and recovery of sight to the blind, and to let the oppressed go free (Luke 4:18). Jesus came to serve the least, the last, the littlest, and the lost. When Jesus' disciples engaged in a debate about who among them would be the greatest, Jesus contrasted Gentile authorities and standards of greatness with those expected among God's people: "Whoever wishes to become great among you must be your servant, and whoever wishes to be first among you must be slave of all. For the Son of Man came not to be served but to serve, and to give his life a ransom for many" (Mark 10:43-43).

The authority by which men and women today claim and fulfill their roles in ministry is given by the triune God who in the beginning authored creation, and who through the work of Jesus Christ has established a new creation. Men and women, created in the image of God, were first called to represent God as servants, and given the authority to be caretakers of creation and to develop the whole creation to its fullest potential. In Jesus Christ, beginning and end find their center and fullness. Through Jesus Christ the first creation is completed in the new creation which lives and pulses beyond every power which seeks to destroy it.

Now women and men and children are joined by baptism to Jesus Christ, who in serving them re-creates them and restores to them the authority to be God's servants in the world. The authority of all believers is recognized as the authority of Jesus Christ insofar as its exercise reflects and makes visible in the church and the world the servant authority of the One who by his death and resurrection has become the sovereign servant.

This authority belongs always and only to Jesus Christ, the only head of the church, who by the Holy Spirit channels that authority to the church, not as the possession of a few, but as a trust which empowers all who are members of the body of Christ. In early Christianity, diakonia, or service, was the term used to describe "all significant activity for the edification of the community" (Eph. 4:11 ff.).[17] The servant authority of Christ is reflected in and represented by the whole congregation. As Reformed Christians the Reformed Church in America confesses that all believers, by virtue of their baptism, share in Christ's anointing and have become prophets, priests, and kings with Christ (HCat, Q/A 32). All believers are called to confess Christ's name; to present themselves as living sacrifices of praise; to begin their reign with Christ, here and now, as they struggle against the powers which seek to destroy creation.

Within this ministry which belongs to the whole people of God, certain ministries are given by Christ to the church "so that the universal ministry of all believers may be enhanced and developed."[18] These unique ministries are located in the offices of elder, deacon, teacher, and minister. These offices do not contain the fullness of the church's ministry; rather, they distill and focus the church's whole ministry. The commision believes that these offices are instituted by Jesus Christ and are sustained in the church by the Spirit's power. At the same time, the commission acknowledges that the Spirit freely organizes and reorganizes the church's ministry in new ways according to the demands of time and place. Today the church in some parts of Latin America is organized into households similar to those of the very early church. These Christians are rediscovering what it means to hold their possessions in common and to be equal partners, men and women, in Christ's ministry.

---

17 Gerhard Kittel, ed., *Theological Dictionary of the New Testament* (Grand Rapids: Eerdmans, 1964), II, 84.
18 CRC, "Report 44, Ecclesiastical Office and Ordination," 693.

The same Spirit who organizes the church's ministry, and who freely calls people together as the body of Christ, also calls and authorizes men and women to engage in every form of ministry in the church. Those who are called and ordained to office in the church are not called to a more elevated position, or a higher status, or a greater authority, or a fuller representation of Jesus Christ than the believer who teaches the children about Sarah and Abraham. Those in office are called to be servants to all servants in the church. They are called to teach, preach, challenge, nurture, lead, prod, heal, and disciple in a way that enables every member of the body to reach their full potential as creatures created in God's image and to claim their calling as prophets, priests, and rulers with the sovereign servant Jesus Christ.

In sum, the authority of women and men in ministry is given to them by the triune God, who is the author of the first creation and the finisher of the new creation which exists within and beyond human history. Those called by God are called to exercise their authority in a way which builds up and makes new and seeks goodness and delight, wholeness and harmony, equality and productivity. As God welcomes and persuades men and women into partnership, so must those who represent God. As God opposes all partnerships which misunderstand or abuse the servant authority made manifest by Jesus Christ, so must women and men who share in Christ's ministry.

But as one contemporary theologian, Letty Russell, concludes, the true nature of Christ's servant authority is not always clear from the church's past.[19] In fact, it is often obscured by its exercise as domination, competition, and power over others in the church. Russell points out that among God's people, "consciously or unconsciously, reality is seen in the form of a hierarchy or pyramid."[20] Spinning out the image of God's kingdom, many have concluded that by divine order God is at the top, men are next, and women are below them. In the name of God's authority as King and Father, women have been placed in submission to men and have been excluded from certain roles in society and the church, and consigned to others. But "the gospel confronts the old image of kingdom as domination and exclusion and replaces it with a new image of kingdom as love and community."[21]

[19] Letty M. Russell, *Household of Freedom* (Philadelphia: Westminster Press, 1987).
[20] Ibid., 33.
[21] Ibid., 83.

Those who seek to understand God's authority must look not only to the past, but also to the future. From the future the authority of God's new creation is breaking into the present. And past traditions find themselves in tension with a future hope, not yet fully realized, but already seeping into the present like cool streams in the desert. Speaking from, and trusting God's future, the church might best describe God's kingdom of love as a household of freedom for all people. It is a household where hierarchies do not divide and oppress. It is a household in which God's hospitality—practiced in the life of the Trinity, revealed in creation and redemption—welcomes all people to full participation. The banquet table of the Lamb is already spread, and people are already coming from east, west, north, and south to share in the feast of God's household of freedom.

The church is a sign in the world of God's new creation—God's household of freedom. God keeps urging women and men, young and old, Jew and Gentile, to be free and equal partners in this household. Right now women and men are being called to new roles as they live out God's alternative future in the present. They are people of God's new creation: "So if anyone is in Christ, there is a new creation: everything old has passed away; see, everything has become new!" (2 Cor. 5:17).

As women and men of God's new creation, the Reformed Church in America has been given new ears for hearing. The Reformed Church can hear in the story of the first creation a call to live in God's image as equal partners caring for creation. In the stories of the widow of Zarephath, Miriam, and Deborah, the Reformed Church can hear God calling women to serve in the many ways which God intends. In the stories of Mary and Martha, Phoebe, and Prisca, the Reformed Church can hear the affirmation that among Jesus' disciples there is neither male nor female. All are one in Christ. In the stories of Reformed Church women who minister in church school classrooms, in serving at the Lord's Table, in preaching and teaching, God's Spirit can be heard calling women to new roles in this denomination. In all of these stories of women who followed God's call, one can see God's future breaking in, refreshing the view of the past, and transforming the Reformed Church's life in the present.

Among the many arguments offered against the opening of all offices to women in the Reformed Church was the argument that this inclusion of women "might tend to diminish men's sense of responsibility in the life and work of the church."[22] Some feared that if women assumed those roles in the church which traditionally belonged to men, then men would abdicate their responsibilities. The men would have no way to serve in the body of Christ.

In reality, there is no end to the work of ministry. In addition, as women are free to assume new roles, so also are men. Women can preach and men can disciple the children. Women can serve at the Lord's Table, and men can serve at the soup supper. Together, women and men can lead the people of God. Whoever has the gifts can assume the ministry. The commission acknowledges that there are social and practical realities which make such changes difficult for the church. Nevertheless, the commission believes that the Spirit is calling the church now to encourage full Christian freedom and leadership for both women and men.

By the authority of Jesus Christ who was at work in the world's creation, was crucified on the cross, and is the firstborn of the new creation, the whole church has been called to serve in the name of Christ. The Spirit equips every member with unique gifts and calls each to a particular service. The church confesses that "believers one and all share in Christ and in all his treasures and gifts," and that all "should consider it a duty to use these gifts readily and cheerfully for the service and enrichment of the other members" (HCat, Q/A 55). It is the church's duty to encourage the development and use of the Spirit's gifts in the lives of girls and boys, men and women.

Whatever one does in the name of Christ must reflect the servant authority of Christ. Whatever role one assumes in the name of Christ must be assumed with humility and for the sake of building up the body and renewing God's creation. Jesus said, "whoever wishes to be great among you must be your servant, and whoever wishes to be first among you must be slave of all" (Mark 10:42-43). The Reformed Church in America must confess that it has not always welcomed the servant leadership of women in the church. However, the Reformed Church can celebrate the inbreaking of God's new creation and the upbuilding of God's household of freedom in which women and men can fill every servant role authorized by Jesus Christ, who is our Servant and our Lord.

---

[22] RCA, "Reports of the Committee," 5-6.

Bibliography

Balch, David L. *Let Wives Be Submissive: the Domestic Code in 1 Peter*. Society of Biblical Literature Monograph Series; 26. Chico, CA.: Scholars Press, 1981.

Bassler, Jouette M. "The Widow's Tale: a Fresh Look at 1 Tim. 5:3-16." *Journal of Biblical Literature* 103 (1984), 23-41.

Brueggeman, Walter. "Of the Same Flesh and Bone." *Catholic Biblical Quarterly* 32 (1970), 532-42.

Calvin, John. *Institutes of the Christian Religion*. 1536 edition. Translated and annotated by Ford Lewis Battles. Atlanta: John Knox Press, 1975.

"Celebrating Women in Ministry in the Reformed Church in America". *Reformed Review* 42 (Spring 1989).

Christian Reformed Church in North America. *Agenda for Synod*, 1990. "Report 26, Committee To Study Headship," 309-330.

Christian Reformed Church in North America. *Agenda for Synod*, 1973. "Report 44, Ecclesiastical Office and Ordination," 635-716.

Douglas, Jane Dempsey. *Women, Freedom, and Calvin*. Philadelphia: Westminster Press, 1985.

Edwards, Ruth B. *The Case for Women's Ministry*. Biblical Foundations in Theology. London: SPCK, 1989.

Fiorenza, Elizabeth Schussler. *In Memory of Her: a Feminist Reconstruction of Christian Origins*. New York: Crossroad, 1986.

Hayter, Mary. *The New Eve in Christ: the Use and Abuse of the Bible in the Debate About Women in the Church*. Grand Rapids: Eerdmans, 1987.

Kittel, Gerhard, ed. *Theological Dictionary of the New Testament*, II. Grand Rapids: Eerdmans, 1964.

Micks, Marianne H. and Charles P. Price, eds. *Toward a New Theology of Ordination : Essays on the Ordination of Women*. Somerville, MA: Greeno, Hadden & Co., 1976.

Parvey, Constance F., ed. *The Community of Women and Men in the Church: the Sheffield Report.* Geneva : WCC, 1983.

Reformed Church in America. Commission on Women. "Domestic Violence." *MGS,* 1986:93-101.

Reformed Church in America. Commission on Christian Action. "Child Sexual Abuse and the Church." *MGS,* 1987:50-58.

Reformed Church in America. Theological Commission. "The Nature of Ecclesiastical Office and Ministry." *MGS,* 1980:98-109.

Reformed Church in America. Reports of the Committee on the Ordination of Women to the General Synods of 1957 and 1958. [A pamphlet published by the RCA for distribution to its churches, 1958.]

Russell, Letty M. *The Future of Partnership.* Philadelphia: Westminster Press, 1979.

———— *Growth in Partnership.* Philadelphia: Westminster Press, 1981.

———— *Household of Freedom: Authority in Feminist Theology.* Philadelphia: Westminster Press, 1987.

Tetlow, Elisabeth Meier. *Women and Ministry in the New Testament: Called to Serve.* Lanham, MD.: University Press of America, 1980.

Trible, Phyllis. *God and the Rhetoric of Sexuality.* (Overtures to Biblical Theology). Philadelphia: Fortress Press, 1978.

Witherington, Ben. *Women in the Ministry of Jesus: a Study of Jesus' Attitudes to Women and Their Roles as Reflected in His Earthly Life.* Cambridge: Cambridge University Press, 1984.

Van Leeuwen, Mary Stewart. *Gender and Grace: Love, Work & Parenting in a Changing World.* Downers Grove, IL: InterVarsity Press, 1990.

Yarbrough, O. Larry. *Not Like the Gentiles: Marriage Rules in the Letters of Paul.* (Society of Biblical Literature Dissertation Series; no. 80). Atlanta, GA: Scholars Press, 1985.

2

Concerning the Practice of the Laying on of Hands in the Ordination Services of the Reformed Church in America

Introduction

The Commission on Theology prepared this paper in response to an inquiry concerning whether or not elders should be allowed to participate in the laying on of hands in the ordination service of those called to the ministry of Word and sacrament. Although it was tempting to offer a simple "yes" or "no" answer, the commission believes that this inquiry raises fundamental theological concerns which deserve the consideration of the whole church. The inquiry provides an opportunity to explore the following: 1) the place and purpose of the service of ordination to office in the Reformed tradition; 2) the meaning of the laying on of hands in such services; 3) the relationship between the several offices of the Reformed Church in America (deacon, minister, elder); and 4) the relationship of these offices to the ministry of the whole people of God. Although the inquiry which prompted this paper concerned only the laying on of hands in the service of ordination for ministers of Word and sacrament, the commission presents recommendations which can be used to guide the church's practice of the laying on of hands in all ordination services.

1. In the Reformed tradition, the service of ordination is understood as part of a larger process.

To begin, it is helpful to gain perspective on the place and purpose of the service of ordination. In the Reformed tradition the service of ordination to any of the church's offices takes place at the end of a larger process. Without the larger process a service of ordination cannot take place. The process begins in God's initiative, that is, in God's call of and bestowal of spiritual gifts on persons to serve in the ordained offices of the church. God's call is made manifest and efficacious through the call of the whole people of God. This pattern is clear in the stories of the early church. When the work of the ministry became too much for the Twelve apostles to bear alone, they directed the whole community of disciples to select from among themselves seven who were of "good standing, full of the Spirit and of wisdom" who could share in the leadership of the church (Acts 6:1-6). The whole community identified those among them who were already full of the Spirit and the wisdom of God, those already set apart and equipped by God for the work of ministry.

In the Reformed Church it is the responsibility of the whole congregation prayerfully and thoughtfully to discern God's prior calling in their election of elders and deacons. Following their election, the names of elders and deacons are published over several weeks in order to ensure that the calling of the congregation truly reflects God's calling. At the end of this process, undertaken by the whole congregation, those elected for the first time are ordained to the offices of elder and/or deacon.

The Reformed understanding of call as a process which begins in God's initiative and is finally affirmed and effected through the service of ordination is undoubtedly made clearest in the case of those who are called to the office of minister of Word and sacrament. Persons who believe themselves to be called to this office must receive the affirmation of a local church through the consistory; be welcomed into the care of a classis; engage in supervised ministerial preparation; be tested through the public examination of gifts, learning, and overall fitness for ministry; be called by God's people to a particular ministry within the universal ministry of the church; and finally, be confirmed by the Holy Spirit through the church in the solemn and celebratory service of ordination.

The service of ordination to office in the Reformed Church is a public affirmation of God's work in calling and equipping a person to serve. The service completes the church's own critical task of discerning and calling those whom God has set apart to minister in the offices of the church. Through the service of ordination, those called are publicly authorized by the church to begin their labors as elders, ministers, and deacons with the commission of Jesus Christ, the blessing of God, the empowering of the Spirit, and the support of the church.

2. The service of ordination in the Reformed tradition has always been a public worship service characterized by a variety of practices, such as fasting and prayer, preaching, exhortation concerning the office, public questioning of the ordinand and the congregation, the offering of the right hand of fellowship, and/or the imposition of hands.

Again, as established above, the service of ordination to office is but one part of a larger process which begins in God's call and continues through the discernment, preparation, calling, and authorization of God's church. In the Reformed tradition the orders for ordination themselves included many parts. One can find remarkable consistency of practice in these early Reformed orders. Fasting and prayer, preaching, exhortation concerning the office, and public questioning of the one being ordained appear historically to be the consistent components of any Reformed service of ordination.

Through the practice of fasting and praying in advance of the actual service of ordination, the whole church—ministers, elders, deacons, as well as the entire laity—demonstrated the seriousness with which they engaged in the action of calling and setting apart an individual whom they believed to be called by God. Through their fasting and praying, they sought assurance that their actions truly reflected the will and call of God and not simply their own desires. Within the actual service, preaching, prayer, teaching concerning the office(s), and the public questioning of the candidate(s) for ordination served to edify, to instruct all present, and to confirm the intent of God to set the candidate(s) apart, the desire of the candidate(s) to be set apart, and the wisdom of the church in discerning and making visible God's own desires and purposes.

Concerning the necessity of the laying on of hands as part of the ordination service, the earliest orders for the ordination of ministers in the Reformed tradition illustrate that there was no apparent agreement on the matter. Some thought it was essential, while others thought it better to omit the practice so as not to introduce the kinds of superstition which they cited in the Roman Catholic sacrament of ordination.[1] Although John Calvin believed the practice was biblical and could even serve as a helpful outward sign of ordination, his own Genevan "Ordonnances" excluded the gesture in order to avoid promoting superstitions among the people.[2] In John Knox's Genevan *Form of Prayer*, there is "a procedure for the election and examination of ministers, elders, and deacons, but there is no ritual for their ordination or installation."[3] It appears that for Knox, "the election itself was regarded as the initiatory act."[4]

[1]   Ainslee, 159.
[2]   Ainslee, 159. Cf. Calvin, *Institutes*, 4:3:16.
[3]   Meeter, 401.
[4]   Idem., 401.

In one of the most fully developed sixteenth-century Reformed directories for the election and installation of pastors, the instruction is that "all the Elders put their hands on the head of the candidate, giving prayer to God that he will send his Holy Spirit that he may be able faithfully to serve in this ministry, to the glory of his name and the edification of his church."[5] In the case of the ordination of elders, following their interrogation, "the Pastor and all the Elders [laid] their hands on their heads" and the pastor invoked the Holy Spirit on them.[6] Similarly, in the case of deacons, the pastor and elders laid hands on those being ordained and invoked the Holy Spirit.[7] In another early Reformed order developed for Dutch refugees in London, the form for the ordination of ministers directs that following the main prayer and the Lord's Prayer, the presiding "Minister of the Word with the other Ministers" lay hands on the heads of the chosen, invoking on them "the Spirit's enlightenment, strength, and government."[8] It appears that in some Reformed orders for ordination, the offering of the right hand of fellowship by elders and ministers to the newly ordained minister served as a sign of consent and a worthy substitute for the laying on of hands.[9]

Where the laying on of hands was included in the service of ordination, there is evidence of diversity on the question of who could be included in this gesture. As was shown above, in some of the early Reformed orders the entire presbyterian eldership, elders and ministers together, participated in the laying on of hands in the ordination of ministers, elders, and deacons. Other orders directed that only ministers of the Word participate. Over time, some Reformed orders, which once allowed for the whole eldership to participate in the laying on of hands, began to restrict this gesture only to "preaching elders" or ministers, allowing the other elders to participate in the ordination service only through prayers and exhortations.[10]

---

5 Valerandus Pollanus, *Liturgia Sacra,* ed. A. C. Honders (Leiden: Brill, 1970), 224 (English translation for this paper by Daniel J. Meeter).
6 Ibid., 229.
7 Ibid., 231.
8 Meeter, 406. The author is delineating the practice presented in Micron's *Christlicke Ordinancian,* 1554.
9 Ainslee, 156.
10 Ainslee, 189.

It is not clear why the practice shifted over time, but it is regrettable. Calvin and other Reformers feared that the rite of the laying on of hands would introduce confusion and superstition among the people. They were anxious not to suggest that those laying on hands *themselves* transmitted the office and/or Spirit of God. They wanted instead to present ordination as an act of the whole church. That is why some, to avoid confusion, eliminated the ritual action from the service of ordination altogether. By restricting to ministers a ritual action which had once belonged to ministers and elders together, some early Reformed orders obscured the more broadly representative nature of ordination and may have thereby introduced the very superstitions they had hoped to avoid.[11]

3. The liturgy for the ordination of ministers of the Word and sacrament in the Reformed Church in America has always included the laying on of hands, although there have been changes concerning who should participate in this liturgical gesture.

Turning from this general survey of Reformed practice concerning the laying on of hands to the practice in the Reformed Church in America, the commission finds both constancy and change. This section examines the forms for the ordination of ministers of Word and sacrament. The section which follows focuses on the forms for the ordination of elders and deacons. There is not, nor has there ever been, in the Reformed Church's liturgy a form for the ordination of those elected to the office of professor of theology.

The 1767 "Form for Ordaining the Ministers of God's Word" prescribed that either the minister who questioned the ordinand, *or* another minister, if present, "shall lay his hands on his [the ordinand's] head" while praying for the enlightening of the Spirit, the strengthening of God's hand, and the governing of the ordinand's ministry. By 1814 the liturgy prescribed that the presiding minister, "*and* other ministers who are present shall lay their hands on his head," while the presiding minister says the prayer as above.

In his *Notes on the Constitution of the Reformed Church in America*, William Demarest explained concerning the laying on of hands that "ministers alone fulfill this duty for the classis in the procedure laid down by the

11 Ainslee, 190.

church, as especially qualified for it by their holding the office to which the candidate is now admitted."[12] In this explanation Demarest granted that ministers lay their hands on the ordinands on behalf of the whole classis, which always acts on behalf of the whole church, but restricts the action to ministers because they alone occupy the office.

The rubric authorizing only ministers to participate in the laying on of hands remained unchanged until 1952, when the liturgy included this proviso: "Since ordination to the Ministry is a prerogative of a Classis, ordinarily only ministers of the ordaining Classis will take part in the laying on of hands." It is not altogether clear what is meant by the use of the word "ordinarily." One might conclude that sometimes ministers from another classis or even another denomination might be invited to participate. Or, one might conclude that sometimes elders and ministers of the ordaining classis might be welcomed to share in this liturgical and pastoral action. Unfortunately, there are no documents available which might help one to understand the intent in this change of wording. Regardless of the original intent, one can conclude that this change in the rubric accompanying the laying on of hands opened the door to the possibility that other ministers and elders might be invited by the classis to join in this action and the prayer for the Spirit which accompanies it.

The next major change in practice was rubricated in the liturgy presented at the 1982 General Synod and approved the following year.[13] Following the interrogation of the candidate by the presiding officer of the classis, which could be either a minister or elder, the liturgy directs that "the presiding officer shall ask the members of the classis to come forward. Those the classis shall invite may join in the laying on of hands."[14] At the very least, this direction has elders and ministers standing around the kneeling candidate. But, it is hard to imagine why all these folks would be invited forward at this point in the service if not to participate in the laying on of hands, elders and ministers together. The added direction that "those the classis shall invite may join in the laying on of hands" appears to apply to persons who are not members of the classis. Although it is not absolutely clear, the 1983 liturgy appears to welcome

---

12 2nd ed. (New Brunswick, N.J.: Printed at Thatcher-Anderson Company, 1946), 41.
13 "Order for the Ordination and Installation of Ministers of the Word," *MGS*, 1982:146-51 and *MGS*, 1983:41.
14 *MGS*, 1982:148.

both ministers and elders of the classis to share in the laying on of hands, along with others that the classis may invite from the larger church.

However, when the 1983 liturgy was published in 1987 in *Worship the Lord*, the direction read: "the presiding officer shall ask the ministers of classis to come forward," presumably as above, to join in the laying on of hands, along with "those the classis shall invite."[15] What happened between 1983 and 1987 which resulted in this change to the liturgy? The commission does not know. In 1988 the Classis of South Grand Rapids and the Particular Synod of Michigan, assuming that the published change was simply an error, presented overtures in which they requested that the liturgy be corrected to read as approved by the 1983 General Synod (*MGS*, 1988: 221-22). They received assurances from the persons responsible for the printing of the church's liturgical resources that the error would be corrected. As of the fall of 1994, this error appears not to have been corrected in current editions of the *Liturgy and Confessions*.[16]

If it is assumed that the liturgy approved in 1983 has been subsequently printed with an error in the invitation to those who may lay on hands, and further, that the error will be corrected, one can say with some certainty that the intent of the 1983 liturgy for the ordination of ministers of Word and sacrament was to invite elders and ministers together to participate in the laying on of hands. This change in practice would align the Reformed Church in America with its Presbyterian brothers and sisters who share with the Reformed Church a presbyterian church order, but who more clearly hold together the offices of minister and elder by referring to the former as the "teaching elder" and the latter as the "ruling elder" and by including both in the laying on of hands when persons are ordained to either office. These offices together constitute the eldership of the church, and therefore there is every reason in the Reformed Church for these two types of elders—ministers and elders—to participate together in laying hands on those ordained to either office.

4. The liturgy for the ordination of elders and deacons in the Reformed Church in America has not always included the laying on of hands, but now does.

---

15 "The Ordination and Installation of a Minister of the Word," in *Worship the Lord* (Grand Rapids: Eerdmans, 1987), 52.
16 Letter to the RCA Commission on Theology from the Rev. Tom Stark, December 1994.

Although John Calvin pointed to the example of the New Testament church to argue that the laying on of hands is an appropriate and even helpful sign of ordination for those elected to the church's offices, and the most fully developed early orders for Reformed ordinations included the laying on of hands for those ordained as ministers, elders, and deacons, the Reformed Church's liturgies from 1767 to 1904 did not include the gesture. Where one might expect to find it, following the interrogation of those who have been elected, there is only this simple prayer: "The Almighty God replenish you all with his grace that you may faithfully and fruitfully discharge your respective offices. Amen" (*Liturgy*, 1767-1860). The prayer is followed by exhortations to the elders, deacons, and congregation.

The laying on of hands in the service for the ordination of elders and deacons first appeared in the 1904 edition of the liturgy. Here it was presented as an option which may be exercised by the presiding minister, but which was not considered "essential to full and proper ordination" (*Liturgy*, 1904). Accompanying the laying on of hands in the service for the ordination of ministers, there is a prayer for the Holy Spirit to enlighten, strengthen, and govern the ordinand. In the service for elders and deacons, the original prayer disappears, and in its place appears this directive and declaration: "Take thou authority to exercise the office of Elder (or Deacon) in the Reformed Church in America: in the Name of the Father, and of the Son, and of the Holy Ghost. Amen. In the Name of the Lord Jesus Christ, the Head of the Church, I now declare you to have been ordained and to be duly installed in your offices of Elders and Deacons, and I now commend you to the grace of God in the discharge of all your duties" (*Liturgy*, 1904). Then follows a benediction.

No changes were made to this liturgy until 1968. In the 1968 revision of the liturgy, the laying on of hands became a requirement which is fulfilled by the presiding minister. No longer is it stated that this gesture is not considered "essential to full and proper ordination." Also included in the 1968 service for the ordination of elders and deacons is the prayer for the Spirit which accompanies the laying on of hands in the service of ordination for ministers. However, in the case of elders and deacons, the prayer does not accompany the laying on of hands. Instead, the prayer is offered just prior to the "ordination and installation" section of the service, which includes the laying on of hands along with the directive given in previous liturgies. In 1983 the service for the ordination of elders and deacons brought together the laying on of hands, the prayer for the Spirit, and the declaration of ordination. These same elements are found in the service for the ordination of ministers, although in slightly different order. Since 1983 this service of ordination indicates that those persons who have been ordained to the same office should be invited to lay their hands on those being ordained.

The commission's survey of the actual practice of the laying on of hands in the Reformed Church in America's liturgies for ordination demonstrates that there has been confusion in the Reformed Church's history concerning this gesture. Why has it always been practiced in the ordination of ministers, but only since 1904 in the ordination of elders and deacons, although there is biblical and historical support to do it in all cases? Why is it that ministers are invited to lay hands on those being ordained to any office, while the current published liturgies only allow elders and deacons to lay hands on those being ordained to the same office?

5. The laying on of hands in the New Testament and the Reformed tradition properly signifies a kind of apostolic succession in the church's ministry.

In part, the questions raised above are connected to one's understanding of what is actually being done when hands are laid on those being ordained. It is little surprise that the Reformed Church in America's own practice has been somewhat confused. The question of precisely what is signified by the laying on of hands has long been debated in the church universal, and there remains today a great diversity of opinion on the matter.

The practice of the laying on hands in the early church found its roots in the practice of Israel. Among the Israelites, the gesture was most frequently found in the context of the presentation of animals for sacrificial offering. Those presenting large sacrifices placed a hand on the head of the animal in order to signify to the priest that this offering was being presented on their behalf. Similarly, in placing their hands on the Levites (Num. 8:10), the Israelites showed that these persons were "their 'offering' to God and that the benefits of the Levites' service [would] accrue to them."[17] Following God's instruction, Moses placed two hands on Joshua's head in order to set him apart as the new leader of Israel (Num. 27:23). The gesture served to make clear to the people that Joshua was the leader designated by God. In all of these instances, the laying on of hands demonstrates "who or what is the focus of the ritual action."[18] The action also makes clear the important bond between the one who lays on hands and the one who is thereby set apart.

In the New Testament the laying on of hands functions similarly, as a way of setting apart certain persons to specific tasks (Acts 6:6). Where the laying on of hands is done for the purpose of setting apart leaders for the church's ministry, it is done by the apostles and is accompanied by prayer (Acts 6:6). Some elders were set apart by the community's appointment, their prayers, and fasting, without the laying on of hands by anyone (e.g. Acts 14:23). In the case of Timothy, the laying on of hands which he received from the council of elders (1 Tim. 4:14) and the apostle Paul (2 Tim. 1:6) served to set him apart and to pass on to him a gift from God. This may be a reference to the gift of the Spirit or the gift of the continuing ministry of Jesus Christ.

The New Testament by itself does not provide one with a clearly articulated theology concerning the laying on of hands in relation to the designation of church leaders, nor a consistently articulated practice. The available examples are few and diverse. In order to arrive at his own understanding of the matter, Calvin relied on the witness of the Old and New Testaments together and concluded: "The apostles,...signified by the laying on of hands that they were offering to God him whom they were receiving into the ministry...In this way they consecrated the pastors and teachers, and the deacons."[19] In this simple and appealing explanation Calvin says nothing about the transmission of the Spirit or the office through the gesture, nor about the relationship between the laying on of hands and the notion of apostolic succession which was being debated all around him.

In the tradition of the Roman Catholic church, apostolic succession is understood as the succession of bishop to bishop, in an unbroken chain

---

[17] Robert F. O'Toole, "Hands, Laying on of," *Anchor Bible Dictionary* (New York: Doubleday, 1992), 3:47.
[18] Ibid.
[19] *Institutes*, 4.3.16.

which reaches all the way back to the first apostles. It is believed that the true teaching of the gospel of Jesus Christ is guaranteed by the long unbroken chain of properly ordained bishops who lay their hands on those being ordained to office in the church. This notion of apostolic succession created serious difficulty for the reformers. Practically speaking, it was difficult to insist that one was a part of the apostolic chain when in fact one had broken with the Roman Catholic church and had been ordained outside the chain of bishops which reached back to the apostles. So, rather than locate the guarantee of apostolic succession in the hands of bishops, the Reformers preferred to speak of apostolic succession in terms of faithfulness to the teachings of the apostles. They were interested in maintaining the unbroken succession of the true doctrine originally derived from the apostles. They were convinced that this doctrinal succession did not depend on the handing on of doctrine in a formal line, from predecessor to successor, beginning with the apostles through a line of bishops.

The reformers believed that the succession of apostolic doctrine was assured in two ways. From one perspective, they taught that those who preach and teach the true doctrine of Christ are the true successors of Christ, regardless of whether or not they are part of an unbroken chain formed by the laying on of hands and the transmission of apostolic authority. Doctrinal succession was carried on by "all those in the official ministry of the Church who, from the earliest times to the latest, had held forth the same Word of God, deriving it,...from Christ and the Apostles, from the most authentic sources available to them at any time, and of course, from the Scriptures in so far as they might be known."[20] Those who do not preach and teach the true doctrine of Christ are not in the succession, but their failure does not break the succession. This Reformed view of true doctrinal succession reflects a high view of the office of ordained ministry which is responsible for the "pure preaching of the gospel" and "the pure administration of the sacraments" (BConf, Art. 29).

But this perspective on the ordained ministry was bound to another, equally important. The Reformers also trusted that the succession of pure apostolic doctrine was vouchsafed in the very existence of the whole

[20] Ainslee, 219.

church. They confessed that the church which was created by Christ would always continue through "the succession of true Christians, generation after generation."[21] They believed "that the Son of God through his Spirit and Word, out of the entire human race, from the beginning of the world to its end, gathers, protects, and preserves for himself a community chosen for eternal life and united in true faith" (HCat, Q 54). The whole church, not just a part of it, could bear witness to the risen Christ through its life and doctrine, thereby claiming for itself continuity with the apostolic doctrine as the most authentic form of apostolic succession.

Within this dual perspective of Reformed tradition, one sees that the succession of apostolic doctrine in the church depends on the pure teaching and preaching of the gospel which cannot occur apart from the ordained ministry. Reformed theology teaches that the continuity of the true church is maintained, in large part, "through the gift of the ordained ministry."[22] But this continuity within the ordained ministry flows out of the succession of the church, the succession of true Christians from generation to generation. The succession of the church and its ministry from the apostles to the present does not depend on unbroken chains of individuals, nor on the power, perfection, infallibility, or faithfulness of the church. Rather, "the decisive point is always the faithfulness of Christ who remains with his church" and makes it faithful.[23] It is the continuous presence of the risen Christ through the Spirit within the ministry of the whole church, from the apostles until now, which guarantees the continuity of the church's ministry with the ministry of Christ. On the matter of apostolic succession, the commission concludes that in the gesture of the laying on of hands there is symbolized the continuity of apostolic teaching within the ministry of the whole church which is confessed in the lives of all God's people and dependent on the particular gifts of the church's ordained offices which flow from the ministry of the whole church.

6. The laying on of hands in the Reformed tradition also signifies God's blessing of and God's setting apart of the one being ordained.

[21] Ainslee, 223.
[22] Eugene P. Heideman, *Reformed Bishops and Catholic Elders* (Grand Rapids: Eerdmans, 1970), 36.
[23] Ibid., 198.

It is God who calls, nurtures, blesses, and ordains the church's ministry.[24] As partners in this work, God is pleased to use the church to make manifest what God has already done. In the service of ordination, the church prays for God's blessing and lays hands on those being ordained in an act of blessing. The laying on of hands finds its meaning in the prayer for God's grace and the Spirit's presence in the lives of those called to office. The ordination prayer and the laying on of hands together present an appeal for and an affirmation of God's blessing. In the service of ordination, the prayer for God's grace is an essential act of intercession on behalf of those called and ordained by God. Joined to this prayer, the laying on of hands makes visible the reality of God's call, blessing, and Spirit on those set apart to serve.

7. Who then shall participate in the laying on of hands in the various services of ordination in the Reformed Church in America?

Classes and the Service of Ordination for Ministers of Word and Sacrament

In the case of the ordination of ministers of Word and sacrament, all those who are members of the classis, both ministers and elder delegates, should be invited to join in the laying on of hands. The classis oversees the entire process of call, preparation, examination, election, and ordination for ministers. Elders and ministers of Word and sacrament together take responsibility for discerning and fulfilling God's will in relation to every person who presents him or herself as a candidate for ordination to ministry of Word and sacrament. Together elders and ministers receive ministerial candidates into the care of the classis, together they pray for and nurture candidates, together they guide and examine candidates, together they judge whether candidates are gifted and fit to assume their ministries within the Reformed Church in America, together they supervise the election of candidates to particular ministries, and together they approve and participate in the candidate's service of ordination.

This shared responsibility of elders and ministers at the classis level reflects and grows out of their shared responsibility for the preaching and teaching of the true gospel, for the pure administration of the sacraments, and for the proper practice of discipline on behalf of the whole church.

---

[24] Ibid., 192.

Without the elder, the minister cannot complete his or her calling. Without the minister, the elder cannot complete his or her calling. Given their mutual responsibility in the life of the church, within the local congregation and the classis, it is improper to exclude either ministers or elder delegates from any activity through which such responsibility is properly exercised and demonstrated. Therefore, both should lay hands on those being ordained to the office of minister of Word and sacrament.

Consistories and the Ordination of Elders and Deacons

In the case of the ordination service for elders and deacons, all who are members of the consistory of the church in which these officers are being ordained should be invited to participate in the laying on of hands.[25] The consistory is responsible to oversee the entire life of the congregation. Among its many duties, it is called to supervise the process of the election of elders and deacons to membership in the consistory. It is given both spiritual and administrative oversight in these matters and is expected to seek the wisdom and guidance of the Spirit, among its members and in the congregation as they elect new leaders. Given the consistory's responsibility to oversee the entire process of nurturing and electing elders and deacons, it is fitting that all members of the consistory participate in every part of this process which concludes in the service of ordination and includes the laying on of hands.

The Whole Church and the Ordination of all Officeholders

Further, the commission concludes that classes and consistories should be encouraged to invite other persons from the Reformed Church in America, nonordained and ordained, along with nonordained and ordained persons from other denominations, to participate with all the members

---

[25] The offices of minister of Word and sacrament and elder depend on the office of the deacon in order to carry our their own ministries within the whole ministry of Jesus Christ. The ministries of elder, deacon, and minister of Word and sacrament are united in Christ, and together these officers form the consistory which "continues the full ministry of Christ in our day." There is equality between the offices, and therefore, between the office-bearers. Together they participate in the one ministry of Jesus Christ and are subject to the authority of Christ, who is the only head of the church. Cf. "The Ordination and Installation of Elders and Deacons" in *Worship the Lord*, 23-26.

of the classis or consistory in the service of ordination, including the gesture of laying hands on those who have been called.

This conclusion grows out of two Reformed convictions. First, the laying on of hands in services of ordination is linked to prayer and God's blessing. The symbolic action does not signify the transmission of office. Second, ordination is an act of God and the whole church. This second point has been made at several previous points, but it bears elaboration. Although the service of ordination and the laying on of hands mark the entrance of those being ordained into the company of those who hold the same office in the church, the service ought not suggest some mysterious rite of initiation into a guild of office holders. Every service of ordination is a public service and celebration which bears witness to the fact that ordination is an act of the church universal—all Christians, both nonordained and ordained—in the church around the corner and on the other side of the world. Those who are ordained to the church's several offices exercise their ministry out of the call of the whole church and on its behalf. Officeholders serve as representatives of the whole people of God.

Representation and Participation in Services of Ordination

The Reformed Church in America has a representative form of government. This means that when consistories and classes act, they act not for themselves but as representatives of those who have elected them. These representative governing bodies make decisions and act on behalf of the whole. When elders, deacons, and ministers of Word and sacrament lay hands on a candidate for ordination, they do so representing the whole church. This is in keeping with the understanding of Reformed Church government and is in many ways appropriate. There are numerous occasions when the only possibility is to act in precise keeping with these principles of representation. However, there are ways in which Reformed Church practice in services of ordination has obscured this representative principle. This is most clearly the case at classis' ordination services. Very often the classis invites all ordained ministers who are present to come forward and join in with the ministers of classis in the laying on of hands. While these ministers participate as representatives of the larger church they serve, it might appear that they are allowed to participate in the laying on of hands because they hold the same office as the one being ordained.

It might be perceived that they are invited forward because they represent the office of minister of Word and sacrament, not because they represent the ministry of the whole people of God, nonordained and ordained together. This perception obscures the unbreakable link between the laying on of hands and the prayer for God's grace which is offered by the church.

Moreover, elders, deacons, and nonordained people often do not feel represented in services of ordination, although they may be present in large numbers. They feel particularly excluded during the laying on of hands. The commission has said in this paper that the laying on of hands is a symbolic act in which the church affirms what God has done and expresses faith in what God will do in the life of the one being ordained. It does this through the prayer which is lifted up with the laying on of hands. Here God blesses and promises blessing through the prayers of God's people. God acts through human actions. God touches through human hands. Here the careful process of call and ordination comes to completion. Since ordination is an act of the whole church, and since the laying on of hands finds its only meaning in the act of prayer which accompanies it, broad participation in the service of ordination, whenever possible and appropriate, can helpfully remind the gathered church of these realities.

It is important that any service of ordination be marked by dignity and proper decorum. Since classes and consistories are responsible for services of ordination, they are the ones who have responsibility to invite others to participate. In addition to the participation of their own membership, classes and consistories may wish to invite specific individuals to participate in the entire service of ordination as representatives of all the church's offices, the laity, and other denominations.

When classes and consistories invite other baptized Christians, nonordained and ordained together, to lay their hands on the heads of those being ordained and to pray for them, the invitation signals three important realities. First, those who hold office in the church and serve on consistories and in classes have unique responsibilities for the church's ordained ministry, and they serve as representatives of the whole church. Second, it makes clear that the one being ordained will be effective in ministry only by the grace and blessing of God and the prayerful support of God's people. Third, it is a vivid reminder that the whole church is responsible in various ways for the recognition and nurturing of the gifts of those who are elected by God to engage in the servant ministry of the church through the offices of deacon, elder, and minister of Word and sacrament. This responsibility precedes the service of ordination and continues after the service is complete. It is by the Spirit's presence and power that the shared ministry of all believers becomes the ministry of the risen Christ for the sake of the world.

8. If a broad representation of people shares in the service of ordination, it is good for the members of the classis or consistory to extend the right hand of fellowship to the new office holder.

In some early Reformed church orders, the gesture of extending the right hand of fellowship served as a worthy substitute for the laying on of hands. In both classes and consistories, the action signals a theology of shared ministry and unique responsibility for the one ministry of Jesus Christ who is the only head of the church. This is entirely in keeping with its biblical usage in Galatians 2:9. The action also implies consent on all sides to support one another in order to further the ministry of the whole church. Along the way, this support may be expressed through such things as intercessory prayers, the sharing of concerns and wisdom, and cooperation in particular programs. Particularly where the right hand of fellowship serves as a welcome into the membership of classis, it also signals the minister's consent to submit to the authority of the classis and to share in its particular responsibilities, including the care and discipline of its ministers.

If the liturgical gesture of offering the right hand of fellowship is practiced along with broadly representative participation in the laying on of hands accompanied by prayer, the liturgies for ordination in the Reformed Church in America might more clearly demonstrate that ordination does mark the office bearers' entrance into a ministerial collegium and into the governing structures of the church. Offering the right hand of fellowship also demonstrates that the whole process of ordination is the work of the whole people of God in confirmation of God's prior gracious action and in trust of more grace for ministry through the abiding presence of the Holy Spirit in the church.

Bibliography

Ainslee, James L. *The Doctrines of Ministerial Order in the Reformed Churches of the 16th and 17th Centuries.* Edinburgh: T. & T. Clark, 1940.

Calvin, John. *Institutes of the Christian Religion.* 2 vols. Edited by John T. McNeill, translated by Ford Lewis Battles. Library of Christian Classics, vol. 20. Philadelphia: Westminster Press, 1960.

Demarest, William. *Notes on the Constitution of the Reformed Church in America.* 2d ed. New Brunswick, New Jersey: printed at Thatcher-Anderson Company, 1946.

Esther, James, and Bruggink, Donald J., *Worship the Lord.* Grand Rapids, Michigan: Eerdmans, 1987.

Heideman, Eugene P. *Reformed Bishops and Catholic Elders.* Grand Rapids, Michigan: Eerdmans, 1970.

Pollanus, Valerandus. *Valerandus Pollanus: Liturgia Sacra (1551-1555).* Edited with an introduction by H. C. Honders. Kerkhistorische Bijdragen, no. 1. Leiden: E. J. Brill, 1970.

Küng, Hans, ed. *Apostolic Succession: Rethinking a Barrier to Unity.* Concilium, vol. 34. New York: Paulist Press, 1968.

Meeter, Daniel J. "The 'North American Liturgy': A Critical Edition of the Liturgy of the Reformed Dutch Church in North America, 1793." Ph. D. diss., Drew University, 1989.

Reformed Church in America. Commission on Theology. "The Nature of Ecclesiastical Office and Ministry," *MGS*, 1980: 98-108.

3

The Commissioning of Preaching Elders

The Context of the Question

The Commission on Theology received from the 1995 General Synod a request to study the question of the licensure or certification of lay preachers (*MGS*, 1995:218). This question arose by way of an overture from the Classis of Mid-Hudson presented to the 1994 General Synod (*MGS*, 1994:248-49).

This question has now been explored for some time in the Reformed Church. In 1984 a Committee on Plurality and Flexibility of the Ministry issued a report to the General Synod which, among other things, called for changes in the *Book of Church Order* to create a position of a licensed elder, authorized to preach and administer the sacraments. The recommendation was not adopted by the 1984 synod (*MGS*, 1984:174-82). In 1988 a Committee on Ecclesiastical Office and Ministry issued a report that affirmed the importance of lay ministry in general, and while it made no recommendations regarding lay preachers, it did say that "the RCA may also want to consider opening the ordained ministry of the Word to gifted elders who have proven their effectiveness in the area of pastoral leadership for an appropriate period of time" (*MGS*, 1988:135).

A number of general observations were arrived at as the commission discussed this referral from the 1995 Synod and heard reports about areas of the church's life where this issue has arisen. It is clear that some congregations, classes, and regional synods have already begun various strategies for using nonordained people in preaching ministries and also for training and recognizing them in a variety of ways, even though there are currently no provisions for such practices within the *Book of Church Order*. This seemed a genuine cause for concern to the commission and underscored the need to address the situation both theologically and in terms of church polity as quickly as possible.

The commission also noted the complex and diverse ways in which the question of lay preachers has arisen within the life of the church. Because the question has arisen in a number of very different contexts, there are a variety of issues which must be addressed in a comprehensive way if the problem is to be addressed adequately on a denominational level.

One of the issues is financial. Many small-membership congregations may find it difficult to afford a full-time ordained minister of Word and sacrament but may find that there are lay people with gifts of preaching in their midst. Such congregations may believe that the presence of such gifted persons offers not only an opportunity for ministry, but also a way out of a difficult economic constraint. From the perspective of one licensed to such a ministry, the possibility of such licensure raises additional questions. Would such a person be classified as a minister for federal and state tax purposes, with the accompanying economic benefits and/or burdens such classification would bring? Would such a move evoke legal challenges from federal, regional, or local governing authorities?

In other congregations the issue is empowerment of the laity. Some churches seek to use lay preachers, not as a substitute for the preaching ministry of an installed pastor, but as a supplement to that ministry and as a sign of the priesthood of all believers and the giftedness of all God's people.

Another issue may have to do with difficulties some candidates for ministry experience in obtaining formal theological education. Lay people with gifts for preaching and church leadership may feel called to exercise those gifts but may find it difficult or impossible to pursue theological education to fulfill ordination requirements. Such persons may find the option of a certified or licensed lay preaching ministry an attractive one. This may be particularly true among immigrant congregations where access to theological education in one's own language is difficult.

The relationship between "licensed lay preachers/preaching elders" and other avenues into ministry which are currently provided for in the *Book of Church Order* is an issue in some Reformed Church in America judicatories. For example, the *Book of Church Order* currently allows for a person without formal theological education to seek a dispensation and be ordained as a minister of Word and sacrament (chapter 1, part II, Art. 10, Sec. 2). The request for a different kind of licensure or other authorization apparently arises, however, out of a desire to authorize a ministry of preaching which is not as broad as that of the minister of Word and sacrament, and which does not involve the need to pursue a dispensation from the requirements of the Certificate of Fitness for Ministry.

A final issue has to do with the integrity and high standards which the Reformed Church seeks to maintain for the Office of Minister of Word and Sacrament. Concerns have been raised regarding the long-range impact upon that office as a result of the addition of a second preaching office or role with less stringent requirements.

Lay Preacher or Preaching Elders?

Recently in the life of the Reformed Church in America, two different approaches have been proposed for an authorized preaching ministry exercised by those not ordained to the Office of Minister of Word and Sacrament. Some have requested the Reformed Church to establish a process for licensing or certifying "lay preachers." Others have requested a process for certifying or licensing "preaching elders." The commission believes that the choice of terms is significant and must be clarified before further action is taken. In what follows, this report will argue that the term "lay preacher" is inappropriate within the Reformed tradition and that any action taken in this area would be more helpfully taken under the category of "preaching elder."

Preaching as the proclamation of the gospel and as a witness to God's action in the world is a function of the whole Christian community. Preaching in this broad sense arises from the experience of divine power and life, to which the believer is constrained by God to bear witness. In this broad context, it is inappropriate and theologically dubious to speak of any kind of "licensure," "authorization," or "certification" to announce the gospel. This would restrict the freedom and obligation of all Christians to proclaim the good news by word and deed. Ultimately, the authorization to witness to the gospel is granted by the Holy Spirit, who moves men and women to bear witness to the reality of God's reign in their lives and in their world.

The Office of Minister of Word and Sacrament is intended to guide and direct the whole church in its proclamation of the gospel in word and deed. The minister of Word and sacrament does not preach as a substitute for the congregation's proclamation. Rather, the preaching office exercised by the minister of Word and sacrament empowers the congregation to witness to the presence and power of God. The ordained preaching ministry has this particular focus and responsibility as one part of the broader mandate given to all Christians to bear witness to God's power and presence disclosed in the gospel. The preaching office is thus a particular means of grace by which God's salvation extends to the church, and through the church to the world.

Why then are not all Christians "ordained"? In a limited sense, all Christians are, since they are set apart from the world and charged by God with the task of offering themselves to God as spiritual sacrifices. But ordination also commonly refers to something more specific. The church recognizes certain gifts and sets certain people apart for specific ministries through the laying on of hands and prayer. (For further discussion, see the report on the laying on of hands in the *MGS*, 1995:369-81.) The church has found it expedient to single out certain gifts and ministries for special treatment—those which pertain to the overall health, welfare, and functioning of the church itself. These gifts and ministries require the acknowledgment and consent of the church in order to be exercised effectively. The church formally and publicly acknowledges these gifts and ministries, not because they are more important, but because such acknowledgment and consent by the church is essential if these ministries are to be exercised effectively by those who hold them.

The question of the certification of lay preachers or preaching elders needs to be viewed in the context of this understanding of the place of ordination. All Christians are witnesses, since the announcement of God's reign is the work of the *laos*, the people. Yet this does not obviate the need for the Office of Minister of Word and Sacrament, which is devoted to guiding and equipping the church for this central task. Yet if one speaks of the certification or licensure of "lay" preachers, there is a danger of losing this crucial distinction, since the people of God, the laity, need no additional "certification" or "licensure" to carry out their basic task of announcing the reign of God. Such language is unhelpful and should be avoided.

The language of "lay preachers" is unhelpful not only because it weakens the involvement of all God's people in witnessing to the gospel, but also because it confuses the distinction in role between the ordained and nonordained. In 1988 the Committee on Ecclesiastical Office and Ministry urged that the word "lay" be used consistently to refer to the *nonordained* ministries of the church, meaning those ministries which are not directly involved with the oversight and guidance of the church in its mission in the world (*MGS,* 1988:131). The laity is called to witness to the gospel in encounter with the world; it is not called to the oversight and guidance of the church in that mission. That is the responsibility of the ordained offices.

However, the Office of Minister of Word and Sacrament is not alone in its responsibility to guide and direct the whole church in its proclamation of the gospel. The elder also bears special responsibility, along with the minister of Word and sacrament, for evangelization, catechesis, discipline, and the proper interpretation of Scripture. Hence it may be more helpful, in achieving the intent of language about "certification of lay preachers," to speak of a process whereby elders might receive some form of authorization to preach in a local congregation.

But why, in the first place, should the Reformed Church in America consider a second preaching role at all? Why should elders be authorized to preach at all? Is not the Office of Minister of Word and Sacrament sufficient to guide and direct the church in its mission in the world? In 1984 the General Synod rejected a proposal for licensed preaching elders, arguing that such a move would remove the need for a congregation to call a minister of Word and sacrament, that it would bypass normal supervision of theological education, that it would weaken opportunities for alternatives such as yoked congregations, that it would weaken the Reformed concept of an educated clergy, and that it would make the (then) present oversupply of ministers even worse (*MGS,* 1984:181-82).

The Reformed Church must continue to discern whether these reasons are of sufficient weight to prevent it from proceeding with the creation of a second preaching role. This paper will not offer all the answers to these issues, but is intended to guide the denomination in its consideration of them. While this paper will address some of these practical concerns, it will also address the theological issues at stake in the question. From a theological perspective, the subject provides an opportunity to address the question of the relationship of elder to minister of Word and sacrament in more detail than has been done in the past, and further to clarify the church's understanding of ordination and its relationship to lay ministries.

From a practical perspective, although there may be an oversupply of ordained ministers in some parts of the Reformed Church in America, this is not at all universally the case now, particularly in some rural areas and among racial/ethnic congregations. Several sectors of the denomination have spoken out with some urgency about the need for strategies which will effectively deal both with a shortage of ordained ministers and with the need for classes to oversee effectively the preaching of the Word in their bounds. The present wording of the *Book of Church Order* grants extraordinary freedom to local consistories to invite unordained people to preach "in occasional or special circumstances" (chap. 1, part I, art. 2, sec. 6e). The frequent appeal to "special circumstances" in the use of nonordained preachers leaves classes needing more guidance from the church in overseeing such situations. The commission felt that these concerns were of sufficient weight to deem the question of authorized preaching elders worthy of fuller exploration.

Some Basic Assumptions Regarding Preaching Elders

The idea of a "preaching elder" requires some clarification regarding the nature of such a function and its relationship to the offices, life, and polity of the church. This understanding varies, even within the Reformed family of churches. Some Presbyterians, for example, speak of ministers as "teaching elders" and elders as "ruling elders." This distinction has not played a significant role in the polity of the Reformed Church in America, however, and it does not seem to be helpful in addressing the issue now faced. In what follows, this report attempts to clarify how such a function should be interpreted within the context of the offices, life, and polity of the Reformed Church.

Elders authorized to preach should continue to be elders, and the distinction between ministers and elders should be maintained. Yet this distinction has not always been articulated with theological precision in the Reformed Church's history. In general, however, Reformed theology understands that a crucial role of the elder is to participate in the *oversight* of the preaching of the Word, whereas the minister's role is the actual *preaching* of the Word itself. In traditional Dutch Reformed practice, these roles were often expressed by a handshake extended to the minister by the senior elder after the sermon, indicating the judgment of the elders that the sermon was in accordance with the Word of God. While this practice has now fallen into disuse, its theological underpinning persists in the use, for example, of the constitutional questions which must be answered by the elders and ministers (*BCO*, chap. 1, part II, art. 7 sec. 1). In this way, discernment and proclamation complement each other in the governance of the church by the Word of God.

If elders were to preach, it must be recognized that this distinction of role would become somewhat blurred. The commission does not believe that such blurring distorts the function of the offices unduly if other safeguards are in place. Nevertheless, preaching elders must realize that when they enter the pulpit they relinquish their supervisory and discerning role and become subject to the discernment and supervision of their preaching by the board of elders.

There are other important distinctions between ministers of Word and sacrament and elders as well. In one of the few General Synod reports where this distinction is addressed, the 1980 study on the nature of ecclesiastical office and ministry states that the elder stands beside the minister in connection with both sermon and sacrament, but is distinguished from the minister of Word and sacrament by virtue of the elder's continued involvement in the world. The elder does not forsake a worldly calling to engage in ministry but represents the "sanctification of the world," the leavening of Christian faith in all of life (*MGS*, 1980:104). While this distinction should not be interpreted to preclude a "tent-making" approach to the Office of Minister of Word and Sacrament, it does suggest that preaching elders should not be entirely dependent on the church for their livelihood but should maintain a vocation in the world, though they should be able to receive a stipend for their preaching ministry. Congregations should not view preaching elders as an inexpensive way to obtain a preacher. A full-time preaching ministry should continue to be exercised only by ordained ministers of Word and sacrament.

Another important distinction between the Office of Minister of Word and Sacrament and that of elder has to do with the scope of the office. Through the granting of the Certificate of Fitness for Ministry, ministers are certified for their calling, not merely by a local congregation or classis, but by the General Synod, acting through one of the Reformed Church in America seminaries or the Theological Education Agency as its agent. The ordination of an elder takes place in a local congregation; the ordination of a minister of Word and sacrament takes place in the classis and is preceded by a denominational certification.

Because of this difference, ministers of Word and sacrament are empowered to represent the whole church and to serve the whole church in a way that elders are not. The state recognizes their authority to solemnize marriages and their distinctive social role in its tax code. The state does not recognize elders in these ways, nor has the church ever sought such recognition for elders. Moreover, although ministers are often invited to preach or celebrate the sacraments in congregations where they are not the installed pastor, elders are rarely if ever asked to exercise their functions in other congregations. Rather, the elder has always been centrally concerned with a particular local congregation and its life, though the elder also represents that congregation in the assemblies and judicatories of the Reformed Church. To put it a bit differently, the difference in the process of ordination means that the authority of the elder is bound more closely to a local congregation than the authority of a minister of Word and sacrament. The commission believes that this distinction should be preserved if elders are to be authorized to preach. Elders should be authorized to preach *in a particular congregation* rather than in the Reformed Church as a whole or even in the classis as a whole. (In unusual cases such as yoked parishes, it might be appropriate for the classis to authorize a preaching elder to preach in more than one congregation.) The authorization of a preaching elder is distinguished in this way from the license to preach granted by a classis to a candidate for ministry, which does not carry the same restriction.

The congregational preaching done by elders ought to be carried out under the supervision of a classis in order that the Scriptures might continue to guide the local congregation with their full depth and richness. In some cases such supervision could be delegated by the classis to the installed minister of the congregation in which the elder is preaching.

Careful consideration should be given to a case where there might be an authorized preaching elder in a congregation with no installed minister. Since the celebration of the sacraments is already within the purview of elders, no particular authorization would be required here. However, any authorization of an elder to preach should not imply permission or authority to exercise any other pastoral functions beyond those normally exercised by elders.

Finally, since the authorization to preach does not inhere in the Office of Elder as it does in the Office of Minister of Word and Sacrament, an elder should be authorized to preach *for a particular period of time, in a particular place*. In other words, the authorizing of elders to preach should not be construed as another ordination or office which would continue to be valid until it is demitted. Rather, it is a commissioning and authorizing of an elder for a specific task, in a specific time and place.

"Licensure," "Certification," or "Commissioning"?

The Reformed Church in America has also heard different proposals regarding how such preaching elders should be authorized. While some proposals have spoken of "licensure," others have used the term "certification." The denomination has also begun to use the term "commissioning" to speak of a special commitment to a task which does not involve ordaining or installing into an office of the church. The Commission on Theology believes that "commissioning" is a better term than either "licensure" or "certification" for this authorization. Both licensure and certification are currently used with respect to the Office of Minister of Word and Sacrament. (A license to preach is given to candidates for ordination during their seminary training, and the Certificate of Fitness for Ministry qualifies ministerial candidates to take their final theological examinations for ordination.) The use of "commissioning" avoids confusing the distinction between preaching elders and ministers of Word and sacrament. Moreover, it emphasizes that the authorization of elders to preach is for a particular time and place.

Some Suggestions for Implementation

With the considerations above in mind, the commission suggests that the following guidelines might be a useful starting point for a denominational discussion regarding the commissioning of preaching elders. The commission suggests that the implementation of such a policy be guided by the following considerations:

1. The congregation must petition the classis to commission a preaching elder, and if the preaching elder is to serve where there is no installed minister, the congregation must demonstrate in its petition that its circumstances make the calling of an ordained minister of Word and sacrament impossible.

2. Ordinarily, the person seeking commissioning as a preaching elder must already be an ordained elder and a member of the great consistory of the congregation in which he or she will be preaching. If the elder is not already serving on the active consistory and is commissioned to a regular preaching ministry, he or she becomes a member of the consistory for the duration of the commission when commissioned by the classis.

3. Commissioned preaching elders must maintain their vocation in the world and must not be primarily dependent on the church for their financial support.

4. The classis must examine the candidate prior to commissioning as a preaching elder in order to determine whether the requisite gifts, knowledge, and skills are present. Such examination must be based on a program of study in the following areas: New Testament introduction and history, Old Testament introduction and history, biblical exegesis and interpretation, sermon composition and delivery, systematic theology, and Reformed Church in America's doctrinal standards. The particular form and content of this program of study must be approved by the classis. The classis may waive all or part of the program of study if the elder can demonstrate that such study or its equivalent has already been completed. In no case, however, shall the classis waive the examination.

5. Since the normal safeguards of education and certification are not present for elders in the same way they are for ordained ministers, the classis must supervise their preaching ministry more closely than that of ministers of Word and sacrament. Such supervision should be regular, careful, and thorough; in the case of congregations where there is no installed minister, this supervision should entail a minimum of one personal meeting with the preaching elder per month.

6. The commissioning must be reviewed and renewed on an annual basis, including an evaluation by the local consistory and the supervising classis. Commissioning is renewed only at the request of the local congregation. When the commissioned preaching elder has primary responsibility for preaching in a local congregation, commissioning is to be renewed only when the

calling of an ordained minister continues to be impossible. The classis may revoke or refuse to renew a commission for the preaching elder if the classis believes that the Word of God is not being rightly proclaimed.

7. Commissioning is only for preaching in specific places designated by the classis, under the supervision of the classis and the local consistory. It does not qualify the preaching elder to accept invitations to preach regularly in places not designated by the classis, nor to engage in any other form of ministry outside the normal functions of an elder.

8. Because the commissioning is within the context of the office of elder, the authority of which is located in the local congregation, commissioned preaching elders are not permitted to exercise ministerial functions which assume recognition by the larger society. That is, they may not act as ordained ministers in the solemnizing of marriages. Likewise they should not be classified as ministers for tax purposes. They may be voting delegates to classis only if they are regular elder delegates from a local congregation. They also may serve as nonvoting delegates to classis at the discretion of the classis. In their preaching ministry they are amenable to the classis through the commissioning and supervision process; in all other matters, they are subject to the discipline of their local consistory in the same way that all elders are.

9. The addition of the role of commissioned preaching elder requires a variety of modifications to the *Book of Church Order*. In addition to changes reflecting the policies above, the commission recommends that Chapter 1, Part I, Article 2, Section 6e of the *Book of Church Order* be amended to read (deletion in brackets): "However, a consistory may authorize, in occasional [or special] circumstances, other persons to preach." The new role of preaching elder would remove the need for consistories to appeal to "special circumstances" in order to justify asking a person who is not a minister of Word and sacrament to preach on a *regular* basis. The assumption would be that consistories should be free to allow nonordained persons to preach on an occasional basis, but that a regular preaching ministry should be carried out only by ordained ministers and commissioned preaching elders.

4
Moral Standards for Holders of Church Offices

Introduction and Background

The 1997 General Synod instructed the Commission on Theology, in consultation with the Commission on Church Order, to prepare revisions to the *Book of Church Order* that address moral behavior, including sexual purity as it relates to qualifications for all four offices of the church, for report to the 1998 General Synod (*MGS,* 1997:405, R-5).

The commission believes there is merit in this action of synod. Currently, the *Liturgy* and the *Book of Church Order* say a great deal about theological faithfulness and commitment to the good order of the church for officeholders (professors of theology, ministers of Word and sacrament, elders, and deacons). But they say much less about faithfulness in behavior. In a time and context where the esteem with which church leaders are regarded continues to decline in the culture as a whole, and when confusion over moral standards is pervasive, the commission believes the church's life and witness may be strengthened by a greater attentiveness to these issues.

It is interesting that the 1987 "Order for Ordination and Installation of a Minister of the Word" makes no references to behavior, apart from ministerial and ecclesiastical functions, in its interrogation of the candidate prior to ordination. Currently, however, the Commission on Christian Worship is proposing a new order for ordination that includes the question, "Will you pray for God's people and lead them by your own example in faithful service and holy living?" The Commission on Christian Worship notes in its comments on this section, "This question contains important personal disciplines (adapted from the Evangelical Lutheran Church in America) and recovers the attention to godly/holy living found in the *Liturgy* of 1968, 1908, and 1882."

It is certainly true that the liturgical tradition of the Reformed Church in America includes a concern with godly or holy living on the part of officeholders. The 1968 form for ordination inquired of the candidate, "Do you promise to discharge your office faithfully according to this doctrine and to adorn it with a godly life?" The 1908 form used similar language, as did the 1882 *Liturgy*. Moreover the 1882 form, in the charge to the minister, urged the candidate to exercise ministry "not for filthy lucre, but of a ready mind" and offered the following exhortation: "Be an example of believers, in word, in conversation, in charity, in spirit, in faith, in purity." The concern for moral behavior and sexual purity has a long history in the Reformed Church in America, a history that should not be forgotten or lost.

At least some of the concern behind the above instruction to the commission, however, arises from the perception that the Reformed Church in America needs to be more explicit in the moral standards it establishes for officeholders in the church. In a time of moral relativism and confusion, officeholders in the church need to have a clear standard to which they may aspire and by which their behavior can be measured.

Christ the Standard

At the most basic and important level, this standard is Jesus Christ himself. Officeholders represent the various ministries of Christ to and for the church, and in so doing they must live lives in conformity with Jesus Christ. Conformity with Christ involves receiving Christ's righteousness, a righteousness imputed by faith and expressed in our lives through the sanctifying work of the Holy Spirit. As recipients of Christ's righteousness, Christians are called to live out their identity in Christ through lives patterned after Jesus' example. This focus on Christ as the center and standard must never be forgotten or eclipsed. Nor should the church ever fall into the trap of believing that Christ alone is insufficient as the standard to govern life and ministry. Paul declares that no foundation can be laid other than the foundation of Christ (1 Cor. 3:11). Any attempt to make more explicit the ethical norms of behavior that should guide and govern officeholders in the Reformed Church in America should begin and end with Jesus Christ, the living Lord whom we are called to follow.[1]

---

1 Calvin writes, "But Scripture draws its exhortation from the true fountain. It not only enjoins us to refer our life to God, its author, to whom it is bound; but after it has taught that we have degenerated from the true origin and condition of our creation, it also adds that Christ, through whom we return into favor with God, has set before us as an example, whose pattern we ought to express in our life. What more effective thing can you require than this one thing? Nay, what can you require beyond this one thing? For we have been adopted as sons by the Lord with this one condition: that our life express Christ, the bond of our adoption" (*Institutes*, 3.6.3).

This is the pattern of Scripture itself. Paul, for example, frequently offers explicit and focused ethical exhortation to his readers, but these exhortations are always grounded in the believer's relationship to Jesus Christ. In the same way, while it is appropriate for the church to spell out more specific ethical norms for officeholders, such norms should always be guided by Scripture that is drawn from Christ's life and leads us into deeper union with Christ. This is entirely in keeping with the distinctively Calvinist emphasis on a positive role for the law of God: the law is a guide for how we are to live out our new life *in Christ.*

Money, Sex, and Power

But it is not enough merely to assert that Christ is our standard; we also must describe how that standard actually shapes the way we live. What difference does it make for us, in our everyday lives, when our lives are grounded in Christ? The commission believes that both our present context and the ancient history of the church point to three central areas of life where we need to describe the moral implications of our life in Christ. Those areas are money, sex, and power.

In the early periods of the church's history, the church spelled out the ethical implications of the gospel—especially its approach to money, sex, and power—under three headings: poverty, chastity, and obedience. Thomas Aquinas describes these as the three virtues intended to counteract the threefold description of the world found in 1 John 2:16: "the desire of the flesh, the desire of the eyes, the pride in riches." The same threefold concern appears repeatedly throughout the history of the church. Calvin speaks in similar terms of the danger of the longing for money, sex, and power:

> Now our blockishness arises from the fact that our minds, stunned by the empty dazzlement of riches, power, and honors, become so deadened that they can see no farther. The heart also, occupied with avarice, ambition, and lust, is so weighed down that it cannot rise up higher.[2]

The ancient virtues of poverty, chastity, and obedience focused attention on the need to control three driving appetites that can dominate our lives

2   *Institutes*, 3.9.1.

and lead us away from faithfulness to Christ: the love of money, which Scripture places at the root of all evil (1 Tim. 6:10, cf. Luke 16:13-15); the drive for sexual satisfaction, which if left out of submission to God can result in terrible pain and impurity (cf. the extensive instruction on sexual ethics throughout Scripture), and the hunger for power, status and prestige (e.g. Matt. 18:1-4). Scripture repeats in countless ways the basic warning that our longings for money, sex, and power can be our undoing as we seek to follow Jesus Christ.

Between Asceticism and Laxity

This is not to say that there is anything inherently wrong with money, sex, and power. These are good gifts of God, and they are unavoidably part of our lives; everything we do and are is touched by them. They enrich all our joy, health, and strength. Too often in the past, the church pursued an impossible attempt to flee from these realities entirely, resulting in the formation of reclusive and repressive enclaves rather than active mission. The churches of the Reformation resisted the tendency of earlier times to emphasize asceticism—the complete abstinence from money, sex, and worldly power. Rather, Calvin emphasized the importance of moderation, gratitude for God's gifts, generous stewardship, and trust in God.[3] But Calvin also points out that mistaken strictness is not the only danger. We can also fail through mistaken laxity. Precisely because money, sexuality, and power are so deeply woven into our lives, and because our longings for money, sex, and power can be so strong, the pursuit of these desires can all too easily displace the lordship of Jesus Christ and dominate our lives, to our own destruction. That is why the church has always called Christians to special vigilance in these areas.

The challenge for church leaders to handle responsibly the desire for money, sex, and power is no less formidable today. Faithfulness to Christ demands of us today, not that we seek to avoid these realities altogether, but that we cultivate a vigilance and discipline over our hearts in these areas, with a deep awareness of our frailty and of the powerful ways in which our culture tries to persuade us to turn these good aspects of creation into false gods that dominate and control our lives. The commission believes that explicit attention to these challenges, and the

3   See, *e.g.*, *Institutes* 3.10.

cultivation of specific virtues to counteract the seductive allure of money, sex, and power, is essential to healthy leadership in our time and place.

Of course, it is not only officeholders in the church who need to be vigilant over the temptations of money, sex, and power. These are concerns to which all Christians must attend. Yet it is particularly incumbent upon officeholders to live as "examples to the flock" (1 Pet. 5:3). Effective leadership in the church is primarily a matter of actions and behavior, and only secondarily a matter of words. Therefore, it is particularly appropriate to invite leaders to consider the moral standards that should guide their behavior—behavior which, in turn, will help to guide the church as a whole.

A Proposal for the Reformed Church in America

How can such goals be attained within the context of the polity of the Reformed Church in America? The commission suggests that a sentence be added to the declarations for licensed candidates, ministers, and professors of theology which are part of the formularies of the *Book of Church Order*. The commission is also proposing that a similar promise be added to the orders for the ordination for elders and deacons. In all these cases, the sentence would read, "I promise to live a holy and exemplary life, guided by the Holy Scriptures as interpreted by the Standards of the Reformed Church in America, in generosity, chastity, and humility." Each of the words or phrases in this promise needs at least a brief commentary.

The promise to live a "holy and exemplary life" recalls first of all the consistent summons of all of Scripture to holiness. While many people think of holiness only as purity, the biblical meaning originates with the notion of being "set apart" to God. The purity associated with holiness flows first from a Christian's special relatedness to God in Christ that stands at the center of holiness. All Christians share in this holiness because of their union with Christ by faith. Church leaders are called not to greater holiness than other Christians, but rather to live out the holiness that is theirs in Christ and to base their ministries on the power of God that accompanies such holiness. The reference to an "exemplary" life arises from the fact that church offices are at their very heart offices of leadership. The pastoral epistles urge that church leaders live their lives as examples to the flock, "in speech and conduct, in love, in faith, in purity" (1 Tim. 4:12). Ordained officeholders in the Reformed Church in America should aspire to nothing less.

The next phrase, "guided by the Holy Scriptures as interpreted by the Standards of the Reformed Church in America," identifies the Bible as our only rule of faith and practice. At the same time, it affirms that the interpretation of Scripture is not a private matter but an exercise of discernment in which the church engages corporately (2 Pet. 1:20). In this phrase, the candidate promises to be guided by the whole church in interpreting the Scriptures and applying them to his or her life.

The next three words, "generosity, chastity, and humility," attempt to give positive expression to the need for vigilance and restraint over the fundamental appetites that so often threaten to lead us away from discipleship to Christ. The central thrust here is not the attempt to avoid money, sex, or power. This is not a new asceticism. Rather, it is the voluntary commitment to moderation, self-restraint, and faithfulness in these areas, so that they will not dominate or control our lives.

"Generosity" entails a basic posture in which giving to others, rather than acquiring for oneself, is the goal of life. As such, it is a posture of resistance to consumerism and the pursuit of affluence that is so intoxicating and pervasive in our culture. It turns the acquisitiveness of our culture on its head and seeks to imitate, in the handling of money and resources, the very graciousness of God. A commitment of officeholders to generosity is a commitment to a lifestyle of contentment, simplicity, compassion, and service.

"Chastity" is not merely, or even primarily, the avoidance of sex. The first definition of the word in all the major English dictionaries refers to abstention from unlawful or religiously proscribed sexual intercourse. For Christians, chastity is the commitment to place one's sexuality under the authority of Scripture and to direct one's sexuality toward faithful, committed, love and toward the good of the other. At the most basic level, it is the exercise of restraint over one's impulses in order to give space for love, commitment, and concern for the other to grow. Chastity is thus just as important in marriage as it is in singleness. For leaders in the church, the cultivation of chastity is a necessary antidote to the pervasiveness of sexual misconduct and sexual impurity in our culture.

"Humility" means neither excessive deference nor low self-esteem. It is rather the exercise of restraint on our natural desire for power, control, and prestige. In Matthew 11:28-29, Jesus bases his invitation, "Come to me, all you that are weary and are carrying heavy burdens," on the fact that he is "gentle and humble in heart." Paul speaks of boasting only in his weaknesses. Moses is described as "very humble, more so than anyone else on the face of the earth" (Num. 12:3). Officeholders need humility, both to submit to the discipline and guidance of their peers and to avoid the tendencies toward the abuse of power that are rampant in our culture.

By including this promise in the ordination vows, the Reformed Church in America affirms an explicit moral framework for officeholders while avoiding the problems of legalistic interpretation that might accompany definitional language placed elsewhere in the *Book of Church Order.*

5
The Constitutional Inquiries

Introduction

In a 1998 overture to General Synod the Classis of Illinois requested the General Synod to direct the Commission on Theology to study and prepare recommendations concerning the purpose, appropriateness, and wording of the "constitutional inquiry questions" in the *Book of Church Order* for report to the General Synod (*MGS*, 1998: 477, R-6). The reasons given in the overture had to do with the purpose of the inquiries, recent controversy over proposed additions to them, and a concern about the type of inquiries that belong on the list. Other concerns were the lack of uniformity in how these questions are asked and what course of action should be taken if any of them is answered in the negative.

A Brief History of the Constitutional Inquiries

The constitutional inquires have their origin in Article 44 of the Articles of the Synod of Dort, 1619. E. T. Corwin described Article 44 as instructing classes to authorize two of their most experienced and best-qualified members to make annual visits to each of the churches within the classis boundaries. It was their business:

> To inquire whether the ministers, consistories and schoolmasters do faithfully discharge their offices; whether they adhere to sound doctrine; whether they observe in all things the received discipline, and promote, as much as possible by word and deed, the edification of the congregation in general and of the youth in particular, so they may in a reasonable…manner admonish those who…may be found negligent; and…assist in directing all things to edification and the prosperity of the churches and schools.[1]

The practice of the classis sending visitors to local congregations was in place in the Reformed churches of the Netherlands from the time of the Synod of Dort in 1619. This practice was continued in the classes of the

---

1   Corwin, E. T., *A Digest of Constitutional and Synodical Legislation of the Reformed Church in America* (New York: The Board of Publications of the Reformed Church in America, 1906), 723-4.

Reformed Church in America, but Corwin noted that this practice of visitation was not very effectively carried out in America.[2]

The constitutional inquiries were first introduced in the Constitution of 1833, replacing the visitation system of the classes.[3] The Constitution of 1833 listed six inquiries that were to be sent from the classis to local congregations. Answers to these inquiries were to be sent from the churches to the classis. The influence of Dort can be seen in the emphasis on sound doctrine, the faithful discharge of the offices of the church, discipline in the church, and care for young people:

1. Are the doctrines of the Gospel preached in your congregation in their purity agreeably to the Word of God, the Confession of Faith, and the Catechisms of our Church?
2. Is the Heidelbergh Catechism regularly explained, agreeably to the Constitution of the Reformed Dutch Church?
3. Are the catechizing of the children and the instruction of the youth faithfully attended to?
4. Is family visitation faithfully performed?
5. Is the 5th Sec., 2d Art., 2d Chap. In the Constitution of our church carefully obeyed? [*This refers to the moral inquiry of the members of the congregation prior to the celebration of the Lord s Supper.*]
6. Is the temporal contract between Ministers and people fulfilled in your congregation?

A seventh question was added in 1874.[4]

7. Is a contribution made annually by your congregation to each of the Benevolent Boards and Funds of the Church?

Some editorial changes have been made to these seven inquiries over the years, but their essential content has remained the same for over 150 years. Recently, three additional inquiries have been added, bringing their total number in the current *Book of Church Order* to ten. In 1986, the inquiry about the performance review of ministers was added. This was subsequently amended to include all three offices in the local congregation. The next inquiry, emphasizing evangelism, was added in 1989. It was

2   Ibid., 724-5.
3   Ibid., 725.
4   Ibid., 1v.

amended in 1991, and the current inquiry reads, "Is your church engaged in significant, regular activities which faithfully witness to the gospel and which challenge others to respond to God s Spirit in a faith commitment to Jesus Christ as personal Savior and Lord?" The last inquiry to be added came in 1995. It asks, "Has the consistory prayerfully considered persons within the congregation, especially the young people, in order to identify with them their gifts for ministry of Word and sacrament, to encourage the development of these gifts, and to pray for those individuals on a regular basis?"

The Purpose of the Constitutional Inquiries

Historically, the purpose of the constitutional inquires has been twofold. They have provided a means by which classes can exercise pastoral authority over their congregations and a means by which individual congregations can live in responsibility to the greater church.[5]

The primary concern reflected in the inquiries has been for the spiritual well-being of congregations. Spiritual well-being is developed through the faithful preaching of the Word of God, sound teaching based upon the confessional standards of the church, the exercise of spiritual discipline, the nurture of young people, and the responsible exercise of office. In asking congregations to respond to these inquiries, classes are providing pastoral oversight of congregations. The inquiries provide guidelines for congregations in the development and maintenance of their well-being, both spiritually and materially.

The three questions most recently added to the *Book of Church Order* are consistent with the original purpose of the constitutional inquiries. While "performance review" is a concept that comes from the corporate business world and is not altogether compatible with a theological process of evaluation, officeholders need to be accountable for the responsible discharge of their duties. Evaluation of the exercise of office contributes to the spiritual and material well-being of the congregation.

The inquiry that asks congregations about their faithful witness to the gospel and their evangelism efforts direct congregations to look beyond their internal concerns so as to give consideration to the larger mission

---

5   This understanding has been developed by the Rev. Allan Janssen in an unpublished paper.

of the church. In so doing, this inquiry links spiritual well-being with a vital engagement of the church in mission.

The inquiry that asks congregations to assist persons in discerning their gifts for pastoral ministry reflects a concern for the future well-being of the church and suggests a process whereby individuals can be encouraged to develop their gifts for ministry and thus contribute to the ongoing work of the church.

Recent Concerns Regarding the Constitutional Inquiries

In 1996 the General Synod considered an overture that proposed adding confessional language to the first constitutional inquiry (MGS, 1996:399). This resulted in the adoption of a recommendation that a subsection iii be added to the first inquiry (MGS, 1996: 401, R-2):

a. Are the doctrines of the gospel preached in your church in their purity in conformity with
   i.   the Word of God?
   ii. The Standards of the Reformed Church in America?
   iii. The truth that divine redemption from sin is only by grace through faith in the perfect work of the Lord Jesus Christ alone, the only mediator between God and humankind?

When this proposed change in the *Book of Church Order* was sent to the classes for approval, it failed to receive the required two-thirds vote. It was discovered, however, that the words "by grace" had been inadvertently omitted from the text as circulated to the classes for approval, so the synod of 1997 sent the proposed change a second time to the classes (MGS, 1997:63). The recommendation again failed to receive the necessary approval.

Attempts to add confessional language to the constitutional inquiries confuse the purpose of the inquiries and run the risk of suggesting that they may take the place of the church's existing confessional standards. The confessional faith of the Reformed Church in America is expressed in the Reformed Church standards (the Heidelberg Catechism, the Canons of the Synod of Dort, and the Belgic Confession). The purpose of the constitutional inquiries is to provide for pastoral oversight of congregations by classes and to foster spiritual growth and well-being. Confessional statements do not belong in the constitutional inquiries.

The 1998 overture from the Classis of Illinois asked, in effect, "What type of questions belong in the constitutional inquiries?" The historical response to this is: questions that have to do with classes spiritual and pastoral oversight of local congregations. Each of the ten inquiries currently in the *Book of Church Order* concerns itself with the spiritual well-being of the local congregation. The making of these inquiries by classes reflects their pastoral responsibility for fostering and maintaining the spiritual well-being of their congregations.

The overture also raised concerns about how the inquiries are asked and about the lack of a course of action if any of them are answered in the negative. These are matters of church order. The Commission on Theology believes that these matters are more appropriately addressed by the Commission on Church Order.

5

Church and Witness

Introduction

Christian Witness to Muslims: An Introduction to the Issues

After the General Synod of 1981 approved "A Study of the Biblical Perspective on the Evangelization of the Jews," it directed that "a parallel study be made on the relation of the church to the Muslim people" (*MGS*, 1981: 113, R-3). Responses by the Commission on Theology to this directive presented to the General Synod of 1986 and 1990 were referred back to the commission for further study and report. The General Synod of 1994 received a draft of the paper "Christian Witness to Islam," and following discussion, referred it back to the commission "for further precision of expression." The revised text of that paper was brought to the General Synod of 1995 under the title and subtitle above.

In order to assist members of the Reformed Church to have an intelligent witness to their Muslim neighbors, the paper addresses the issues of Islamic origins and fundamentals, similarities and differences between Islam and Christianity, and foundations of Christian witness. The historical material traces the course of Islam from its origins among the Arab people, through the life of Mohammed and the birth of the Qur'an, to its status as a worldwide religion with an estimated 600 million

232

to 1 billion followers. The second section offers such points of contact between Muslims and Christians as revelation, monotheism, prophets, and the five pillars, along with such points of difference as the Trinity, the Holy Spirit, the person of Christ, human sinfulness and redemption, and the relation between religion and the state. The final section on witnessing commends a balanced witness through evangelization in word and deed, and through a genuine, informed, sensitive dialogue that reaches out in the name, the spirit, and the love of Christ. An annotated bibliography accompanies the paper.

The synod adopted the commission's recommendation to commend the paper for educational purposes in congregations, institutions, and agencies of the Reformed Church in America and to encourage these bodies to put its principles into action.

Guilt, Responsibility, and Forgiveness in the Farm Crisis

In April of 1985, the General Program Council of the Reformed Church in America received a report on the economic crisis that had shaken American agriculture. The council's concern was subsequently reflected by General Synod in its instruction to the Commission on Theology to explore and comment upon the moral, legal, and personal dimensions of the current crisis (*MGS,* 1985: 79).

In 1986 the commission brought to the General Synod a draft entitled "Guilt, Forgiveness, and Responsibility in the Farm Crisis." Its recommendation to invite responses from individuals, consistories, and classes for use of the subsequent draft was adopted.

The final report under the title above was brought to the General Synod of 1987. As a backdrop to the urgent need for appropriate pastoral counsel in this crisis the paper aids the church in understanding the crisis and suggests what theological understanding might say to its unique and mounting problems. After documenting the economic reality of the farm crisis, the paper describes the human toll and the erosion of being and self-worth experienced when the farmers' bond with their land is broken. Theological issues of guilt, responsibility, faith, success and failure, forgiveness and reconciliation come to the fore in bewildering patterns of complexity. The pastoral challenge to the church is described and four tasks are suggested as concrete actions to meet that challenge.

The commission's recommendations did not ask the synod to approve the paper, but rather to take a series of actions to address the farm crisis. Following a mixed response to these specifics, the synod instructed the commission to develop a broad theological basis from which the farm issue could be viewed. After careful consideration the commission reported to the General Synod of 1988 its conclusion that such a study of the theological basis for economic life, private ownership, and world community more properly falls within the interest and expertise of the Commission on Christian Action, since much of the foundational theological investigation is already contained in its 1984 paper, "Biblical Faith and the Economic Life" (*MGS,* 1984: 51-67).

The Papers

1

Christian Witness to Muslims: An Introduction to the Issues

Introduction

The writer of the Letter to the Hebrews states:

> Long ago God spoke to our ancestors in many and various ways by the prophets, but in these last days he has spoken to us by a Son, whom he appointed heir of all things, through whom he also created the worlds (1:1-2).

This, indeed, is the essence of the Christian faith as revealed in the Bible. What, then, shall be a Christian witness to a people who believe that God's self-revelation took place in a different way?

Simply by bearing the name "Christian," every believer is a witness to Christ whether he or she wants to be or not. Hence, bearing witness is not a choice for a Christian. The Scriptures are full of this challenge, opportunity, and duty. "God so loved the world"—all of it, all people in it including Muslims—"that he gave his only Son" (John 3:16). One of Christ's last words before he ascended into heaven gives Christian believers the responsibility of carrying that love to everyone in all the world (Acts 1:8). Failure to bear witness is failure to obey Christ's command.

Yet, one cannot talk about a witness to Muslims unless one has some understanding of Islam. In spite of the fact that the Reformed Church in America has had work in Muslim lands for over a century, and Islam is found in practically every one of the Reformed Church's mission fields, as well as in the United States and Canada, there is still much ignorance of Islam and hostility toward Muslims. Such ignorance and hostility are born of misunderstanding, apathy, and cultural differences. Furthermore, it is increasingly clear that this ignorance and hostility are deeply damaging to the church's mission. With the presence of so many Muslims in North America now, including areas in which Reformed Church in America congregations are located, it is crucial for the membership of the Reformed Church to have a more intelligent witness to its Muslim neighbors. Therefore, this paper will addresses Islamic origins and fundamentals, similarities and differences between Islam and Christianity, and foundations of Christian witness. An annotated bibliography follows the paper for the convenience of those who want to do further study.

Islamic Origins and Fundamentals

Islam had its historical origins among the Arab people. Ethnically, the Arabs are Semites like the Jews. Arabs consider themselves to be children of Ishmael, son of Abraham by Hagar. This means that Muslims, Jews, and Christians share a common sense of spiritual descent from Abraham. According to the Christian Scriptures, Ishmael was born when Abraham was eighty-six years old. Abraham loved Ishmael dearly. When Abraham was promised a son by Sarah, his response was, "O that Ishmael might live in your sight!" (Gen.17:18). God promised to make a great people from Ishmael (Gen. 16:10). Ishmael received the sign of the covenant, circumcision, when he was thirteen years old, at the time when Abraham's whole household was circumcised (Gen. 17:23-27). While Ishmael and Hagar had to leave Abraham's house, they apparently were not far away, since Ishmael joined Isaac in burying their father (Gen. 25:9).

The sacred scripture of Islam, the Qur'an (or Koran), traces the roots of the Arab people back to Abraham through Ishmael. According to a widely accepted tradition in Islam, Ishmael rather than Isaac was the "gentle son" whom Abraham was told to sacrifice (Surah 37:83-113). Another tradition holds that Abraham and Ishmael built the *Ka'aba*, the present center of pilgrimage in Mecca (Surah 2:122-125). According to Islamic belief, Abraham shared his faith in the one God with this son whom he loved, and this faith continued among at least some of the Arab people (the *hanifs*, or monotheistic prophets and reformers).

Historically, Islam as an organized religious system stems from the life and ministry of the prophet Muhammad, who was born in 570 A.D. in Mecca, an important commercial city on the Arabian peninsula. In 595 he married a widow, Khadija, owner of a caravan business. Estranged from the polytheistic religion of his clan, Muhammad began to seek the solitude of a cave outside of Mecca for meditation. About 610, during his meditations, he began having what he believed were revelations from the one true God. Because of hostility from the citizens of Mecca, he left Mecca for Medina in 622, in what was called the *Hijrah*, or migration. This date marks the official beginning of the Islamic calendar. In 630 Muhammad returned in triumph to Mecca, where he died in 632.

In Islam, Muhammad is considered to be a prophet and an apostle or messenger, following in the line of all the prophets of Judaism and Christianity. He was, in their view, the "seal" of all the prophets, confirming their message and providing its definitive interpretation (Surah 10:38). He is not considered divine and is not worshiped in Islam. Muhammad's greatest miracle was receiving the Qur'an in Arabic, the full revelation of God, dictated to him by the angel Gabriel. According to Islam, the Qur'an fulfills, completes, and supplants the Old and New Testaments. Muslims consider it as the direct word of God, and hence as beyond the limitations of human history. The orthodox Muslim view of the Qur'an is probably a stronger view of verbal inspiration than any inerrantist view held in evangelical Christianity. God is the one who speaks in the Qur'an; its underlying theme is the oneness of God. Muslims believe that the Qur'an reveals the will of God for their lives.

After Muhammad's death, his followers found that there were important matters not explicitly dealt with in the Qur'an. Traditions (*hadith*) were then collected by believers concerning what they had heard Muhammad say and what they had seen him do. These were carefully checked as to the credibility of the witnesses involved. While they do not have the validity of the Qur'an, which is regarded as the very word of God, they do have a secondary validity because they come from the mouth or actions of the one who was used by God at this point in history as God's messenger. These two sources then, the Qur'an and the Hadith, constitute the major sources from which Muslims derive the religious law (shariah), their rule of faith and practice.

Muslims believe that their religion was directly revealed by God; and it is incumbent upon Christians who live and talk with Muslims to be sensitive to their beliefs regarding Muhammad, the Qur'an, and the origins of Islam. On the other hand, historians discern in Islam a synthesis of elements from Judaism, Christianity, and pre-Islamic Arabic religion. Without denying the profound originality and genius of Muhammad, one should also consider some of the historical influences which shaped the Qur'an and which influenced the rise and rapid spread of Islam. There were many Christians and Jews in Arabia at that time, and it is evident from the Qur'an that Muhammad was familiar with some forms of both Christianity and Judaism. One of his wives and an intimate friend were Christians. He traveled throughout the area in charge of his wife Khadija's caravan business. In these travels he may have lodged in Christian monasteries, a common place for travelers to stay. Muhammad's familiarity with Judeo-Christian Scriptures and themes probably originates in these types of contact.

Islam spread rapidly in a region where Christianity had been strong. Certainly one reason for this was the weakness of the church. Christianity was deeply divided at that time, especially over the issue of the person and work of Christ. A series of schisms and excommunications had greatly weakened the church and obscured its central message. In this situation, the teaching of Muhammad could be seen as a restoration of the power and simplicity of Judeo-Christian monotheism. He offered a message that was strong and clear: there is no deity except the one true God, a God who has sent his revelations to the world through his prophets and apostles. In the Qur'an, Muhammad proclaimed, God has now set forth his definitive instructions for faith and practice, both in the religious life and in the secular world.

After Muhammad's lifetime, armies under the banner of Islam began a series of conquests which would spread Islam from the Atlantic to the borders of China within a century. These conquests were aided by political instability in the Christian world. The Christian Byzantine Empire, which controlled much of what is now the Arab world, had been at war with Persia for many years. The empire had been oppressive, conscripting soldiers for its army and taxing the people heavily. The Muslim invasions, therefore, seemed to offer these Byzantine subjects a way to escape oppression. Eventually, Muslim armies conquered a vast region which had been predominantly Christian, including Syria, Palestine, Egypt, North Africa, and Spain. Christians and Jews, the so-called "people of the book," were tolerated by the Muslim authorities, and significant Christian communities have survived to the present day in some of these regions. Gradually, however, Islam and the Arabic language became dominant.

During the Middle Ages, European Christians acting on both political and religious motivations attempted to invade and conquer Palestine. The ensuing struggle, known in the West as the Crusades, stretched over two centuries. It ended in defeat for Christendom and dramatically heightened the hostility between the Muslim and Christian worlds. Understandably, many Muslims came to see the Crusades as the first in a long series of imperialistic attacks on their civilization and religion. Conflict continued on the borders of the Christian and Muslim worlds. Spain, reconquered by Christians during the late Middle Ages, continued to have a significant Islamic minority until the Muslims were expelled in 1609. The remnants of the Byzantine Empire were destroyed in 1453 by the Ottoman Turks, who also took control of much of the Arab world. The Turkish Empire eventually dominated much of southeastern Europe before it began to recede in the eighteenth century; its weakening led European nations in turn to establish colonial dominance over Islamic peoples. Many of the political and ethnic conflicts of the present—Cyprus, Bosnia, Azerbaijan—have their roots in the religious divisions between Christians and Muslims in this border region.

Since Muhammad's death, Islam has spread throughout the world. In modern history, much of this growth has occurred not through conquest but through peaceful missionary efforts. Estimates for the number of Muslims today range from six hundred million to one billion, meaning that one out of every five or six people in the world is a Muslim. (In comparison, the number of Christians is estimated at 1.5 billion.) The Arabs today are a minority in the world of Islam, with the Arabic language a minority language, even though it is the language of the Qur'an. The majority of Muslims today come from Asia, especially from Pakistan, Bangladesh, India, Indonesia, China, and the former Soviet Union. Through immigration, Muslims have become a significant presence in Europe as well as in North America, where they may soon constitute the largest non-Christian religious group. Some of the growth of Islam in North America is also due to conversion, particularly in the African-American community, where highly disciplined forms of Islam have enjoyed significant success in dealing with the problems of urban poverty.

The majority of Muslims subscribe to *Sunni* Islam, which recognizes the full authority of the Hadith, or traditions concerning Muhammad. The largest non-Sunni group is *Shi'ite* Islam, which is dominant in Iran and strongly represented in Iraq, Syria, and Lebanon. The Shi'ites tend to place more emphasis on divinely guided spiritual leaders (*imams*), and look forward to a future in which religious and temporal leadership are completely reunited. On most fundamental issues, however, Sunni and Shi'ite Muslims are in accord.

Christianity and Islam: Similarities and Differences

In order to witness effectively to Muslims, it is important to have some familiarity with the Qur'an. Translations are available in inexpensive paperback editions in most bookstores. (See the bibliography for recommended editions.) One should approach the Qur'an with an open mind, understanding that it differs from the Bible in its style, subject matter, and arrangement. The Qur'an refers frequently to persons and events from the Bible, although these references in the Qur'an may differ in some respects from the corresponding accounts in the Bible.

Understanding the beliefs and practices of another religion is a complex process requiring patience, empathy, and objectivity. The temptation exists to view that religion exclusively through the lens of one's own faith. This can produce a very inaccurate picture, in which points of resemblance are over-emphasized, and beliefs central to the other religion are obscured. Nonetheless, one can make a beginning effort to understand Islam by noting some important points of similarity and difference between Muslim and Christian beliefs.

Important similarities between Islam and Christianity include the following:

Revelation. Both claim to be religions revealed by the one true God. For Muslims, of course, it is the Qur'an which is God's final revelation to humankind, revealed to Muhammad by the angel Gabriel.

Monotheism. Islam is one of the three great monotheistic religions, along with Judaism and Christianity. The basic tenet of Islam is monotheism, the worship of the one true God. The Arab word for God, Allah, is used by both Arabic-speaking Muslims and Christians to refer to the one true God. (Linguistically, the word is related to the Hebrew words *El* and *Elohim.*) At the same time, one must realize that the Islamic perception of the identity and activity of God is not entirely the same as the Christian perception. In Islam, as in Christianity, God is the creator and sustainer of the universe and all that is in it. God is all-knowing and all-powerful. God will be the judge on the day of judgment, granting eternal life to believers and condemning unbelievers to hell. God is the forgiver of sins, merciful and compassionate. Yet Islam teaches that God demands complete obedience and submission, or surrender (the meaning of the Arabic word "islam") to God's revealed will as it is found in the Qur'an and the Hadith.

Prophets. The Qur'an has a high regard for the prophets who came before Muhammad, including the patriarchs in the Old Testament, and Jesus and John the Baptist in the New Testament. It adds the names of other prophets from the Arabic tradition. These are all men whom God chose to bring his messages or guidance (*huda*) to the peoples of the world. God chose a few prophets to be his special messengers or apostles. A messenger is a prophet to whom God has "sent down" a book. According to Islam, God sent down the Torah to Moses, the Psalms to David, the Gospel to Jesus, and the Qur'an to Muhammad.

The Qur'an gives a special place to Jesus. It states that he was born of the Virgin Mary, without a human father. He was the greatest prophet and teacher before Muhammad. He did many miracles, healing the sick and raising the dead, miracles which even Muhammad did not do. Jesus is in heaven today with his human body; he will return at the end of history to vindicate Islam and usher in the final judgment. Jesus is called "the Messiah" in the Qur'an; other names are "Son of Mary," "the Messenger of God," "a word from God," and "a spirit from God."

The five pillars. Surrender to God is made possible through sincerely practicing the five pillars of Islam. Some of the ideas behind these pillars are common to Judaism and Christianity. They provide contact points for dialogue between Muslims and Christians.

The first pillar is witness. A believer must make public confession of his or her faith in God and Islam before credible witnesses. For the Muslim this means to "bear witness that there is no deity except the one true God, and that Muhammad is his messenger."

The second pillar is worship, or prayer. After ritual washing, the believer recites prescribed prayers and verses from the Qur'an while facing in the direction of the Ka'aba in Mecca. There are instructions for the position of the body at various points in the worship. This worship is to be offered five times every day. There is time allotted for personal prayers at the conclusion of the worship experience, but they are not mandatory. While worship is possible anywhere, the recommended place is the mosque or *masjid*.

The third pillar is fasting during the month of Ramadan, the month in which Muhammad began receiving his revelations. During this month, Muslims are forbidden to take anything into their body from dawn to sunset. Much time should be spent in the contemplation of God, worshiping God, and reading or listening to the Qur'an.

The fourth pillar is the giving of alms to the poor, especially during the month of Ramadan. This practice emphasizes that the believer's possessions must also be submitted to God by being shared with the poor.

The final pillar is the pilgrimage (*hajj*). If possible, all Muslims should make the pilgrimage to Mecca at least once in their lifetime. Preferably, this should be done in the pilgrimage month, arriving in time to observe the first ten days of the month in Mecca.

Along with these five pillars, there is a strong emphasis in the Qur'an on doing good deeds and living a righteous life, walking the straight path which God has revealed. Whatever Christians may think of the origin and nature of Islam, it is evident that there are many sincere, upright Muslims who are sincerely seeking to serve the One they know as God.

While there are a number of similarities between Islam and Christianity, there are also basic differences which people must eventually deal with, whether in evangelization or in dialogue. Christians can retain the respect of those who differ with them only as Christians truly know their own faith and are able to explain it to others. This means that Christians understand others' beliefs in addition to their own, and how others' beliefs differ from their own.

Important differences between Islam and Christianity include the following:

Revelation. Christians believe that the Bible came into being over a span of centuries through the Spirit of God dwelling within the writers, inspiring them, yet working through their own personalities. Although the original text of the Bible is written in Hebrew and Greek, the Bible is given for all people in all ages, and should therefore be translated into all languages in order that everyone can understand and profit from its message. This revelation became incarnate in Jesus, the "Word made flesh," so that Christians understand the Bible as finding its fulfillment and meaning in Christ.

Muslims believe that the Qur'an was revealed in Arabic to one person over approximately twenty-two years, dictated to Muhammad by the angel Gabriel. Muhammad recited it word for word to his followers, who wrote it down. After the death of Muhammad, the messages were eventually brought together in a single book. Muslims believe that it is impossible to translate the Qur'an exactly into any other language. What Christians would regard as a translation of the Qur'an would be called by Muslims an "interpretation" or a paraphrase. In Islamic worship services, the Qur'an is to be read only in Arabic.

From these differences in the concept of revelation, one can easily understand why the proliferation of translations of the Bible raises questions in the minds of Muslims as to the authenticity of the Bible. Because languages continually change, Christians feel translations of the Bible must be updated in order to convey the ideas that God gave to the original writers. The Muslim believes that the ideas of the Qur'an remain clear only as the original Arabic words are retained.

Trinity. Muslims reject the Christian doctrine of the Trinity, holding it to be an unacceptable qualification of the monotheism which is central to Islam. In fact, many Muslims understand the doctrine in a way which is closer to "tri-theism" than to a declaration of the "tri-unity" of the one God, which, of course, offends the powerful Islamic conviction of the oneness of God. Apparently for this reason, among the ninety-nine beautiful names for God in Islamic tradition, the term "Father" is never used, and the term "Son of God" is never used for Jesus. The Holy Spirit is mentioned frequently in the Qur'an as an instrument of God's revelation to his messengers. But the Spirit is not understood in Islam as a personal presence within all believers, empowering them to live faithfully before God.

The Person of Christ. Even though Muslims believe that Jesus was born of the Virgin Mary, without a human father, he is not considered divine.

Neither does the Qur'an contain the idea of the incarnation, that "God was in Christ." Kenneth Cragg, in his book *The Arab Christian: A History in the Middle East*, writes that the theological task for Christians lies "in bringing together what Islam means by *Allahu akbar* (God is the greatest) and what the New Testament understands by 'God in Christ'" (Philadelphia: Westminster/John Knox, 1991, 283).

Human sinfulness and redemption. Another major difference between Islam and Christianity lies in the Muslim view of the human predicament and its solution. According to the Qur'an, humans were created weak and imperfect. God then sent his prophets in order to guide them on "the straight path" which would lead them to Paradise. This path includes becoming a Muslim and practicing the five pillars of the faith. As long as a person does this, and does not become a worshiper of more than one god, he or she will enter into Paradise. There appears to be no word for, or idea of, "sinfulness" in Arabic. According to Islam, although Adam was weak at creation, humans are not "born in sin." Basically, to sin is to wander from the straight path, or to commit mistakes. When people sin they must ask God's forgiveness, seek to make amends for the wrong done, and return to the straight path. There does not seem to be the sense of alienation between God and humanity as a consequence of sin which Christianity expresses in its doctrine of original sin.

Since Islam's view of the human predicament is more optimistic than Christianity's, it should not surprise Christians that Islam sees no need for a divine act of redemption. Hence, for Muslims the death of Jesus has no saving significance. Through the mercy of God, individuals can be saved by means of the five pillars. This is illustrated where the Qur'an (Surah 4:157), describing the persecution of the prophets, says about Jesus, "They slew him not nor crucified him, but it appeared so to them." The Arabic in the last part of the sentence is ambiguous, and Muslim scholars disagree on its interpretation: either the crucifixion happened with the one crucified appearing to be Jesus, or the crucifixion only appeared to happen. The main point is that Islam feels no need for a savior or redeemer. It was not, in their view, necessary for Jesus to die in this way. On the other hand, as Cragg says, "Christianity must hold on to the central Christian conviction, as the heart of its scripture and its liturgy, of the God whose sovereignty fulfills itself in the love that comes, suffers, and reconciles, in the measures we can identify in Jesus and the cross" (*The Arab Christian*, 293).

Religion and state. Islam makes no separation between religion and the state. It is a complete way of life, including politics, culture, economics, and all other aspects of life. Islam in its pure form is not a state religion, but rather a theocracy, a religious state. Christians and Jews have continued to live under Islam as *dhimmis*, or tolerated minorities; they are allowed to have their own laws and courts and to carry on their own affairs without interference from the state. But the ideal situation, in the Islamic view, is one in which religious and political power are closely linked. Many of the movements in contemporary Islam which are described as "fundamentalist" are attempting to move the Islamic world closer to that ideal.

Islam and Christianity are both monotheistic religions worshipping one God; many of the words and ideas are the same. Yet the two are not one, and nothing will make them one. Christians and Muslims fail to understand each other's religion in their own integrity when one says that both religions are following the same path in their worship of this one God. People of both faiths will profit, however, as they become better acquainted with one another and seek to live together in love and peace, respecting each other's faith while giving witness to their own.

Foundations of Christian Witness

How then shall Christians witness to their Muslim neighbors in the light of Christ's statement, "You are my witnesses"?

A Question of Balance

Christians today often find themselves divided between two conceptions of witness, one focusing on *evangelization*, the other on *dialogue*. Witness through evangelization assumes that the eventual goal of sharing one's faith with another is to convert the other to Christianity. This approach takes very seriously Christ's command to "make disciples of all nations." It assumes that religions are not all fundamentally the same or equally valid, and that the gospel is the answer to the deepest spiritual needs of every individual and every culture.

The emphasis on evangelization captures important aspects of the mission which Christ gave to the church. Without it, Christianity is seen as a mere product of the culture rather than as a proclamation of God's universal truth and love. Yet, it may also present Christians with temptations: First, there is the temptation to assume that one's culturally shaped version of Christianity is equivalent to the gospel itself. Second, there is the temptation to manipulate any encounter with non-Christians so that the Christian message will prevail. Third, there is the temptation to forget that it is God, not Christians, who regenerates, saves, and sanctifies, and that Christians must await God's work while avoiding pressure and manipulation.

Some Christians have reacted to these temptations by expressing their witness through the model of dialogue. These believers want to see Christian witness expressed in a nonmanipulative and generous way, which respects the integrity and freedom of the other. For too long, they argue, Christian witness has been used as a tool of dominance by Western imperialism; now it is time for Christians to listen as well as speak, to learn as well as teach. This perspective also captures an important element of the attitude required of Christ's followers, that they offer the gospel in a way which reflects Christ's nonviolent and self-sacrificial love. In view of the history of conflict and colonialism which has shaped relations between Christians and Muslims, this is a vital insight. Yet here, too, there are a trio of temptations to be avoided: First, there is the temptation of an easy relativism, which assumes that whatever anyone believes is "right" for them. Second, there is the temptation to see evangelization only in coercive terms, and in the context of western imperialism. Third, there is the temptation to neglect the universal scope of God's gracious act of reconciliation in Christ.

A balanced view of Christian witness will incorporate both evangelization and dialogue. It will lead Christians to obey the command of Christ to share the gospel with the whole world, even while treating the convictions of others with understanding and respect. It will teach Christians to be sensitive to the ways in which the Christian mission can be perceived by others as coercive and dominating, without losing confidence in the goodness of God's purpose in Christ for all people and all nations. What follows is an attempt to provide guidance for Christians who seek to provide a balanced witness to the good news of Jesus Christ.

Witness through Evangelization in Word and Deed

Offering an authentic witness to the Christian faith in the contemporary world is never an easy task. But it is made more difficult by the fact that both here in North America and around the world, the media, especially through movies and videos, as well as newspapers and books, present a false picture of Christianity. Just as most North Americans know about Islam only from the media, even so, most Muslims also know Christianity in the same way. Christians are combating a strong foe in North America, which presents a very warped picture of Christ and Christianity, as well as of Islam. Compounding this problem is the negative witness provided by the behavior of Americans, whom most people around the world consider as "Christians." It is taken for granted that Americans do what they do because they are Christians, just as most Americans think Palestinians, Iranians, and Saudis do what they do because they are Muslims. Of course, neither supposition is accurate.

This means that the first challenge for Christians bearing witness to Muslims is to counteract negative or inaccurate stereotypes of the Christian faith which may exist in the minds of Muslims (as well as dealing with the stereotypes of Islam which exist in the minds of Christians). If such stereotypes are to be overcome, it will not be by words but by example. The way in which Christians live their lives will have a far greater impact on the fruitfulness of their witness than the words they use to express their beliefs. In fact, apart from their lives, their words are of little effect. The greatest example in witness is the person of Christ. Christ came to proclaim and demonstrate God's love for all people. Christ lived that same love as God's Word incarnate, so that people could see and experience it. Surely one of the main things that attracted people to Jesus was his life among them. Jesus challenged them to believe in him because of the works he did (John 10:37-38). In order to witness to Christ, then, Christians must witness as Christ did, embodying Christ's love in their lives.

The Book of Acts says of the apostles that people "recognized that they had been with Jesus" (Acts 4:13b, RSV). Being with Jesus made a difference. Their lives were different since they had submitted to Christ. They became credible witnesses because they were different. This has to be the basis of one's Christian witness, especially in the Muslim world.

Most Muslims are content with the life they have in Islam. Do Christians have anything better to offer them? Do Christians show this in their relationships with them? Are Christians loving, forgiving, caring people? Do Christians have something in their personal lives that Muslims do not have in Islam? Only in the context of such a living witness can Christians meaningfully share their reasons for living as they do.

If Muslim friends indicate an interest in reading the Bible and especially the New Testament, it would probably be best to read with them, or give them, the Gospel of Luke first. Luke starts with the annunciation to Elizabeth and Zechariah, the annunciation to Mary, and the birth of Jesus, all of which are mentioned in the Qur'an. Of course, other elements of the Gospel may be disturbing for Muslims, particularly references to Jesus as the Son of God. Remember that an abstract discussion of the Trinity or the divinity of Christ at this point will not help a Muslim reader to understand and appreciate the character of Jesus as portrayed in the Gospel of Luke. Also, remember that the Muslim denial of these doctrines is intended to avoid an idolatrous confusion of the world with its Creator, a goal that Christians share.

After having established a good relationship and understanding of one another, other parts of the New Testament may be explored. Meaningful dialogue will come about only when there is mutual confidence. This can then lead to discussions of more complex issues such as sin and salvation, the person of Christ, and the Trinity. These discussions should be respectful of Muslim convictions, but should also serve as an opportunity to express the heart of the Christian faith "God has spoken to us by a Son," not merely communicating with humankind, but entering into our reality and triumphing over the sin and despair of the human predicament.

Witness through Dialogue

Christian-Muslim dialogue refers to conversation between individuals or groups about the beliefs and practices of the two religions, as well as about issues of common concern to the Christian and Muslim communities. An important goal of dialogue is to help people of one faith understand people of another faith, not as exotic "foreigners," but as neighbors who share many hopes, concerns, and interests. Another goal is to learn more about one's self through opening one's self to the insights and responses of others.

Genuine dialogue is not a substitute for the proclamation of the gospel, but rather a special form of witness with distinct goals. It does not require glossing over one's beliefs in order to avoid offense to the other. Rather, it requires honest sharing of basic convictions from both faiths in order to come to a better mutual understanding. Members of each religion must respect the other for who they are and what they believe. Dialogue is not argument, and the participant in dialogue must set aside any intent to "win." To be effective, there must be an openness on the part of both sides to ask and answer honestly questions about the deep matters of each other's faith. Group dialogue is valuable in bringing people together for a better understanding of each other's religion and their own. It can also lead to the opportunity to work together to meet common social needs. Muslims are as disturbed as Christians are by the problems of crime, terrorism, the collapse of public morality, the conflict between science and religion, and the decline of education. These are all common concerns in which Christians and Muslims can be involved together, since these concerns pertain to problems faced by both.

It is important, of course, for Christians who enter into dialogue to know the Christian faith and to have a thorough knowledge of the Bible. Those Christians who have the opportunity to engage in dialogue should first ask themselves whether they can clearly explain the Christian life and salvation to someone who has never heard it. It is especially important to be able to discern what is essential to the Christian faith, as distinguished from elements which are peripheral or cultural. In addition, Christians in dialogue need at least a basic understanding of Islam. This requires some familiarity with the Qur'an and with the history of Islam. Christians must be aware of those things that will offend Muslims as well as those things on which there is agreement. Eventually, basic differences must be dealt with, including such theological matters as the divinity of Christ, human sinfulness, the cross, and the Trinity. Christians must also be prepared to deal with social issues such as the relationship between religion and politics. These differences should not be evaded, although there is no need to emphasize them at the beginning of the dialogue. When they do arise, Christian participants should make it clear that they respect the sincerity and the concerns of their dialogue partners even if they cannot agree.

Few Christians have the opportunity to be involved in group dialogue. However, personal dialogue is open to all who have contact with Muslims where they live and work, and this may prove to be more challenging, enjoyable, and beneficial than group dialogue. As Christians caring for other people, Christians may often have the opportunity to begin the dialogue. It is an opportunity to reach out in the name, the spirit, and the love of Christ. As the parable of the Good Samaritan makes clear, Christians must not merely say, but also demonstrate, that Christians are neighbors to Muslims in their midst.

Conclusion

The world draws closer every day. Those whom we thought at one time were far away have become our neighbors. The Scriptures encourage Christians to show their love for God by loving their neighbors (1 John 4:20-21). The greatest gift Christians have to share with Muslims is the life and peace that comes through faith in Jesus Christ as Savior and Lord. Christians should not hesitate in sharing this precious gift with Muslims. Yet the gift must be shared in a way which reflects the mind of Christ, "who, though he was in the form of God, did not count equality with God a thing to be grasped, but emptied himself, taking the form of a servant" (Phil. 2:6-7, RSV). As Christians serve their Muslim neighbors in Christ's love, the Holy Spirit will open up opportunities for genuine and effective witness.

Annotated Bibliography

First time students of Islam might read *The Call of the Minaret*, by Kenneth Cragg (New York: Oxford University Press, 1956); *Muhammad: Prophet and Statesman*, by Montgomery Watt (London: Oxford University Press, 1961); *An Introduction to Islam*, by Frederick M. Denny (New York: Macmillan, 1985); *Islam: The Straight Path*, by John Esposito (London: Oxford University Press, 1990); and *History of the Islamic Peoples*, by Carl Brockelman (New York: Capricorn, 1960). Two highly regarded English versions of the Qur'an are *The Meaning of the Glorious Koran*, by M.M. Pickthall (New York: Mentor, 1955) and *The Koran Interpreted*, by A. J. Arberry (New York: Macmillan, 1955).

For basic elements of a Muslim world view, read *The Teaching of the Qur'an*, by H.U.W. Stanton (London: SPCK, 1919/1969); *The Formative Period of Islamic Thought*, by W. Montgomery Watt (Edinburgh: Edinburgh University Press, 1973); *The Dome and the Rock*, by Kenneth Cragg (London: SPCK, 1964); *How to Understand Islam*, by Jacques Jomier (New York: Crossroad, 1991); *Toward Understanding Islam*, by Harry Dorman (New York: Columbia University Press, 1948); and *Islam from Within*, by Kenneth Cragg and Marston Speight (Belmont, California: Wadsworth, 1980).

Resources for understanding Islam's interaction with modernity are found in *Introduction to Islamic Civilization*, by R.M. Savory (Cambridge: Cambridge University Press, 1967); *Islam in the Contemporary World*, by C.K. Pullapilly (Notre Dame, Indiana: Cross Roads, 1980); *Islamic Values in the United States*, by Yvonne Haddad and Adair T. Lummis (New York: Oxford University Press, 1987); and *Neighbors: Muslims in North America*, edited by Elias Mallon (Cincinnati: Friendship Press, 1989).

The history of Muslim-Christian relations is traced in *Muslim-Christian Encounters: Perceptions and Misperceptions,* by J. Montgomery Watt (New York: Routledge, 1991). Interaction between Christians and Muslims is discussed in *Islam: A Christian Perspective* (Exeter: Paternoster Press, 1983) and *Frontiers in Muslim-Christian Encounter* (Oxford: Regnum Books, 1987), by Michael Nazir-Ali; *Christian-Muslim Relations: An Introduction for Christians in the United States*, by Marston Speight (Hartford, Connecticut: Task Force on Christian-Muslim Relations, National Council of the Churches of Christ in the USA, 1983); *Striving Together: A Way Forward in Christian-Muslim Relations*, by Charles Kimball (Maryknoll, New York: Orbis); and in books by Kenneth Cragg, *Sandals at the Mosque; Christian Presence Amidst Islam* (London: SCM, 1959); *Muhammad & the Christian: A Question of Response* (Maryknoll, New York: Orbis, 1984); and *Jesus and the Muslim: An Exploration* (London: Allen & Unwin, 1985).

The record of Protestant missions in the Islamic world since 1800 is deserving of study. *Mission to Muslims: The Record*, by Lyle Vander Werff (Pasadena, California: William Carey Library, 1977), focuses on Reformed and Anglican efforts in proclamation and presence.

For useful insights on evangelization, see *Sharing Your Faith with a Muslim*, by Abdiyah Akbar Abdul-Haqq (Minneapolis, Minnesota: Bethany Fellowship, 1980); *Design of My World*, by Hassan Dehqani-Tafti (London: Lutterworth, 1959); *A Christian Approach to Muslims: Reflections from West Africa*, by James Dretke (Pasadena, California: William Carey Library, 1979); *New Paths in Muslim Evangelism*, by Phil Parshall (Grand Rapids, Michigan: Baker, 1980); from the Lausanne Committee for World Evangelization, *Muslims and Christians on the Emmaus Road* (Monrovia, California: MARC, 1989), edited by Douglas Woodberry; and *The Christian Approach to the Muslim*, by G.E. Morrison (London: Edinburgh House, 1964).

A variety of views on dialogue and evangelization are represented in *Faith Meets Faith*, edited by Gerald Anderson and Thomas F. Stransky (Grand Rapids, Michigan: Eerdmans, 1981). A Presbyterian approach to dialogue is found in *Christians and Muslims Together*, by Byron L. Haines and Frank L. Cooley (Philadelphia, Pennsylvania: Geneva Press, 1987).

2
Guilt, Responsibility, and Forgiveness in the Farm Crisis

An Economic Reality

The continuing sharp decline in America's agricultural economy or the farm crisis, as it is often called, has placed many farm families in precarious financial situations, many times resulting in failure and bankruptcy. The hard realities of the predicament are no longer in question. For example, in Iowa in 1985

a. rural banks closed their doors in numbers rivaled only by the Depression;

b. farmland values plummeted 30 percent;

c. Governor Terry Branstad invoked a moratorium on farm foreclosures, a measure not taken by state government since the Depression;

d. the good news of a bountiful harvest resulted in the erosion of corn and soybean prices to the lowest level in several years;

e. farm bankruptcy filing continued to rise; and

f. mounting personal and social violence drew national attention (*Des Moines Sunday Register,* 19 January 1986: XIff).

In addition, the national cooperative Farm Credit System, which holds one third of the national farm debt, this year turned to Congress for a multi-billion dollar financial bailout. Upon his recent retirement from office, United States Secretary of Agriculture John Block conceded that his six years in office saw the worst agricultural downturn since the Depression (1.26.86). All of this bad news is perhaps best summarized in the fact that since 1971 Iowa alone has lost 22,000 farms (*Des Moines Register,* 21 January 1987: A12). And while in the last year the farm crisis has not significantly worsened, its long-standing dire condition has not perceptibly improved. Indeed, it is now perhaps no longer accurate to talk of the dire predicament of America's agricultural economy as one of crisis—a term that usually connotes a brief and decisive turning point. Rather, the crisis has now become perpetual—a deep, lasting, and seemingly insoluble depression.

To be sure, the continuing "crisis" in American agriculture is real, deep, extensive, and not likely to end very soon. Current forecasts predict that in each of the next few years five to ten percent of current Iowa farmers will lose their farms. The crisis has fallen on both large and small farmers and has radiated outward to affect the well-being of the innumerable small communities supported by the farm economy. To a large extent, its causes remain inscrutable and will remain shrouded in three decades of complex federal farm policy and the tangled caprices of international finance and politics. Nor do immediate or long-term solutions seem clear or forthcoming either from economic theorists, the financial establishment, or Congress. The only foreseeable certainty is more hurt and confusion for all those involved, whether as farmer, businessperson, bureaucrat, or banker.

Through much of this distress, the farmer and farm communities remain peculiarly alone. During the catastrophic Depression of the 1930s, virtually every section of the United States suffered enormous economic dislocation. Reeling from a deteriorating national economy, farmers endured a further blow from drought and widespread crop failure. During those hard years, the farmer was in the same soup, so to speak, as everyone else. Adversity afflicted the land as a whole, and citizenry and government alike struggled to endure and recover. Perplexity and a sense of impotence—and then perhaps resolve and hope—were common states of mind. In the current crisis, in spite of oceans of publicity, the farm industry stands relatively alone, not sure that the country or the government grasps its plight. In an industry more vital than defense, American agriculture continues to provide an abundance of food, becoming ever more productive, and all the while flounders financially. The land and its workers supply more and more, and markets for the rich harvests seem only to diminish. Hard questions about compensation for risk, service, and labor quickly enter any discussion of the farm crisis, as do questions of simple fairness and justice.

A Human Toll

The great misfortune of the farm crisis is not confined to ledger books of economic loss or gain; the current difficulty is not a momentary, financial aberration from regularly mounting agricultural prosperity. Rather, the deep economic crisis in agriculture in the Midwest has imposed great and lasting financial burdens on farmers and their communities, and with the erosion of the economic foundations of agriculture there has been a mounting psychological, social, and spiritual toll. In the farm crisis, one witnesses a deep human tragedy whose contours and effects are far-reaching. To be sure, statistical data, news stories, benefit concerts, and Hollywood movies do offer some glimpses—some of them poignant—into the experience of farm families. However, it is also to some extent true that, given the unique character of farm life, the real toll of the farm depression remains stubbornly subjective and elusive, and those outside an agricultural setting, no matter how they might strive, cannot grasp the full personal and family burden of economic peril and failure.

The prospect of leaving agriculture often shakes farmers, marriages, and families to their emotional and spiritual foundations. For these people, economic failure entails far more than the loss of property and employment. Rather, most often farming offers a cherished way of life—in short, a calling or vocation that engages the full devotion and commitment of persons and families. Indeed, more than many careers in the modern work world, farming can elicit a deep sense of personal vocation, meaning, and identity. So it is that economic failure often brings prolonged grief, as in the loss of a loved one, and agonizing uncertainty about self-worth, personal responsibility, and the trustworthiness of God. Incomprehension and shame often result, thus threatening the well-being of otherwise responsible, stable, and resourceful members of the church and local social and economic life.

Agricultural life in rural America seems to have fostered a distinct tradition of self-understanding, one that differs markedly from the ethos of contemporary mobile urban life. While these qualities are inward and personal in nature and consequently somewhat elusive, it is nonetheless possible to identify dearly held, perhaps irreplaceable values and traits that the farm crisis has endangered. The uniqueness and centrality of these attitudes and "habits of the heart" to some extent explain the severity of personal emotional trauma.

A Sense of Being

Foremost among these is veneration of the land. Perhaps more than other segments of contemporary American labor, the vocation of farming affords the development of a special sort of bonding between the person and the land, which is a central, productive, and tangible facet of the glory and work of the creation. In the creation narrative, God declared the landscape and its natural plenitude to be both aesthetically pleasing and physically nourishing—in short, to be "very good" (Gen.1:31). And insofar as farming in a general sense helps the earth to flourish, the farmer's activity with the land—in ways more direct than most careers allow—reflects and extends the original work of the creation. Further, the farmer is quite specifically engaged in carrying out some of God's first direct commands regarding humankind's life and home on the earth: "to till it and care for it" (NEB, unless otherwise indicated) or, as the King James Version nicely puts it, "to dress it and to keep it" (Gen. 2:15). The centrality of agriculture is further indicated in the fact that after God creates botanical nature, he goes on to fashion night and seasons in order to mark the festivals that will celebrate the fruition of God's intentions for the earth and creation (Gen. 1:14). Finally, throughout the creation account there runs the strong suggestion that the earth and creation are not themselves complete and "good" until humanity bestows love and labor upon the land by tilling it (see especially Gen. 2:5). It is not romantic sentimentalism, then, to point out that many farmers rise early in the morning not primarily to do their chores but to enjoy the sunrise and its light upon the frost.

In the work of agriculture, then, there is a particular moral significance, something primal and attractive, and a particular pleasure. In peculiar and ultimately mysterious ways, at least some of the pain of the farm crisis arises from the loss of relationship and a unique vocation; that is, the separation of the tiller from the soil, from the beauty and rhythms of the earth, and from humankind's original calling to be "dressers" and nurturers of the earth for God and people alike. The sorrow of losing land and a deeply felt calling often resembles mourning after the sudden and tragic loss of a family member or well-loved friend.

Very often additional grief comes in the loss of a patrimony or an esteemed family heritage in which a place and a work has tied together and sustained generations. Land and community relationships have passed from one generation to another. Bonds of trust and mutual support have grown up over decades. In this instance one might speak of a quality of "rootedness," a generational stability and legacy that is fixed geographically in region and locality, socially in kinship and community, and attitudinally in gratitude and devotion. Acutely conscious of these time-moored networks of inheritance and obligation, loss or disruption occasions intertwined reactions of guilt and self-doubt and anger and recrimination. These consequences profoundly affect self-esteem and social attitudes, appearing most often in personal depression, tense marriages, and social animosity among children.

More frustration results from the threat to habits of rural self-reliance. Even with modern technology and federal subsidies, farmers have labored over the years with considerable ingenuity in a risky and capricious marketplace. And they have usually made a go of it without failure or resort to special assistance from government or bank. Most farm families maintained a life of modest material comfort without discontent or desire for wealth. However, the volatility of national and world politics and economics, beginning with the Russian grain embargo of 1978, have struck their economic sector particularly hard. The evidence of the toll is abundant. What a few short years ago seemed to be endlessly escalating land prices have dropped by half. Similarly, not too long ago government, bankers, universities, and media encouraged farmers to borrow at high interest rates to expand holdings and modernize equipment. Since then crop and land values have plunged by as much as sixty percent. Thus, unforeseen forces beyond personal or local control have played havoc with this basic sense of self-sufficiency and equity.

With these factors in mind, it is not difficult to understand why many in farm communities feel bewilderment and impotence. As the jaws of economic reality close, frustration and anger mount, as do disappointment, guilt, and grief. Needless to say, such a frontal siege on economic survival attacks as well the values and habits at the very center of agricultural life. Hard-hit farm families wrestle in perplexed wonderment with their recent surprising fate, for which there is often no explanation or solace. Frequently such experiences are, in a fundamental sense, profoundly disorienting, demoralizing, and dispiriting. Families feel rage and confusion about their present circumstance and especially about their options for the future, which seem limited at best. In the midst of such loss, family leaders often struggle with enormous guilt, no matter how unavoidable or uncontrollable a given predicament might seem.

An unpredictable world has routed patterns of responsibility and self-sufficiency at the heart of rural traditions. Fear, shame, and fatigue sap the drive necessary to change professions and shift to a wholly new way of life. For many farmers, as for businesspeople, bankers, and government officials, the farm crisis has, in short, provoked disheartening if not debilitating questions about personal worth and meaning. This profound shaking of the roots of personal being surfaces in questions about Providence and the justice and trustworthiness of God. Seemingly God has not rewarded personal faith and discipline, but, as government and banking, has fully abandoned farm families to their plight. More than that, in the apparent economic caprice that characterizes the farm crisis, it seems that Providence has been arbitrary if not vindictive.

Theological Directions

It is to this crisis of vocation, morale, and belief that the church must minister. Farm families confront wrenchingly difficult financial, psychological, moral, and religious challenges. There are no easy or quick solutions to the complex troubles of their predicament. To suggest otherwise would be to deny obvious realities, to play with hopes, and ultimately to bring still greater damage. Nonetheless, biblical and theological notions and commitments can console and inspire those stricken and ultimately work to clarify and redeem the tragedy. The church is called to mediate in behalf of Christ the suffering of its members and neighbors, and thus it must undertake a demanding venture in caring that will tax its personal, program, and financial reserves.

The Problem of Guilt

A major and seemingly inevitable consequence of economic failure comes in sizeable burdens of guilt. Carefully laid plans have fallen on disaster, and even though bankruptcy may in fact result from uncontrollable forces, farm couples still feel enormous responsibility—to one another, to a lost future for their children, and oftentimes to several generations of family heritage. A syndrome of self-accusation in endless "what-if" conjecture sometimes results. Or immovable guilt and frustration find no relief or recourse, often finding temporary vent in blaming others—from government to bankers and spouses—or self. Entangled in guilt, justified or otherwise, the individual loses hope and the capacity to persevere.

Scripture deals with the loss of land in the Levitical prescription for a Year of Jubilee (Lev. 25:8-55). The law prescribes that every fifty years those who, for whatever reason, have lost land since the previous Jubilee shall have that land returned to them. A portion of land for self-support, a gift in effect from God, seems to be a natural right in Israel. If climatic or economic conditions or poor management choices cause the sale of that land, the individual and his heirs do not lose the right or the gift. In time it is returned to them as a gift for use. Moreover, the notion of accumulating or hoarding quantities of land for selfish purposes seems contrary to common sense ideals of economy and God's demands for social obligation and interdependence. The remarkable salient feature of the Year of Jubilee for application to the current farm crisis is that Scripture understands the loss of land and property to be the inevitable product of an imperfect society and fallen world. Nowhere does the discussion mention economic failure as a moral defeat meriting guilt. Guilt only incurs to those who failure to extend mercy to those in misfortune. Further, the concept of Jubilee affords some comfort that a just and compassionate society, for which all are enjoined to strive, recognizes in full the special status of land and patrimony or the right of inheritance. The wisdom of Jubilee, then, consoles the stricken and petitions for mercy from the powerful.

Central to this perspective is God's unequivocal assertion that all belongs to God ("the land is mine") and that on it humans are but "aliens and settlers," inhabiting the land in the first place by the good grace of God (Lev. 25:23b). That being the case, those tenants who use it in loan from God should care more for what God cares about than about individual ownership. It is, after all, common sense to keep the landlord happy. And as the Levitical discussion makes more than clear, God cares above all for compassion and justice, especially in the distribution of land and wealth. While it might in fact be impossible to implement the Jubilee legislation in our complex economic individualism, its spirit should nonetheless serve as a prescriptive guide in extending innovative and sacrificial economic mercy.

Success, Faith, and Self-Worth

It is important to note as well that the Bible does not tie economic success to human worth. If anything, just the opposite holds true. While the goodness of the creation is a grand gift to be enjoyed, private excess or hoarding of its plenitude in wealth is usually considered to be an encumbrance and barrier to a genuine apprehension of God and divine love. Nor does Scripture suggest that wealth is a consistent reward for hard work or faith. In general, there is no one-to-one correspondence between hard work and financial success. Rather, when wealth does come, its arrival often resembles in logic the inscrutable timing and logic of bad fortune; explanations do not abound. Others work as hard as the rich and do not prosper. Given the current extent and depth of self-recrimination among farmers, this biblical perspective is both crucial and pastoral and can hardly be overstated. It is a notion that preachers should go out of their way to impart.

Just as work and discipline are not guarantors of success, great faith does not insure material well-being or life without tragedy. To suggest that faith functions as a holy rabbit's foot—the more one rubs it, the more it works—distorts biblical understandings of faith and providence. As the Commission on Christian Action has observed, American society often "views the possession of wealth as the appropriate reward for virtue and a mark of God's favor" ("Biblical Faith and Our Economic Life," *MGS,* 1984: 54). Within this milieu, economic failure tragically carries with it the stigma and incubus of immorality or lack of faith.

The biblical record well indicates that faith does not bring success or protection from adversity. The Psalms attest over and over again to the affliction and tumult that can befall the faithful. The stories of almost every leader and prophet of faith are long tales of woe and calamity interspersed with moments of gladness and reconciliation: Abraham, Jacob, Joseph, Moses, David, Jeremiah, Amos, Jonah, and, of course, Job. The triumphalist and utilitarian belief of much contemporary Christianity exalts paths of easy faith as means to achievement. Faith often becomes an instrument or vehicle to goals other than the beatitude of God. In some circles, faith is seen as an investment in a secure economic future, as a sort of holy stock market portfolio. Unfortunately, such renditions of the purpose and significance of faith do not conform to the hard evidence of an often tragic biblical record. Many "health and happiness" credos overlook the inevitable periods of misfortune and darkness that often prominently accompany, if not directly result from, the holding and living of faith. We cannot overlook God's sorrowful pictures of Jesus agonizing in the desert, in the garden, and finally upon the cross, abandoned by friends and even by God. We know also the hard fate of the apostles of Jesus who endured shipwreck, persecution, prison, and execution. The church celebrates still its history of holy martyrs for faith. Paul urges perseverance as a cardinal spiritual and moral principle not only because the Christian faith itself is demanding, but because life itself is more often than not beset by innumerable troubles and afflictions. In sum, material circumstance bears little or no correlation to one's spiritual or personal worth.

Thus it is that in a tragic world, with its ample causes for despair, faith offers light with which to walk through spiritual and moral darkness and by which we may make ourselves and others whole. That is the task and end of redemption. The desire for conspicuous palpable signs of God's care is natural and constant, but Paul points toward a different orientation. Amid the groans and agonies of the universe, even the people of faith groan "inwardly while we wait for God to make us his sons and set our whole body free. For we have been saved, though only in hope. Now to see is no longer to hope: why should a man endure and wait for what he already sees? But if we hope for something we do not yet see, then, in waiting for it, we show our endurance" (Rom. 8:23-26). Faith imparts assurance of things not seen or yet received in full. What divine signs we might receive lie in the harvest of the spirit, and by that mysterious work of renewal and love done in us, we can confirm the living presence of our Lord the Redeemer (Gal. 5:22). Faith is trust, in the midst of bad times, that in love "all things are held together" in Christ (Col. 1:17). The Spirit pleads our case in God's own way and "co-operates for good with those who love God and are called according to his purpose" (Rom. 8:27-29). And always while we look through a dark glass, "nothing in all creation...can separate us from the love of God in Christ Jesus our Lord" (1 Cor. 13:23; Rom. 8:39). We know too that our Lord addresses our woe, for he walked in a human skin in paths like our own and ministered to and comforted others, even when he was without consolation.

Forgiveness and Reconciliation

Surely one of the most difficult of human burdens is guilt, especially amid tragedies that seem to have resulted from human agency. The bewildering economic and social complexity of the farm crisis provides innumerable occasions for anger and recrimination—against self, family, neighbors, clients, bankers, government, and even God. If fault can be found at all, it can be ascribed to a variety of implacable sources. While the mind can usually grasp the idea and necessity of forgiveness, taking its reality into the self, into heart and soul, often proves tortuously difficult. The Christian community can be grateful that forgiveness is not only a promise but a command; it is, first and last, the very pivot and end of God's approach to a fallen humanity. Reconciliation is after all, as hard and impractical as it may often seem, the chief hallmark of God's kingdom.

In light of God's forgiveness, the church of Christ must labor to reflect upon and to extend acceptance and love to all beset by anger and defeat. Judgment and accusation are always out of place, but especially so in situations of loss and grief. Those caught in misfortune know too well if blame and error apply to their circumstance. Even if unwise business decisions or greed may have in some cases led to circumstances that later brought failure, it is not the business of whole parishes to accuse and judge the afflicted but to restore them. Whatever the case, Christians must labor to accept the struggling and mistaken, to reassure self-worth, and to foster renewal and healing. Matters of individual responsibility and guilt are best dealt within pastoral counsel, consistories, and support groups. In all that it seeks to do, the church should know that its spiritual work must mediate the healing grace of God to broken and suffering emotions, minds, and spirits, no two of whom are alike. We deal, in short, with grace and psychology.

Economic Failure and Responsibility

This is perhaps one of the thorniest matters in the current crisis. Put simply, those facing bankruptcy have before them numerous legal options that place on them different degrees of obligation to past losses. While lenders should try as much as possible to forgive or renegotiate loans, borrowers should not feel, on the other hand, that they have the unqualified right to walk away from incurred debts simply because market conditions have been unfavorable. Banks fail as well as farmers, and behind those sometime faceless and seemingly powerful entities, other people work, live, and struggle. Wisdom and counsel in this area are complicated and delicate matters of analysis and conscience. Amid the chorus of conflicting perspectives on this matter, there probably is no one single word of general advice in resolving indebtedness. And there is certainly no way of enforcing such advice.

What is necessary perhaps is that the matter of indebtedness and bankruptcy be taken with utmost seriousness by lender, borrower, and the legal profession. Needless to say, justice and fairness in these complicated economic and legal circumstances are elusive at best. The bank needs its money, farmers care about their land and their families, and lawyers generally serve whom they must. The church's role herein is to urge all parties to ponder the questions of morality and justice, questions which often transcend recourses that are legally permissible. On all sides, evasion of moral responsibility to the opposite party—the willingness to let someone else "hold the bag"—falls outside the biblical relational norms (and unfortunately the biblical writers never imagined so complex a legal and economic structure as ours).

The best means to ensure such seriousness about the moral dimensions of financial dealing also proves elusive. Preaching affords one approach, and surely congregations as a whole should ponder the difficulties of all parishioners. Pastoral counsel affords a personal, immediate, and probably more effective route for presenting and probing questions of culpability. At some stage, the matter should be placed on the agenda for discussion by consistories which are usually made up of a diverse lot of professions and opinion. Further, it is suggested that the same be undertaken on the classis level so all clergy and consistories in agricultural regions be apprised of the legal and moral complexities of the issues. Classes might indeed work together to form task forces of farmers, bankers, and lawyers, who might formulate practical moral counsel for all involved.

Individual consistories or local inter-church committees might actively side with the plight of the farmer. Assuming an advocacy role, such bodies might determine which banks may be unnecessarily harsh or impatient with "good-faith" borrowers. Such banks might be encouraged toward forbearance and kindliness. Failing that, local groups might urge boycotts by parishioners of regular banking services and the withdrawal of church funds. Further, congregations throughout the denomination should consider issuing bonds or mortgaging church property at ten percent of valuation. By this means, the enormous economic resources of the denomination might be made available for long-term, low-interest loans.

The Pastoral Challenge

The church must indeed come to the aid of those caught in the farm crisis. Its counsel and solace can be decisive in turning shame, despair, and sorrow to hope and renewal. With significant numbers of its members in travail, when any part of the body suffers, the church's chief task is to bind up the physical and spiritual wounds within the body of Christ.

Connections

The hard experience of the farm crisis and social agencies suggests that just about any gesture of pastoral care to those in crisis, no matter how well intended or developed, depends on the realities of pre-existent trust and intimacy. That is, willingness to accept either practical or emotional counsel depends to a large extent on prior trust and closeness. Emergency aid from churches or social agencies, unless sought out by the sufferer, is not likely to be well received. Such intervention is often seen as insult or an invasion of privacy. A large portion of this suspicious response might result from the depth of self-reliance and even stubborn independence in the ethos of farm communities, attitudes which are pervasive and hard to overestimate. Farm families are, after all, most often autonomous units that are accustomed to working alone and surviving by their own wits and labor. With this mindset, it is understandable that those in economic trouble first deny the reality of the financial threat and then, upon recognition, often withdraw deep into themselves. So great is the shame and self-recrimination of failure that parents and siblings are often kept in the dark until difficulties reach crisis proportions. And sometimes spouses are not told and, if informed, are not allowed to serve as confidants.

This portrait of rural independence and fortitude makes clear the obligation of individual congregations, local and denomination-wide, to take very seriously the Christian calling to care deeply for one another at all times and not only in times of conspicuous need, however praiseworthy that might be. Those who suddenly appear on the scene as soon as tragedy strikes are likely to be resented and sent away. In farm congregations, as in any of the parishes of the church, it is particularly important that members consciously open and extend themselves with caring, candor, and mutual acceptance. Only by establishing such a fabric and texture of caring and concern will an atmosphere emerge wherein the troubled may find solace, help, and hope.

Needless to say, such qualities in congregational life are not easily instigated or realized. Church programming might emphasize opportunities that encourage and occasion the development of such trust within the parish. Sermons might offer an impetus for such, but alone they probably have little chance for deep and lasting effect. Prayer vigils for those stricken and laboring within economic calamity might offer a means to increase awareness and to solidify congregational sentiment. Further, consistories should reflect on appropriate settings and formats, ranging from soup suppers to retreats, that might enhance personal interchange and trust.

While saying the above, it is nonetheless important to assert that it is *never* too late to initiate expressions of Christian concern, no matter how difficult or awkward circumstances might make such expressions. One psychologist tells of a farm family that left their church when no one spoke to them in the wake of their bankruptcy. As the family belatedly discovered, what they at the time interpreted to be disapproval and rejection from lack of concern was in fact reticence and uncertainty on the part of the congregation. They did indeed care very much and grieved with the family but did not know how to express their sorrow. The silence led to great hurt. The point is, however, that *any* expression of concern, even the wordless touch of an arm, does show care and sympathy, which offers indispensable emotional support, however small and incidental such expressions might seem to the giver.

So the whole church, not merely its paid professional staff, must give sacrificially of itself if it is to convey necessary and adequate psychological and spiritual support to those who suffer in its midst. Always the members of Christ's body must see their neighbors as the person of Christ. Too often the church has been the last group, after government, business, and friends, to hear the cries of its own members.

Some responsibility falls too on those who are in need of aid. However painful it might be for them, they should be encouraged to realize that steadfast refusal of aid prohibits others from giving where God and love call them to give. To be sure, this is a hard insight to impart, but grace lies in receiving as well as giving. Indeed, nothing is more fundamental than our humble acceptance of God's love and help for our needy and wayward selves. This holy concern comes in many ways, and not solely in the forgiving mercy of God for our sins. Rather, God's love abides through all dimensions of our lives—personal, social, and economic. Thus, in the acceptance of ordinary or special beneficence, the recipient allows Christians to exercise their calling to charity and their summons to imitate the actions and mediate the love of Christ. Giving and taking are necessary actions of any social world, and ones to which Christians in particular are called. Humility and Christian caring compel us all to receive when in need. To refuse is to rebuke God's loving care through his earthly body, the church. Clergy and counselors might indeed focus on this perspective to alleviate sometimes-acute feelings of shame at the receipt of any sort of kindliness, financial aid, or emotional help.

Tasks

1. Through consistories and congregations, the denomination should seek to implement the stipulations of the Jubilee legislation, especially in economic support of the unfortunate and in encouraging the right and duty of redemption. Needless to say, within existing moral, legal, and financial structures, this is no easy task. No area of the corporate life of the church is in more urgent need of attention and creative and compassionate thinking. Individual congregations and classes must consider the hard difficulties of necessary and appropriate forms of practical financial and legal aid. Individual congregations and denominations are repositories of enormous capital investment, and such resources should, if possible, be brought to bear on real and immediate challenges of the agricultural depression. With this in mind, it seems reasonable to suggest that churches consider mortgaging part of all of their buildings and grounds in order to generate capital for direct financial assistance or interest-free loans. The money from the mortgage might then be used to help farmers in current financial distress or bankrupted others during a period of vocational transition. Certainly, the current situation would warrant from the church such radical gestures of support and caring. Whether the above proves feasible or not, churches and classes

should establish collaborative groups that might improvise short and long-term solutions to the problems in particular areas or families. When most everyone looks to government for solutions, it is perhaps appropriate for churches, especially those of a Reformed heritage, to reassert their historic role of shaping and caring for society and culture.

2. Very often families in the midst of economic and emotional distress cannot effectively deal with family necessities or long-range planning. In such circumstances, consistories and/or classes should offer with speed and charity the technical expertise of church members on agricultural, market, and financial matters. When families are at sea both emotionally and practically, debilitated by the complexity and immensity of their problems, the wisdom, integrity, and charity of the church visible and immediate not only extends indispensable practical aid but promises to renew lost trust and hope. Individual congregations and classes should consider establishing "help groups" whose specific intent and function would be to alleviate in whatever way possible the practical distress and upheaval of farm families. Already beleagured farm families should not need to turn to still more and sometimes untrustworthy highly paid "professionals" for assistance. If the church cannot be trusted in such matters, then there is some question whether indeed it remains the church.

3. Churches should move to provide support groups of farm crisis victims for farmers and businesspeople who are encountering financial stress. Only to such folk, only to those who have undergone like difficulties, the struggling workers can turn for emotional understanding and support, mercies they cannot be sure of receiving from "outsiders." Beyond this immediate function, such groups can also provide valuable counsel in such practical matters as legal strategies and vocational counseling. Emotional bonds and interpersonal commitment can provide an invaluable framework and wellspring for individual and familiar recovery.

4. The church has here the opportunity by God's grace to turn pain and misfortune into blessing. Part of the special responsibility of the body of Christ is to heal and restore the hurt and brokenness of its members. In the midst of despair and misfortune, the corporate prayer, petition, and ministry of congregations can bind the wounds of tragedy toward light, hope, and new life. Important expressions of this dimension of the life of the church might come in prayer vigils and worship liturgies wherein the stricken might find healing and solace. Such public occasions of corporate worship and intercession both acknowledge the sufferer's grief and anger and perhaps thereby further the motions of healing. Such corporate experiences work to effect forgiveness and reconciliation within families and between community members.

6
Church and Sexuality

Introduction

The Church and Homosexuality

The General Synod of 1990 instructed the Commission on Theology "to conduct a new study on homosexuality and submit a report to the 1992 General Synod (*MGS*, 1990: 461, R-12). The pressure of other tasks prevented the commission from responding to this mandate until 1991. The commission then decided the issue could best be dealt with by a task force that would include representatives from specialized fields and different geographical regions of the denomination. The task force began its work in 1992 and submitted its final report to the commission early in 1994.

The commission's paper, "The Church and Homosexuality," brought to the General Synod of 1994 adopted the basic thrust of the task force's report and employed much of its language. The paper's extended introduction describes the unusual mandate from the 1990 General Synod, the passionate diversity of opinions about homosexuality voiced during a "listening session" at the 1993 General Synod, and the rich and enlightening experience the task force coveted for the church as a whole. These factors led the Task Force on Homosexuality to recommend through the Commission on Theology that, instead of seeking another position paper, the Reformed Church in America enter into a season of discovery and discernment that would enable the denomination to make an appropriate Christian response to homosexual persons. The remainder of the paper provides goals, an outline, and a rationale for this process of study, reflection, and discernment.

After extensive discussion of this paper and its recommendation in both the Advisory Committee on Theology and on the synod floor, the 1994 General Synod took a series of actions. Inasmuch as a detailed summary of those actions comprise the introductory paragraphs of this chapter's second paper, "Materials for the Study and Discussion of Homosexuality: A Prospectus," (see p. 279), that record is not repeated here.

Materials for the Study and Discussion of Homosexuality: A Prospectus

The commission introduces the substance of this paper with an opening statement on the issue of homosexuality, a survey of the actions of past General Synods on the issue, and the commission's own response to the three mandates given to it by the 1994 General Synod.

The paper's substance consists of a prospectus outline of the assumptions and the content of the materials that will be produced to fulfill the 1994 General Synod mandates. Its first section attempts under five headings to distill from previous synod statements on the issue a set of clear parameters to guide the production of the mandated study materials. Its second section sketches out in broad form the basic outline which the study materials will follow. The outline's headings are God's creation and human sexuality, is homosexuality wrong?, homosexuality and the Christian life, the church: a safe place for sinners, and homosexuality and society.

The commission's recommendation to instruct the denomination's Congregational Services Unit through its Office of Education, in consultation with the commission, to provide materials and resources in keeping with the above prospectus outline to enable Reformed Church in America congregations, classes, and regional synods more fully to fulfill the 1994 General Synod's call to repentance, prayer, learning, and growth in minister to and with persons of homosexual orientation (*MGS,* 1994: 376) was adopted.

The Papers

1

The Church and Homosexuality

Introduction

The Commission on Theology received an unusual mandate from the 1990 General Synod. The 1990 General Synod voted:

> To adopt as the position of the Reformed Church in America that the practicing homosexual lifestyle is contrary to Scripture, while at the same time encouraging love and sensitivity towards such persons as fellow human beings (*MGS,* 1990: 461, R-11).

However, after making this very clear pronouncement, the 1990 General Synod then reaffirmed the earlier studies of 1978 (see *MGS,* 1978: 229-40) and 1979 (see *MGS,* 1979: 128-35), and also asked the Commission on Theology to carry out another study on the subject (*MGS,* 1990, R-12: 461, R-12). The commission, and the task force appointed by the commission to address this issue, reflected at some length on the unusual sequence of events. Usually studies are made, and then resolutions are adopted! Why in this case was the sequence reversed?

It seems clear that the debate at the 1990 General Synod, as well as this unusual sequence of events, indicated a lack of clarity and consensus around these issues in the church as a whole. That conclusion was powerfully confirmed in a "listening session" organized by the task force at the 1993 General Synod. In hearing from more than 150 people from many different sectors of the church, the task force confronted a passionate diversity of opinions:

> "I find gay persons to be sensitive, caring, loving, persons."

> "I'm not sure if it is a choice or genetic."

> "Homosexual orientation is a result of sin in our world."

> "They are stuck in that lifestyle."

> "The Bible is clear—their lifestyle is anathema. I did not make this rule, God did."

"They are sinful and defy God's Word."

"My son died of AIDS. My son may have made poor choices—not about being gay, but he took risks. Whether genetic or not, the church needs to love gays."

These are just a few of the statements made by Reformed Church people at the 1993 General Synod who responded to the question: "What are your perceptions about people who are gay and lesbian and how did you arrive at them?"

The task force also encountered another phenomenon in these hearings they had not expected: a surprising openness to talk and to listen to each other emerged within the context of very fruitful dialogue. In fact, not only did such openness appear in the listening sessions, but the task force found themselves deepened and stretched in their own understanding of the issues they were addressing, despite the fact they reflected a wide diversity of viewpoints on the question of homosexuality.

These experiences lead to the following assessment of the Reformed Church in America's current situation. It seems clear that there is a significant majority within the church who are convinced that the question of homosexuality is quite clearly and easily settled: one must simply and firmly condemn a practicing homosexual lifestyle as sinful. On the other hand, there are in the Reformed Church parents of gay children, pastors who are trying to work compassionately with gay people, and gay people themselves, who voiced, in one way or another, a frustration with the church's position and a longing for a more open conversation. Among all these people there is a deep commitment to Christ, to Scripture, and to the church.

The church is attempting to do justice to four basic concerns: 1) a concern for faithfulness to the Word of God; 2) a concern for the unity of the church; 3) a concern for homosexual persons; and 4) a concern for the integrity of the church's moral witness in the culture. Yet many Christians fear this issue cannot be resolved without one of these values being lost or compromised. The commission firmly believes, however, that this need not be the case. Rather, the commission believes the Reformed Church in America faces an opportunity to engage in a fresh and more pastoral approach.

How should the Reformed Church respond to such a situation, where deep and passionately felt differences of conviction emerge? As the task force reflected on this pastoral dilemma, they returned in their thinking to their hearings and to their own interactions. In their report to the Commission on Theology, they said: "We read, discussed, prayed, thought, wondered aloud, and struggled with the Word. It was a rich and enlightening experience, and one we covet for the church as a whole." Those times of prayer and dialogue were moments of fruitfulness and growth for the task force. Why should it not be possible for the larger church to experience that same growth of community and discernment? Why should it not be possible for the people of the Reformed Church in America to learn from each other?

Recommendation of the Task Force

The task force's experience led them to make a rather unusual recommendation through the Commission on Theology to the General Synod. They do not think the most helpful response at this moment is another position paper. What they have learned cannot effectively be shared with the church in such a format. In addition, the Reformed Church has already reaffirmed its earlier position in sending this mandate to the commission. What is needed is a pastoral response.

Therefore, the Task Force on Homosexuality, with the endorsement of the Commission on Theology, recommends that the Reformed Church in America enter into a season of discovery and discernment, guided by study, prayer, listening, and discussion. At the conclusion of the process, feedback to the Commission on Theology is to be used to report to the whole church its emerging conclusions, the insights gained, and concrete experiences of ministry that have manifested Christ's love. Throughout this process it is hoped that congregations which engage in this process for a period of time will learn to express even more faithfully an appropriate Christian response to homosexual persons, a response that has integrity in the face of concrete realities.

This season of discovery and discernment is to be a time for individual congregations and clusters of congregations to participate in moral discernment with the assistance of resources provided by Congregational Services through its Office of Education and Faith Development. These resources are to be developed in cooperation with the task force, using materials gathered during the task force's study. These resources will enable a process of dialogue that brings together real-life narratives, biblical and theological reflection, social science research, and pastoral care. A facilitator's guide is to be developed to assist leaders in guiding congregations through the process.

To revisit the issue of homosexuality in this way does not mean a rejection of the position taken by the RCA in 1978 and 1979 (*MGS,* 1978: 229-40 and *MGS,* 1979: 128-35). Until the General Synod chooses to overturn or replace these statements, and their reaffirmation in 1990 (*MGS,* 1990: 461, R-11), they remain the Reformed Church in America's position. A revisitation does mean that the Reformed Church will again take a fresh look at the questions and issues involved and will be open to new biblical, theological, pastoral, and scientific insights about how it can respond to homosexual persons in its midst in a way that is more faithful to Christ.

Description of the Process

What is described below is a process designed to enable people to learn new things. It avoids as much as possible any semblance of propagandizing, since the primary purpose is to enable Christians to think about the issues in an informed, open, and dialogical way. The process seeks to accomplish the following:

1. Provide an opportunity for the Reformed Church in America to explore the issue of homosexuality with a view toward living out the 1978 and 1979 studies (*MGS,* 1978: 229-40 and *MGS,* 1979: 128-35) of ministering effectively to and with homosexual persons.

2. Engage the Reformed Church in America in a dialogue to help its members learn how to discern the Spirit when dealing with issues such as homosexuality.

3. Assist Reformed Church members in shaping attitudes and actions in ways that inform their life and practice.

4. Prepare a response based on insights gained from the process and share it in usable form with the whole church.

The following outline is intended to provide an example of the kinds of issues the commission believes are helpful in achieving these goals. The precise details of the process are to be determined as the commission, the task force, and the Office of Education and Faith Development work together to produce a resource for use by Reformed Church members:

Outline

Part 1: Homosexuality and the Church

A. Introduce church members to the diversity of opinion on homosexuality within the Reformed Church in America, and provide a process that enables them to tell stories of their experience of someone who is gay or lesbian and to reflect on how that experience has shaped their attitudes and responses.

B. Tell a real-life story of a Christian who is homosexual and who poses the questions to the church: How can the church be a place of grace for persons who are homosexual? How can we learn better to give an understanding and compassionate response?

C. Provide an opportunity for people to raise the serious questions that need to be answered throughout the following segments of the process.

Part 2: Biblical Interpretation and Application

A. Review the biblical texts and the broader sense of the biblical witness dealt with in "Homosexuality: A Biblical and Theological Appraisal" (*MGS,* 1978: 229-240) in light of the full range of biblical scholarship available to date, and begin to formulate a response to the questions: What *do* the texts say? What are the key points at which Christians interpret these texts differently? How are we to understand their impact for Christian life today?

B. Engage in an exploration of how we in the Reformed Church in America understand the authority of the Bible for our faith and life. If different assumptions arise from this exploration, then what implications might this have for how we understand the ways in which God speaks to us and guides our lives through Scripture?

Part 3: Social Science

A. Review findings of the scientific community subsequent to the 1978 and 1979 studies (*MGS*, 1978: 229-40 and *MGS*, 1979: 128-35) about the incidence and causes of homosexuality.

B. Review therapeutic approaches to dealing with homosexual orientation and practice in order to discover what we know about its effects on the whole person and its potential for reversibility.

C. Consider the relationship between scientific findings (what is) and moral norms (what ought to be).

Part 4: Ministry Approaches

A. Review congregational life and practice in light of "Christian Pastoral Care for the Homosexual" (*MGS*, 1979: 128-135), in order to evaluate the ways in which we in the Reformed Church in America have or have not learned to live the current denominational position.

B. Discover models of ministry being carried out by other Christians in order to assist congregations to develop their own responses.

C. Explore ways that each Reformed Church congregation, in light of its own location and character, can develop specific plans and goals for ministry among homosexual persons and their families.

Part 5: Final Stage

The Commission on Theology envisions a final stage in which the commission will gather feedback from congregations and individuals who have participated in the process. Using this material, the commission will prepare a report aimed at furthering the ministry of the church.

Rationale for the Process

The broader ecumenical church community has grappled with the issue of homosexuality for some time. Task forces are faced with the daunting task of discerning the will of God in relative isolation from the body of believers who have to live with the interpretation. It is not uncommon for a study group, after long and arduous study, to see its ideas and recommendations rejected by the denomination. Often the debate becomes polarized and divisive, with severe costs to the life and ministry of the church.

As frustrating and alarming as this phenomenon may be for the church, it should not be seen in isolation from its larger context. In fact, a broader view suggests that what may seem to be an isolated problem peculiar to North American Protestantism may be symptomatic of the more general condition in the culture. Recent thinking about the relationship between the church and society points to several factors which might frustrate an attempt on the part of a denomination to locate and articulate consensus on a controversial issue.

The first factor is the declining power of denominations. More and more congregations (even in the Reformed Church in America) are beginning to adopt a more localized mentality which may have little connection with a broader sense of denominational identity. A second factor is the increasingly pluralistic complexion of this society. Ethically, this new pluralism tends to erode any consensus as to what is "right" and "good." People may respond to this by becoming more entrenched in their previously held positions, or they may succumb to a sense of moral relativism, the belief that says "Whatever I decide is right for me." Third, study after study has concluded that the individual has become the fundamental unit of modern North American society. As Donald Luidens, a sociologist at Hope College, observed:

> In this highly privatized faith, the church plays a secondary role; it is no longer the prevailing authority or mediator of the true faith. Historic creeds and doctrines of the church are rendered inconsequential in the face of personal witness. Ecclesiastical judicatories are irrelevant in matters of personal faith. If one is unfulfilled in one church, another sanctuary waits around the

corner to welcome the seeker with open arms ("What's a Denomination to Do?" *Church Herald* [January 1994], 10).

In this context, it is not at all clear that the typical strategy of addressing the morality of homosexuality by a general synod pronouncement works effectively to draw the denomination together into deeper insight and more consistent ministry. The centripetal forces affecting the church can, in this case, best be addressed by a process of study, reflection, and discernment beginning at the level of the local congregation.

Equally significant, however, is the sense the Reformed Church in America has not yet learned to live out the position statements adopted by the General Synod in 1978 and 1979 (*MGS,* 1978: 229-40 and *MGS,* 1979: 128-35). The commission observes that it is not uncommon to hear people characterize the 1978 and 1979 reports by emphasizing either their exegetical conclusions, which stressed a biblical condemnation of a "homosexual lifestyle," *or* their pastoral concerns which counseled a compassionate response to homosexual persons. Neither emphasis on its own reflects the denomination's complete position. The commission believes churches can better learn to live out a complex moral stance by developing it in the context of their own lives and practicing its application. Only a concrete community of Christians can show what such a stance might mean and how it might be possible.

The emerging literature on the use of the Bible in moral decision-making indicates that such merging of faith and practice is best fostered in local communities of Christians, as they grapple with biblical texts in the light of both their tradition of Christian nurture and the challenges of contemporary life. If any supplementation or change in the Reformed Church in America's denominational position results from the process the commission is recommending, it should arise out of the process, and not at its beginning. "Having" a denominational position on such an issue is of little use if we have not yet learned to live out that position. Far more important is the process by which we as Christian communities and individuals learn to live out the gospel in the complex circumstances of our lives.

2

Materials for the Study and Discussion of Homosexuality: A Prospectus

Introduction

Homosexuality is an issue which Christ's church cannot avoid. The challenge arises not because developments within the larger culture in North America make it unavoidable, but rather because the pastoral and theological issues surrounding homosexuality raise fundamental concerns for the church's identity, its sense of what it means to obey God and to minister to people in a broken world. Yet, it is an issue that people often attempt to avoid, because it involves difficult and uncomfortable questions about sexuality, and because for many, attitudes about homosexuality and toward homosexual people are deeply visceral in nature. If Christians are to confront this issue in an honest, informed, and biblical way, however, Christians must learn to open their hearts to God's Word, and in that light to set aside their own assumptions and to listen and talk with each other.

The General Synod of the Reformed Church in America has dealt with the issue of homosexuality several times in recent history. In 1978 the Commission on Theology submitted a paper to the General Synod entitled "Homosexuality: A Biblical and Theological Appraisal." General Synod voted to make the paper available to the churches for study (*MGS,* 1978: 229-40). In 1979 a companion paper from the commission, "Christian Pastoral Care for the Homosexual," was similarly recommended for study, on the grounds that "the report is biblically sound, positive in spirit, and will become a valuable resource to pastors and elders in the discharge of their pastoral responsibilities" (*MGS,* 1979: 128-35). Hence, these papers, while not adopted as the official position of the denomination, did elicit favorable response from two General Synods.

In 1990, responding to an overture which proposed that General Synod adopt the 1978 report "as the official position of the RCA on the subject," General Synod instead voted "to adopt as the position of the Reformed Church in America that the practicing homosexual lifestyle is contrary to Scripture, while at the same time encouraging love and sensitivity toward such persons as fellow human beings" (*MGS,* 1990: 461, R-11). At the same time, General Synod voted to "instruct the Commission on Theology to conduct a new study on homosexuality" (*MGS,* 1990: 461, R-12), and commended the 1978 and 1979 General Synod papers to the churches as "pastoral advice until such time as a subsequent study...is approved by General Synod" (*MGS,* 1990: 461, R-13).

The Commission on Theology appointed a task force in 1992 to help it consider the issue. The task force recommended to the commission that rather than producing a new study, the church should initiate a process of study and reflection at the congregational level. It also proposed an outline for such a study, in which the 1978 and 1979 reports represented the current denominational position. Acting on this recommendation, the commission submitted to the 1994 General Synod a proposal "to urge RCA congregations, classes, and regional synods to enter into a season of discovery and discernment guided by study, prayer, listening, and discussion, aimed at relating to homosexual persons in ways that are more faithful to Christ," using material to be prepared by Congregational Services staff, in consultation with the commission. After extensive discussion in the Advisory Committee on Theology and on the floor of General Synod, the following substitute motion was unanimously approved by General Synod (*MGS,* 1994: 375-76):

> To adopt the following resolution:
>
> The General Synod of the Reformed Church in America recognizes and confesses that the Reformed Church in America has failed to live up to its own statements regarding homosexuality in 1978 (*MGS,* 1978: 229-40), 1979 (*MGS,* 1979: 128-35), and 1990 (*MGS,* 1990: 461, R-11). Few in the Reformed Church in America have creatively and lovingly spoken with persons with a homosexual orientation about the truths of Scripture and the hope of the gospel. Many have participated in or tolerated forms of speech and behavior which humiliate and degrade such persons. Many of the churches within the Reformed Church in America have not provided an environment where persons have felt the acceptance and freedom to struggle with hard issues involving sexual orientation. Many Reformed Church in America members have shown no interest in listening to their heartfelt cries as they struggle for self-acceptance and dignity. For all these

wrongs, this General Synod expresses its humble and heartfelt repentance, and its desire to reflect the love of Christ to homosexual persons. In all that this General Synod does, it seeks to obey the whole of Scripture, demonstrating in its own life the same obedience it asks from others. It calls itself and the whole church to a greater faithfulness to Christ in relationships with persons of homosexual orientation.

To this end, the General Synod calls the church to a process of repentance, prayer, learning, and growth in ministry. This process will be guided by the basic biblical-theological framework presented in the previous statements of the General Synod in 1978 (*MGS,* 1978: 229-40), 1979 (*MGS,* 1979: 128-35), and 1990 (*MGS,* 1990: 461, R-11).

The same substitute motion also instructed the Commission on Theology to develop three resources (*MGS,* 1994: 376):

1. A study guide…[based on] the 1978 and 1979 statements of General Synod on the church and homosexuality. This study guide will include updating of these reports only with respect to factual material.

2. A process of reflection for Reformed Church in America congregations who are seeking to increase their sensitivity and awareness of the ways in which persons of homosexual orientation have wrongly suffered in our churches and in our society.

3. A collection of models for ministry to persons of homosexual orientation…which are in harmony with the Reformed Church in America's stated positions [which say, a) that homosexual practice is wrong, and b) that the church must reach out in love and compassion to persons of homosexual orientation].

The commission was further instructed to submit these materials to the 1995 General Synod for its approval prior to their distribution (*MGS,* 1994: 376).

As the commission discussed the 1994 General Synod mandates, three areas of concern emerged. First, it became clear that there was not adequate time for the careful completion of this entire mandate before the

1995 General Synod. Secondly, the commission felt that the 1994 General Synod's statement that the 1978 and 1979 reports should be updated "only with respect to factual material" (*MGS*, 1994: 376) was ambiguous. The commission believed that its work would benefit from the opportunity to confer with the General Synod on exactly the scope of updating which was appropriate. Finally, there was some concern over the possibility that significant funds might be invested in the production of materials on a controversial topic which might not then be approved by the 1995 General Synod, resulting in a waste of precious resources.

In response to these three concerns, the commission decided to produce a prospectus for the materials requested by the 1994 General Synod, rather than to engage in the full production of materials. This course of action is intended to keep good faith with the 1994 General Synod's desire that the theology of the materials be approved by General Synod. It also allows the commission the opportunity to test its understanding of what is centrally important about the 1978, 1979, and 1990 General Synod statements on homosexuality which should guide the production of materials. Finally, this course of action allows the Reformed Church in America to move ahead with investing in the production of materials, with the confidence that the materials will be distributed and that these will reflect the mind of the denomination. It should be understood that the commission does not submit this paper as a new position on homosexuality for the denomination, but rather as part of the process of the production of educational materials mandated by the 1994 General Synod.

Prospectus Outline

The following is an outline of the assumptions and the content of the materials which will be produced to fulfill the 1994 General Synod mandates. The first section attempts to distill from the previous statements of the Reformed Church in America on the subject of homosexuality a set of clear parameters to guide the production of the Reformed Church study materials mandated by the 1994 General Synod. Though many sentences and passages from the 1978 and 1979 reports are reproduced verbatim, this first section does not attempt to reproduce every detail of the earlier statements, since some of the data and terminology used in these statements is no longer current. Nor does it set out extensively to rethink or revise these statements, though at some points it seeks to clarify the arguments contained in them. The aim is to make available to members of the Reformed Church in America a digest of the earlier statements to serve as a basis for further discussion, and to define the pastoral and theological parameters which will guide the production of study materials to fulfill the 1994 General Synod mandates. The second section sketches out in broad form the basic outline which the materials will follow.

Section I: Guiding parameters for Reformed Church in America study materials on homosexuality (drawn from 1978-1979 General Synod statements, MGS, 1978: 229-40 and MGS, 1979: 128-35)

A. Homosexual behavior is not God's intended expression of sexuality.

Although the Bible gives relatively little attention to the issue of homosexuality, those texts which do refer to homosexual activity are clear in their condemnation of the practices they describe. Some of the passages which are cited to make the case against homosexuality do not in themselves justify a blanket condemnation of homosexuality (e.g., Gen. 19:4-11, the story concerning the men of Sodom). Nonetheless, two passages in the Old Testament clearly prohibit such conduct (Lev. 18:22 and 20:13). Some argue that this prohibition is a result of the need to avoid the "cultic prostitution" practiced by neighboring peoples and is therefore no longer relevant to people today. While this argument has been contested, it is true that these prohibitions appear in a context where there are many commands which Christians no longer regard as binding in light of the broader witness of Scripture and the gospel of Christ. Hence, their status must be weighed by how the issue is dealt with in the New Testament.

The clearest passage in the New Testament bearing on this issue is found in Romans 1:26, 27. Here, the apostle Paul is arguing that human sinfulness is rooted in one's exchanging the worship of God for the worship of the created order. Because this rebellious exchange disrupts the vertical relationship between God and humans, it results in a parallel disruption in one's horizontal relationships with each other. Homosexual behavior is one symptom of the "exchange" of natural for unnatural relationships, although not the only one, nor necessarily the most serious.

The censure of homosexual behavior is rooted in Scripture's strong sense of a natural, created order for human life, which in the arena of human sexuality is manifested in the differentiation and complementarity of the sexes. Human sexuality is created for heterosexual expression, since both male and female appear when humankind is created, and since each is complemented and completed only by the other.

B. Homosexuality is no more nor less serious than other forms of human sinfulness.

The fact that heterosexuality is normative according to Scripture does not mean that there is any excuse for singling out persons of homosexual orientation for extraordinary censure or rejection. *All* human sexuality has been injured by the fall of humanity, and no one may presume that his or her sexual orientation and conduct, by themselves, merit special praise or blame. The compulsive fear and loathing which homosexuality arouses in modern society, therefore, should not lead heterosexuals to place those who struggle with homosexuality beyond the pale of God's grace. While calling homosexuals to repentance, the church must itself repent of its revulsion and fear. The Holy Spirit works among those whose mutual dependence upon God's grace is acknowledged and shared. Only in that climate of grace are persons freed to face themselves honestly and to become open to the transforming love of Christ as it becomes embodied in the fellowship of believers.

C. There are varied and complex causes of homosexual orientation and behavior; hence, simplistic analyses and solutions should be questioned.

Modern research into the phenomenon of homosexuality has introduced the concept of *sexual orientation*. This means that for some people, homosexual behavior arises out of a basic orientation toward members of the same sex. This orientation is not consciously chosen and is generally a matter over which the individual has no control. For people with a homosexual orientation, homosexual attraction does not occur as a deliberate perversion of a heterosexual instinct, but rather is simply discovered or realized in the process of sexual maturation.

The causes of homosexual orientation are still a matter of research and debate in a number of fields, including biology and psychology. There is no consensus regarding the causes of homosexuality, but there is consensus that the causes are to be found in factors over which the individual has no direct control. Various theories point toward genetics, hormonal functioning, psychosocial development in infancy or early childhood, or some combination of these factors. Such homosexual orientation has not lent itself easily to medical or psychotherapeutic redirection. Some Christian ministries report success in helping persons of homosexual orientation to redirect their sexual orientation and their habits of sexual expression, while other Christian ministries report that the problems involved in redirecting sexual orientation seem more intractable.

Recognition of this reality means that the church must learn to deal differently in its pastoral strategies with persons who, apart from or even against their own choice, find themselves having a homosexual orientation. Scripture does not directly address the problem of homosexual acts which emerge in accord with one's conscious sexual orientation and not against it. Most of the texts which address homosexuality focus simply on *behaviors* which are or are not appropriate. (Romans 1:26-27 is an exception, since it refers to men "giving up natural intercourse with women" and being "consumed with passion for one another." Yet this language probably reflects the common understanding in other Jewish and Graeco-Roman texts that homosexual desire was the result of insatiable lust, unsatisfied with only heterosexual relations. It is a matter of debate among exegetes as to whether this text directly speaks about persons of a homosexual *orientation* for whom homosexual attraction may be the only form of sexual attraction they have ever experienced, and who therefore cannot be said to have "given up natural intercourse with women" for homosexual relationships. Though the text clearly condemns homosexual behavior, it is not clear that it has in view the kind of orientation some people experience and report today.) Although this does not mean heterosexuality is less binding as a norm, one must recognize that individuals cannot be blamed for having inclinations over which they have neither control nor choice. Homosexual orientation should be understood as a result of the general problem of evil, rather than of the sin of specific individuals. How a person acts with regard to such orientation is, of course, a matter of personal responsibility.

D. Any expectations for persons of homosexual orientation to experience wholeness should be shaped by both the hope and the realism of the Christian life.

The position of a person with a homosexual orientation in our society is painfully difficult. Trapped in a sexuality one did not choose, and which many in society and the church regard as disgusting, one must cope with the feeling of being unclean and false. Guilt, self-loathing, and a fear of close relations may become a part of one's life. The resulting loneliness may lead one to expect instant, unqualified approval from others, and to suffer despair when it is not forthcoming. Preoccupation with one's homosexuality—or sexuality at all, for that matter—may hinder development of a well-rounded character.

Nevertheless, among those who live with a homosexual orientation, there is a wide spectrum of behavior and psychological responses. Some show a much better pattern of adjustment than others. In particular, there is a wide divergence in the degree of sexual responsibility which is shown by homosexual persons living an active sexual life (as there is, of course, among heterosexuals). The church must adopt a different pastoral strategy toward those homosexuals who become involved only with another adult in the context of a long-term, affectionate relationship, as distinct from those who engage in promiscuous "one-night stands."

In any case, the homosexual person needs the same thing that all Christians need in order to experience God's grace: gracious acceptance of the person and an understanding of the call to repentance and the process of sanctification. This process of sanctification must always be viewed in light of the "already-not yet" tension within Scripture. The Spirit of God is moving in the lives of all Christians to lead them toward greater faithfulness and conformity to Christ. At the same time, Scripture is equally clear that this movement is a lifelong process, often full of failures and dormant times, as well as growth and victory. No one reaches sinless perfection in this life, though all can expect the grace of God to be at work in their lives, accomplishing more than one might ask or imagine.

This doctrine frees the church both from denial and from despair. Christians need not deny the difficulties many homosexual persons experience in coping with or trying to change their sexual orientation and behavior. Nor need Christians despair of God's grace. Rather, Christians live in hope, trusting that the Spirit of God has many ways, both great and small, of forming Christ in them. This hope frees the church, as a healing fellowship, to accept the homosexual person in his or her homosexual orientation, even though it cannot condone the behavior which may result from that orientation. Without such acceptance, the homosexual person is left with the choice of leaving the fellowship, wearing the mask of heterosexuality, or suffering condemnation. Most choose the mask. The effect is to leave the homosexual feeling hypocritical, unwanted, unknown, and in fear of exposure. Sadly, Christian congregations often seem more concerned with "instant righteousness" or the appearance of righteousness than with the patient, often painful process of sanctification.

That process begins with genuine, responsible self-confrontation before God; it is thwarted by self-deception, self-justification, and self-concealment. Unfortunately, these destructive patterns of behavior, so tempting for homosexuals in contemporary society, are reinforced by the difficulty which Christians have in dealing openly with each other about their struggles. The church must learn once more that healing and growth in the personal realm is never smooth, effortless, and error-free. All Christians must be willing to join the homosexual in seeking the hope and help all need in order to become the persons God knows and intends all to be.

The church should expect its members to be open to new possibilities. The homosexual must not place a ceiling on the capacity for growth. This means letting go of the myth of incurability, while at the same time avoiding a facile, overly optimistic view toward change and healing. In order to make this attitude possible, the church must itself be a welcoming place to wrestle with the issues of sexual orientation and behavior, inviting all its members to a deeper wholeness guided by the truth of Scripture.

E. *Homosexual persons should be accorded their full measure of human and civil rights.*

Approval of homosexual orientation or acts is not a prerequisite to firm support of basic civil rights for homosexual persons. Sexual conduct is primarily an ethical question and not the concern of criminal law, except when sexual acts are committed against minors, or when they involve public decency, rape, or prostitution. Criminal laws to deter such acts are in force and applicable to both heterosexual and homosexual persons. Statistical evidence denies any allegation that homosexual persons are more inclined to commit violent crimes than heterosexual persons. Further statistical comparisons indicate, for example, that a child is no more likely to be seduced by a homosexual teacher or youth worker than by a heterosexual in the same role. Therefore, legislation specifically directed against homosexual persons is unnecessary and constitutes a prejudicial attempt to legislate private morality. At the same time, civil rights for homosexuals do not include a right to special protections or privileges for homosexuals which are unavailable to all citizens.

Sincere concern is sometimes expressed by parents and other adults concerning the possible negative effects of homosexual role models on children and adolescents. While this concern is valid in instances where homosexuality is espoused or flaunted, parents should recognize that negative sexual role models abound in this permissive and promiscuous society. Human sexuality is debased and exploited in advertising, in the media, and on the street in many unseemly ways. Inevitably, young people observe some persons who act out their sexuality in an irresponsible manner. Although youth cannot be isolated from such influences, they do need guidance in discerning right from wrong and making moral judgments in sexual matters. Here the teaching ministry of the church as well as the healthy sexual modeling and nurturing role of parents in the Christian home are crucial to a child's maturing sexual awareness and identity. The church should also respond to the need for a constructive Christian social witness in matters of sexual values and conduct. Concern for youth is better expressed in these positive ways than through blanket, discriminatory sanctions against all persons of one sexual orientation.

While the commission cannot affirm homosexual behavior, at the same time the commission is convinced that the denial of human and civil rights to homosexuals is inconsistent with the biblical witness and Reformed theology.

Section II: A prospectus of study materials to fulfill 1994 General Synod mandates (MGS, 1994: 376)

The commission proposes a five-part series, each part to include three components: a) theological reflection in the light of Scripture and contemporary scientific research, b) encounter with lived experience of homosexual persons, their friends, and their families, and c) reflection on models and strategies for the church's ministry to and with persons of homosexual orientation.

The educational goals of the study materials are:

1. To explore the Reformed Church in America's existing theological and pastoral guidance regarding homosexuality.

2. To encourage reflection on how churches and individuals may more faithfully live out this guidance.

3. To assist church members in shaping attitudes and actions in ways which inform their life and practice.

4. To stimulate new ventures in Christian ministry by exploring various models and strategies for ministry to and with persons of homosexual orientation.

The suggested outline is as follows:

Part 1: God's creation and human sexuality.

Explores the goodness of creation, including sexuality, and its distortion by sin.

Explores the difficulties Christians have dealing with problems in the area of sexuality within the context of the church.

Develops a biblical understanding of the divine intention for human sexuality.

Identifies the church as the community which has not fully arrived, but continues on   the way to sexual wholeness as God intended it.

Part 2: Is homosexuality wrong?

Exploration of key passages, focusing on Leviticus 18 and 20, Romans 1, 1 Corinthians 6, and 1 Timothy 1.

Introduction to the notion of sexual orientation and its impact upon ethical reflections regarding homosexuality.

Reflection upon the usefulness and limits of the moral distinction between homosexual orientation and homosexual behavior.

Moral positions versus judgmentalism.

The meaning of forgiveness and acceptance for homosexual persons.

Part 3: Homosexuality and the Christian life.

The Reformed doctrine of sanctification and homosexuality.

An honest assessment of reorientation therapies.

Models for the church's wrestling with the possibilities and limits of transformation.

Part 4: The church: a safe place for sinners.

The problem of bigotry and intolerance.

The church's response to brokenness.

Models for being gracious and truthful in welcoming persons of homosexual orientation into the life of the church.

Part 5: Homosexuality and society.

Issues of human and civil rights for homosexuals.

Christian responses to the gay rights political agenda.

The church as the model of a new community.

The Commission on Theology proposes this prospectus outline as the framework for fulfilling the 1994 mandates given to the commission, and requests that the 1995 General Synod give final authorization for the production of educational materials guided by this prospectus.

Appendix

The following list will assist those who wish to examine the papers of this volume as they appear in the annual Minutes of the General Synod of the Reformed Church in America (*MGS*).

Chapter I Church and Scripture

1. The Use of Scripture in Making Moral Decisions: *MGS*, 1994:359-68.

Chapter II Church and Faith

1. The Challenge of Liberation Theology (with study guide): *MGS*, 1988:357-79.
2. Confessing the Nicene Creed Today: *MGS*, 1991:400-02.
3. The Nicene Creed and the Procession of the Spirit: *MGS*, 1991:402-34.
4. Confirmation and the Reformed Church: *MGS*, 1992:455-66.
5. *Book of Church Order* Conscience Clauses: *MGS*, 1998:470-74.
6. "The Crucified One is Lord": Confessing the Uniqueness of Christ in a Pluralist Society: *MGS*, 2000:124-39.

Chapter III Church and Sacraments

1. Children at the Lord's Table: *MGS*, 1988:380-85.

Chapter IV Church and and Ministry

1. The Role and Authority of Women in Ministry: MGS, 1991:435-49.
2. Concerning the Practice of the Laying on of Hands in the Ordination Services of the Reformed Church in America: MGS, 1995:369-80.
3. The Commissioning of Preaching Elders: MGS, 1996:391-98.
4. Moral Standards for Holders of Church Offices: MGS, 1998:464-69.
5. The Constitutional Inquiries: MGS, 2000:145-48.

Chapter V Church and Witness

1. Christian Witness to Muslims: An Introduction to the Issues: *MGS*, 1995:357-68.
2. Guilt, Responsibility, and Forgiveness in the Farm Crisis: *MGS*, 1987:273-82.

Chapter VI Church and Sexuality

1. The Church and Homosexuality: *MGS*, 1994:370-75.
2. Materials for the Study and Discussion of Homosexuality: A Prospectus: *MGS*, 1995:381-88.

Scripture Index

The following index is for both volume one and volume two of *The Church Speaks*. References to volume one are indicated by Roman numeral I and to volume two by Roman numeral II.

293

Name Index

The following index is for both volume one and volume two of *The Church Speaks*. References to volume one are indicated by Roman numeral I and to volume two by Roman numeral II.

302

Subject Index

The following index is for both volume one and volume two of *The Church Speaks.* References to volume one are indicated by Roman numeral I and to volume two by Roman numeral II.

References to Calvin's *Institutes*